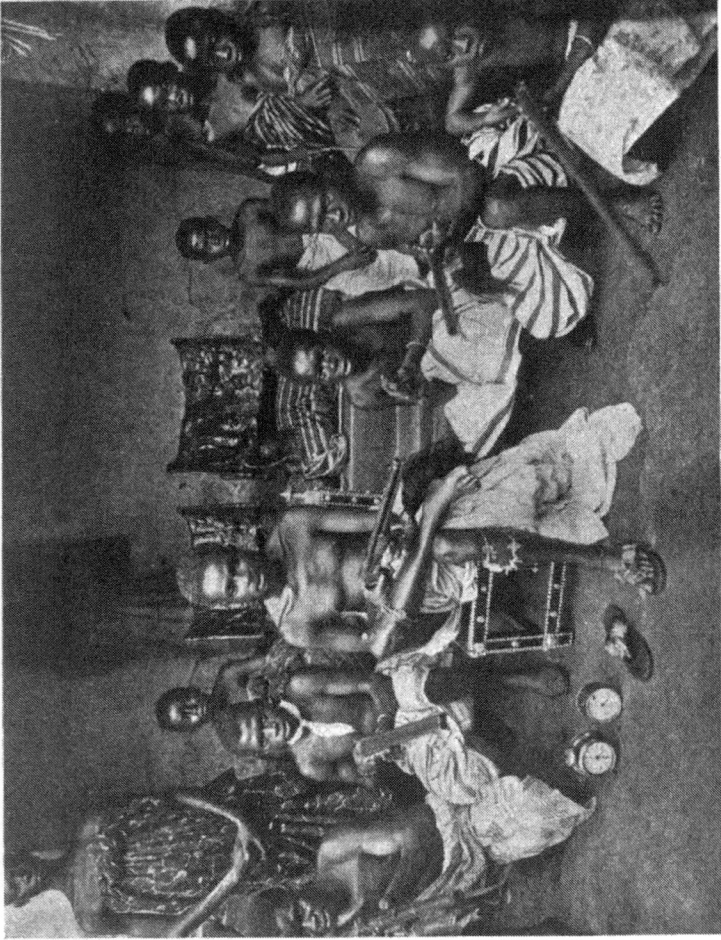

OWUSU SEKYERE, OMANHENE (PARAMOUNT CHIEF) OF
MAMPON, AND HIS SONS

ASHANTI PROVERBS

(THE PRIMITIVE ETHICS OF A SAVAGE PEOPLE)

TRANSLATED FROM THE ORIGINAL

WITH

GRAMMATICAL AND ANTHROPOLOGICAL NOTES

BY

R. SUTHERLAND RATTRAY

F.R.G.S., F.R.A.I.

DIPLÔMÉ IN ANTHROPOLOGY, OXFORD
DISTRICT COMMISSIONER, ASHANTI ; QUALIFIED INTERPRETER
IN HAUSA, TWI (ASHANTI), CHINYANJA, MŌLE
AUTHOR OF ' HAUSA FOLK-LORE ', ' CHINYANJA FOLK-LORE '

WITH A PREFACE BY

SIR HUGH CLIFFORD, K.C.M.G.

GOVERNOR AND COMMANDER-IN-CHIEF GOLD COAST COLONY

OXFORD
AT THE CLARENDON PRESS
1916

OXFORD UNIVERSITY PRESS

LONDON   EDINBURGH   GLASGOW   NEW YORK

TORONTO   MELBOURNE   BOMBAY

HUMPHREY MILFORD M.A.

PUBLISHER TO THE UNIVERSITY

1898

PREFACE

In preparing this volume, to which he has asked me to contribute a preface, Mr. Rattray has performed a considerable service to those of us who are interested in the Tshi-speaking people of the Gold Coast, or who are concerned in the administration of their affairs. He has blazed for us a track through a wilderness which has so far been very imperfectly explored, and has thereby opened the way to further discoveries.

Much has been said and written concerning the difficulty which the European mind usually experiences in comprehending the mentality of Orientals, but it is probable that the difficulties which beset a student of West African thought are far greater than any which are experienced in Asia. Orientalists of many nations have been engaged for centuries in interpreting the East to the West, and their efforts, more especially during the past fifty years, have been attended by a certain measure of success. All the great literatures of Asia are to-day accessible to European scholars, and familiarity with Oriental languages is now common. The philosophies of Asia have not failed to make their strong appeal to many Europeans, in spite of the fact that they are, in the main, distinctive products, dissimilar from anything which the West has evolved on its own account. In the same way, democratic theories of government, which may be regarded as being in some sort the exclusive product of the European intellect, have recently seemed to hold for modern Asiatics, who have been influenced by Occidental education, a very special fascination.

The literatures which enshrine the highest thought of the East are, however, little known to the rank and file of any Asiatic people. They are the fruit of exceptional minds, and as such they are for the most part appreciated by those who are themselves exceptional. A far more faithful mirror of the popular mind is to be found in the proverbial sayings with which the vernacular languages of Asia abound. In the East, the every-day talk of even the most illiterate peasants has what may be called, for want of a more exact term, a certain 'literary' flavour. The attitude of mind of the average Oriental is one of innate conservatism. Decrying the present, he is filled with an immense reverence for the past and for the wisdom which has been transmitted to him by unnumbered and forgotten generations. An ancient proverb accordingly possesses a peculiar force and cogency in the general estimation by reason of its antiquity, and is apt to be accepted as a conclusive summing up of any discussion upon which it bears. Thus it comes to pass that the man who can *quote* has in debate among Orientals a distinct advantage over the man who relies principally upon argument. And the number of these proverbs is as large as their use is constant. The speech of the average Asiatic peasant is, as it were, a sort of mosaic composed of these aphorisms; his mind passes from one to another of them, as pieces are moved upon a chess-board; his thought is at once guided and confined by them ; and it is not too much to say that no one can use a vernacular language of the East with force and finish unless these wise saws have become for him part of his mental furniture. From them, moreover, far more than from the literatures of Asia, is an understanding to be gained of the soul of the people, their character, and their philosophy.

If this be so in the East, it is pre-eminently the case in West Africa, where no literatures exist to record the matured thought and wisdom of the finest local intellects which the centuries have produced; wherefore a study of the proverbial sayings of the natives here furnishes the principal, if not the only, means whereby an understanding of their character and mentality may be acquired by Europeans. It is this fact which gives a special value to books such as this which Mr. Rattray has compiled.

To any one who is acquainted with the proverbial wisdom of the East, the present collection will appear to lack the epigrammatic crispness of thought by which the former is characterized. This perhaps indicates that the mind of the people whose sayings Mr. Rattray is interpreting for us differs from our own more fundamentally than do the minds of the peoples of Asia. Many of the aphorisms will be found to be somewhat cryptic, and it is rather daunting to find the curt dictum that ' When a fool is told a proverb, the meaning of it has to be explained to him '. If this— which is apparently axiomatic to the Tshi-speaking native of West Africa—be applied to the student of Mr. Rattray's book, few of us, it is to be feared, will escape conviction of folly. On the other hand, many of the wise saws appear to the European mind as so trite and obvious that we should hardly esteem them worthy to rank as proverbs at all. At the very outset, therefore, we discover indications of a wide discrepancy of mental outlook and appreciation between ourselves and the people who have evolved these aphorisms, —a discrepancy which seems to exist not only with regard to that which to us is obscure and to them self-evident, but also with regard to what they recognize as wisdom and we should be inclined to class as banal truism. Both, I think, should whet our curiosity, and neither should excite our derision. Our task is to endeavour to understand the workings of the minds by which these sayings have been evolved and of the minds which have adopted them as expressions of the collective experience of a people. To this end nothing can be discarded as unworthy of consideration because it chances to strike only a faint answering chord in us. It is to those who are prepared to approach this study in a spirit of earnest and patient inquiry that I commend Mr. Rattray's collection of proverbs.

HUGH CLIFFORD.

LONDON,
August 8, 1914.

AUTHOR'S NOTE

In the year 1879 a book of *Tshi Proverbs* was published by the Basel Evangelical Missionary Society. This work, which was edited by the late Rev. J. G. Christaller, contained some '3,600 proverbs in use among the negroes of the Gold Coast, speaking the Asante and Fante language'.

The collection, to use the words of the compiler, consisted of proverbs, '*taken down by the missionaries themselves from the oral communications of certain elders or of other old or younger people, or were written by native assistants who increased their previous knowledge by learning from experienced countrymen*'.

The book in question is entirely in the vernacular. It does not contain any translation, notes or other explanatory matter, though had the Editor (the Rev. J. G. Christaller) lived he would have 'added a translation and explanation to the proverbs'.

To the present writer (who, during his four years of service in Ashanti, had acquired a colloquial knowledge of the language), it seemed a misfortune that such a store of interesting and valuable material, and so much '*wit and wisdom*', should have been, for over thirty years, buried in the comparative obscurity in which such a work must needs lie. It must literally be a closed book to all but a very few persons, confined in this case to those missionaries of West Africa, who can understand and speak the Twi or Ashanti language, and to their native teachers and scholars. The present writer, therefore, wrote to the Basel Missionary Society and asked permission to translate some of these proverbs. Sanction was most kindly given by the Rev. B. Groh. It is therefore to the Basel Mission in general, and more particularly to the late Rev. J. G. Christaller (whose name is worthy to rank with that of the late Dr. Clement Scott, and with that of Mr. A. C. Madan, in

the field of African linguistic research), to whom any
thanks from the larger public are now due. The task of
the present writer has been that of commentator and
translator only, from the materials collected by these
pioneers.

The eight hundred odd proverbs given in the present
work have been selected chiefly with a view to showing :—

1. Some custom, belief, or ethical determinant pure and
simple, which may be of interest to the anthropologist.

2. Some grammatical or syntactical construction of
importance to the student of the language.

The notes that are added after each proverb are also for
these two classes of readers.

The writer would crave the pardon of the former class
of student for these brief notices, which are only intended
to 'help out' or explain a proverb when necessary. Any
attempt to go very fully into customs which a particular
saying touches on, is beyond the scope and object of the
present work.

An almost literal translation of each proverb has been
given, as this work is intended primarily for students of the
language. Some attempt has been made to group the
proverbs chosen from the original work (in which all are
alphabetically arranged) under the various heads, suggested
by the person, animal, object, custom, virtue, or vice, &c.,
round which the saying is woven.

The numbers given at *the end* of each proverb are those
under which they will be found in the original collection.

From the environment in which these proverbs were
first collected, one might suppose that they would not be
entirely free from missionary influence, hence the present
writer thinks that a few remarks concerning the people
whose sayings are here recorded seem somewhat necessary.
Of the 3,600 proverbs examined some few seem to bear
traces of European influence. All such have been omitted
from the present work. In translating such as are here
chosen, in no single case has reliance been placed on the
writer's own knowledge of the language alone.

Every saying has been verified and re-verified by actual inquiry among the Ashantis themselves. The result of these investigations has been peculiarly instructive. All the proverbs herein contained are household words among *the old people*, whereas to the younger rising generation of educated or semi-educated natives they are often unknown, and even when repeated to them, unintelligible in many instances. Further reliance, moreover, may be placed in them when it is remembered that this collection was gathered more than thirty years ago, at a time when education and European influence was not so widely felt as is the case now. Again, the field of inquiry wherein the present writer has sought for widespread verification of each and all of these sayings is not even that in which they were originally collected. The dense Ashanti forest north of Coomassie must have been a *terra incognita* to the white man in those days, and it is here the writer's lot is cast. It is difficult to realize that it is little more than a decade since the first European resident came to Coomassie. These people, the true Ashantis of the forest country, present the anthropologist with a peculiarly interesting and hitherto perhaps neglected task. The general idea would seem to be that this is a field of research that is so well trodden by alien feet as to offer little chance or opportunity of retracing thereon the tracks left by the original husbandmen. They have been described by Ellis, and Bowdich, and Cruikshank, some will say. They have been contaminated (for to the anthropologist all civilization affecting his 'pet' people or tribe is contamination) by centuries of civilization, French, Portuguese, Dutch, and English. But in arguing thus, are they not being confused in the popular mind with the natives of the Gold Coast, with whom, it is true, they are politically one? It is further contended that they must be very far removed from that pristine state which would entitle them to be called a 'primitive' or perhaps even a 'barbaric' people. A casual acquaintance with them, which is the most that a person can ever hope to have, who does not speak their tongue,

will show that they had a more or less elaborate and highly
developed system of government, that they were armed
with guns, and that they wore clothes. These indications
of European influence that have filtered through from the
Coast Belt proper, from which region, as already suggested,
Europe seems to have derived most of its ideas of the Gold
Coast native, are in reality little more than the thinnest of
thin veneer. Old and time immemorial customs and beliefs
lie here very close to the surface and even at times right on
the top. The investigator needs only to have that colloquial knowledge of the language which alone is the ' Open,
Sesame ' to the native heart and mind.

Mention has been made of the Ashanti forest ; this has
not only served these people as a natural stronghold against
their enemies (and incidentally perhaps given them a reputation as warriors which they might not otherwise have
gained) but has also reared itself as a barrier against
culture and influence from without. In remote forest
villages, where generation after generation must have
lived and died, and carried on custom and tradition from
some very distant period,[1] the faint echo of the outside
world is barely felt, or heard, or heeded. Moreover it must
always be remembered in dealing with signs of European
influence among the Ashantis that any such influence has
not, in the past, been acquired by direct contact with a race
that had settled and conquered among them (as is the
record of Coast civilization), but rather that the foreign
elements in their social system had been voluntarily adopted
by themselves as conquerors, rather than as conquered.
A few words may also be said about ' the high gods ' or God
of these people, the Ǫnyàmé, or Ńyankǒpǫ ṅ, that figures in
so many of the sayings which follow. That He is *not*
a product of missionary influence, as Ellis would have us
believe,[2] the present writer is absolutely convinced. The

---

[1] The writer has dug up neolithic axe-heads in and near many Ashanti
villages. Vide paper on the Ejura celts by Professor H. Balfour in
October 1912, *Journal of African Society.*

[2] Vide *The Tshi-Speaking Peoples of the Gold Coast,* chap. iii.

late Major Ellis, with all due acknowledgement to his great ability in this field of research had not, as far as can be judged from his writings, even a pretension to be an accomplished linguist in the Twi or Ashanti language, and must have relied for much of his information on his interpreters. Again, he was dealing with a people who had been under the influence of civilization for hundreds of years, and must have so continually been confronted with evidences of this contact that he would be perhaps all too ready to class as exotic the faintest suspicion of any similarity in the native customs and beliefs to those of the European with whom they had so long been in direct communion.

What the present writer has found to be the case with regard to most of these sayings, namely that they appear known to the *old* Ashanti men and women, and strange or unknown among the *young* and civilized community, he has also found to be the case with reference to all inquiries concerning their belief in a Supreme Being. The most (as one would suppose) bigoted and adverse to all Christian influence will be the fetish priests and the old people, who are content to live their lives in the remote ' bush ' villages, not mingling with, or caring about, the new world which is awaking for the younger generation ; but it is this very class, among whom the writer has many real friends, who are surprised if one questions their right to possess and have possessed their own High God; yet this belief in a Supreme Being marches side by side with that mode of thought in which mankind, the beasts, and, to their mind, *animate* nature, are all very much akin. That the present religion (using that word even in the wide sense of Taylor's ' minimum definition') of these people, which is known by that much misleading term ' fetish worship ', is a degenerate form of some much higher cult, perhaps even monotheistic, seems to be indicated.

These few words the present writer has felt in duty bound to say, lest the reader, astonished at the words of wisdom which are now to follow, refuse to credit that a ' savage ' or ' primitive ' people could possibly have possessed the rude philosophers, theologians, moralists, naturalists, and even, it will be seen, philologists, which many of these proverbs prove them to have had among them.

These sayings would seem to be, to the writer, the very soul of this people, as of a truth all such sayings really are. They contain some thought which, when one, more eloquent in the tribe than another, has expressed in words, all who are of that people recognize at once as something which *they* knew full well already, which all the instinct of their lives and thoughts and traditions tells them to be true to their own nature.

In most cases these sayings explain themselves. Perhaps one man will give one interpretation, one another, even in the same tribe. One of another race will almost certainly give yet a third; but, as the Ashantis themselves say, 'The traveller who returns from a journey may tell all he has seen, but he cannot explain all '.

The writer is much indebted to His Excellency Sir Hugh Clifford, K.C.M.G., Governor and Commander-in-Chief of the Gold Coast Colony, for his recommendation that a subvention should be granted to assist in the publication of the present work, and also for the kindly interest and encouragement which he has so courteously shown its compiler. This is the second occasion on which the Colonial Government has by most generous grants assisted in the publication of the writer's works, and he again has the honour to thank the head of that Government, the Secretary of State for the Colonies for his most generous recognition and encouragement of students of West African linguistics and folk-lore.

Grateful acknowledgements are also due to the Delegates of the Clarendon Press, who have once more laid its compiler under a deep obligation to them.

The writer's sincere thanks are given to Mr. A. C. Madan, Student of Christ Church, Oxford, who has undertaken the revision of all the proofs and has, in the absence of the writer in Africa, seen the work through the press. His thanks are also due to Mr. Samuel Kwafo of Mampon, West Africa, who has given him much help with regard to the language and customs of his people, the Ashantis.

R. S. R.

July 7, 1914.

CONTENTS

16 CONTENTS

CHAPTER I

1. *Asase terew, na Onyàmé ne panyin.* (2787)
Of all the wide earth, the Supreme Being is the elder.

Asase. Deriv. possibly *ase*, down, beneath, as opposed to *osoro*, above, the heavens (*asase* reduplication of *ase*). Here means the world, the earth, which is also expressed by *wiase = owia ase*, under the sun ; *owia* being again derived from root *wi*, seen in *wim' = wimu*, in the firmament.

Terew. May be either taken as an adjective, or, if the pronoun *e* is understood, as a verb, ' is wide '.

Na. This particle can often be rendered by the conjunction ' and ', but is often used to give emphasis to a word or clause.

Onyàmé. The late Major Ellis in his *The Tshi-Speaking Peoples of the Gold Coast of West Africa*, writes as follows : ' Within the last twenty or thirty years the German missionaries, sent out from time to time by the mission societies of Basel and Bremen, have made Nyankupon known to European ethnologists and students of the science of religion, but being unaware of the real origin of this god, they have generally written and spoken of him as a conception of the native mind, whereas he is really a god borrowed from Europeans and only thinly disguised. . . To the negro of the Gold Coast, Nyankupon is a material and tangible being, possessing legs, body, arms, in fact all the limits and the senses and faculties of man. . . For this reason no sacrifice was offered to him. . . There were no priests for Nyankupon . . . consequently no form of worship for Nyankupon was established. . . All the rites and practices peculiar to the worship of each deity had the sanction of years of tradition and custom, and it could not be expected that the people would be able to initiate new rites for a new deity. . . There were no priests for Nyankupon. . .'

Though perhaps scarcely within the scope of the present work,

1698   B

the writer can hardly allow these statements to remain unchallenged, as careful research has seemed to him so totally to disprove them. Now the first credentials the present writer would ask of any one who was advancing an opinion, as the result of independent research into native customs and beliefs such as this, would be the state of proficiency that the investigator had acquired in the language of the people whose religion and beliefs he was attempting to reveal.

The standard he would ask would be a high one. Had the investigator real colloquial knowledge of the language of the people whose inner soul he was endeavouring to lay bare ? Such a knowledge as is gained only after years of arduous study and close intercourse, a knowledge that will enable the possessor to exchange jokes and quips and current slang, and to join in a discourse in which some dozen voices are all yelling at once. Such a knowledge of a language is a very different thing from an academic acquaintance with it, which might fit the possessor to write an excellent grammar, dictionary, or some such treatise.

Judged by such a standard the late Major Ellis must have been found wanting.

Perhaps the person most nearly approaching to this standard was one of those very 'German Missionaries' whose evidence is so lightly brushed aside, the late Rev. J. G. Christaller. This missionary pioneer, to judge from his works and local reputation, must have possessed a knowledge of this language and an insight into the minds of the Twi or Ashanti people that has possibly never been surpassed.

Evidence from missionary sources is, however, rather unfairly, the present writer thinks, somewhat discounted, at any rate where questions of religion are at issue. Such being the case the following brief notes, coming from one who has for several years studied this language and people, and who perhaps holds that the unseen and unknown are unknown and unknowable, may be worthy of some little attention as likely to be an unbiased report.

The following titles are used by the Ashantis to designate some power generally considered non-anthropomorphic, which has its abode in the sky (which by metonymy is sometimes called after it).

The derivations given are those generally assigned by the natives themselves, but these cannot be absolutely guaranteed, as the correct ones. While entirely disagreeing with the theory

that this 'High God' is the product of European (i.e. Dutch,
Portuguese, or English) influence *from the South, i.e. the Coast*, it is
of course possible that it may trace its origin from a much remoter
age and a wholly different influence. The Ashantis who came
from the North, may have been influenced by the teachings of
Mohammedans and this 'Supreme Being', Onyankŏpoṅ, Onyàmé,
or whatever title he be known by, be not 'the thinly disguised'
Jehovah of the Christians, but the Allah (which name was itself
that of a famous 'fetish') of the Mohammedans. But even this
extension of some hundreds of years to the life of this 'High God'
would hardly, in the writer's opinion, give him time to have
become such a deeply-rooted part, the very centre in fact, of the
religion of the Ashantis.

The names then of this High God, Supreme Being, God, Creator,
or whatever title we choose to assign to him, are :

1. *Onyàmé.* Deriv. given by natives, *onyã*, to get, and *mĕ*, to be
full, satiated, (by metonymy the sky, which is looked on as his abode).

2. *Onyankŏpoṅ.* The derivation of this word as *Onyàmé-nkŏ-poṅ*
(Onyàmé, alone, great one) seems borne out by noting the word
in the Akyem dialect, where it is *Onyan-koro-poṅ*, (Onyàmé, one,
great).

3. *Tweaduampoṅ.* The derivation of this is almost certainly
twere-dua-ampoṅ (lean on a tree and not fall).

4. *Boṛe-Boṛe.* Derivation *bọ ade, bọ ade* (make things, make
things), Creator.

5. *Otumfo.* *Tumi*, power, to be able, and *fo* the personal suffix.

6. *Onyankŏpoṅ Kwame.* That Onyankŏpoṅ who was born on
Saturday, or came into existence on a Saturday.

7. *Odŏmaṅkŏmã.* Deriv. unknown, but the word is used somewhat as the equivalent of 'inventor'.

8. *Ananse kokŏrko.* The Great Spider, see note on No. 175 on
ananse.

In Ashanti, in remote bush villages, buried away in the im-
penetrable forest, and as yet even untouched by European and
missionary influence, it would seem incredible that the Christian
idea of a one and Supreme Being should, if a foreign element of
only some two or three hundred years' growth, have taken such
deep root as to affect their folk-lore, traditions, customs, and the
very sayings and proverbs with which their language abounds.
These proverbs and traditions, moreover, which speak of and contain

references to a Supreme Being, are far more commonly known among the greybeards, elders, and the fetish priestly class themselves than among the rising younger generation, grown up among new influences and often trained in the very precincts of a mission. Fetishism and monotheism would at first sight appear the very antithesis of each other, but a careful investigation of facts will show that here in Ashanti it is not so.

The religion of these people has been shrouded in misunderstanding and obscurity, much of which has been caused no doubt by the name with which it has been stamped and branded, 'fetishism' (Portuguese *feitiço*, French *fétiche*, from Latin *facere*). This name conjures up a picture of the worship of stocks and stones and hideous idols, yet minute inquiry will serve to show that the underlying idea in these is almost monotheistic in its conception (see notes on No. 17, under *ǫbosom*). It may even have once been entirely so, if any reliance can be placed on the following myth which is universally known among the older people.

Yeṅ tete abere so no Onyankŏpǫṅ wǫ fam anase ǫbɛn yeṅ korā. Sā bere no nso aberewa bi rɛwǫ fufūo na woma a ǫde rewǫ no kopem Onyankŏpǫṅ. Na Onyankŏpǫṅ kā kyerɛ aberewa no sɛ́, 'Adenti na woreyɛ me sā yi? Senea wayɛ nti mɛtǐbɛ̆ makǫ soro', na ampa ara Onyankŏpǫṅ. T'ǐbɛ̆ kǫ soro.

'Long, long ago Onyankŏpǫṅ lived on earth, or at least was very near to us. Now there was a certain old woman who used to pound her *fufu* (mashed yams, &c.) and the pestle (lit. the child of the mortar, as the Ashanti word means) used to constantly knock up against Onyankŏpǫń (who was not then high up in the sky). So Onyankŏpǫṅ said to the old woman, "Why do you always do so to me? Because of what you are doing I am going to take myself away up in the sky". And of a truth he did so.' (Lit. translation of above.)

The myth goes on to relate how the people tried to follow him and bring him back.

Na afei, a nnipa ntumi mmeṅ Onyankŏpǫṅ bio, aberewa no kā kyerɛɛ ne mmanom ṅhīnā sɛ́ mǒṅfǐbefǐbe ṅwaduru pĩ mera na momfa ntoatoa so ṅkǫ soro nkosi sɛ ɛbɛto Onyankŏpǫṅ.

Na ampa ara ne mmanom no yɛɛ no sā, na wǫde awaduru pĩ toatoa so, a ekaa bākǒ pɛ na adu Onyankŏpǫṅ ; na nso bākǒ a aka no, wonnyā bi nti, wǫṅ nana no, anase aberewa no, kā kyerɛɛ ne mma no sɛ, 'Monyi nea ɛwǫ ase no, na momfa ṅkǫkyɛ soro de no mā ennu'. Na nɛ mma no yii ǫwaduru no pɛ na ṅhĩnā perɛw guu fam, a ekŭm nɯ̃ipa pi.

'But now, since people could no longer approach near to Onyankŏpǫṅ, that old woman told all her children to search for all the mortars they could find and bring them, and pile one on top of another, till they reached to where Onyankŏpǫṅ was. And so her children did so, and piled up many mortars, one on top of another, till there remained but one to reach to Onyankŏpǫṅ. Now, since they could not get the one required anywhere, their grandmother, that is the old woman, told her children, saying, "Take one out from the bottom and put it on top to make them reach". So her children removed a single one, and all rolled and fell to the ground, causing the death of many people.' / (Many other legends could be given, and the writer hopes to give a selection in some future work on the folk-lore of these people, the present volume being hardly the place for them.)

To say, as the paragraph already quoted does, 'that there were no priests for Onyankŏpǫṅ . . . consequently no form of worship was established . . no sacrifice was offered him', would seem to point to the fact that the writer must have been unaware of the very root idea underlying the supposed power of, and the rites performed in propitiation of, every fetish or minor deity. So closely connected are the two, a Supreme Being on the one hand, and the cult of the hundreds of fetishes and minor deities on the other, right down to the *suman* (see note on No. 17, *ǫbosom*) in its lowest form, where it becomes the charm or talisman, that it is necessary to repeat here, in writing of Onyankŏpǫṅ, much that is written later under the heading of 'fetish'. The connexion between a Supreme Being and a hideous blood-smeared idol or basin of bones, blood, and fowls' feathers seems remote, but they are really very near akin. Ask any fetish priest, whom you have persuaded to allow you to visit the *body* of the particular spirit, i. e. fetish, of whom he is the custodian (the *body*, mark you, for what *you* see as a wooden image or a mound of mud daubed with blood is exactly such *to the fetish priest*, save perhaps for the added awe or sanctity as having been in the past and being the possible future, *not* necessarily present, abode of a spirit),—ask him what his fetish really is, and whence it came, and from what source comes its power. And this is what he will tell you.

His *ǫbosom*, or it may be *suman* (see note on *ǫbosom*, No. 17),

let us suppose for the sake of example, is a newly-captured deity,
(the number of fetishes are probably being added to daily). He will
tell you how it was sent by Onyankŏpǫṅ or Ǫnyàmé in a blinding
flash of lightning, how he caught it and shut it in a gourd till
he had prepared an acceptable dwelling for it, and let it get used
to its new surroundings (just as one keeps a dog chained up
perhaps for a day or so when taken away from his master, to a new
home). If you ask what the 'it' is he captured, he cannot tell,
but will probably say vaguely ' *Onyankŏpǫṅ tumi* ', or ' *hǫnhǫn* ',
that is, ' the power, spirit, or *mana* of Onyankŏpǫṅ '. And this is
the supposed origin of every fetish; they come from, and have their
power only as part of the power ascribed to, Onyankŏpǫṅ. He is too
remote and too powerful to directly have dealings with mankind,
but he distributes for their benefit a little of his power, and this
spirit or *mana* or power is what is called down by servants specially
trained to know its needs and tastes, and having found a faithful
priest, and a temporary dwelling on earth, consents at times to live
there, and be the intermediary between man and the Supreme Being,
from whom it comes and of whom it is a part. This is what a fetish
really is. It must be clearly understood, however, that the attributes
we ascribe to God are wanting entirely from the native conception
of Ǫnyàmé; he cares nothing for morals, and there is no sign that
any retribution follows for a good or misspent life, though the
departed spirits of persons who have lived on earth would seem to
return to Onyankŏpǫṅ to render some account before being allowed
to enter the spirit world below, *asamaṅ* (see No. 34, *ǫsamaṅ*).
Hence the expression *waye̩ Onyankŏpǫṅ de*, he or she has become
Onyankŏpǫṅ's, never *ǫbosom de* which would have no meaning to
the native mind.

It is thus seen that, *indirectly*, every fetish priest is a priest of
Onyankŏpǫṅ; but *direct* service is also rendered. In every village
in Ashanti may be seen a tree or stick terminating in three forks,
which form a stand on which a pot or gourd is set. The name of
this stick is *Ǫnyàmé dua*, Ǫnyàmé's tree. In the pot, dish, or
gourd, are placed offerings for Ǫnyàmé. Again, a fetish priest will
not infrequently appeal directly to Ǫnyàmé to give increased
power to his fetish. The very name for a fetish, one that is often
given, would also seem to prove its origin, *Onyankŏpǫṅ ǫkyeame*,
the mouthpiece of Onyankŏpǫṅ (see note on No. 481, *ǫmãmpám*).

On the occasion of the installation of a new chief, a ceremony

not likely to be readily influenced or changed because of contact
with European influence, one part of the ceremonial consists in all
the women and girls of the new chief's family parading the town or
village and singing:

'*Oseee / yei !*'

'*Yei !*'

'*Tweaduampon e e e*'

'*Yedase ō !*'

'*Amen*'.

Oseee, (*bɔ ose*) is to 'shout'. Hence perhaps we can translate thus:

'Hurrah, yei!'

'Yei!'

'Supreme Being e e e!'

'We thank you (lit. We lie down at your feet. See note on
No. 712).

'You who appeared on a Saturday.'

One can readily imagine the casual student discarding the above
with scorn on coming to the last word '*amen*' which, were he not
well versed in the Ashanti language, he would be excused in
thinking to be the Heb. *āmĕn*, and the whole song would at once
become stamped as having a Christian origin.

Amen, or *Awene*, is, however, pure Akuapem and Ashanti, and is
derived from *Memeneda*, Saturday, and refers to the belief that
Onyankŏpɔn came into existence on that day. Again, every
Ashanti man and woman knows that he or she has a direct appeal
to Onyankŏpɔn, not necessarily through the fetish priest, as would
be the procedure were the fetish being appealed to. This is a well-
known saying, *Obi kwan nsi* (or *ntwa*) *obi kwan mu*, 'No man's
path crosses another man's path', and here, although there is no
direct mention of the Supreme Being, the universal interpretation
of the saying given is, that 'every one has a direct appeal to
Onyankŏpɔn'. See also note on *twa*, No. 507, where the fact that
the name of the Supreme Being is among the words used by the
drummers is noted.

Ne. This particle or verb seems to give to the noun in apposition with its subject a certain definiteness which almost
supplies the want of the English definite article (not found in the
Ashanti language). *Onyàmê ne panyin*, The Supreme Being is
the elder, not *an* elder, which would be expressed by the verb *ye*.

Panyin. Deriv. *nyin*, to grow up (the word used for 'to reach puberty'), and *apǎ*, old, long lived. The word is used in various senses, e. g. one who is full of the wisdom of years of experience, and as a term of respect. The Chief Commissioner is the *Oboroni Panyiǹ*.

2. *Wope akǎ asem akyere Onyankŏpoǹ a, kǎ kyere mframa.* (2656)
   If you wish to tell anything to the Supreme Being, tell it to the winds.

   Wope. *Pe*, to wish or to want. This verb is either followed by the subjunctive as here, *akǎ*, *akyere*, or by the conjunction *se*, and the verb preceded by the pronoun.
   Onyaǹkŏpoǹ. See note on *Onyàmé* above, No. 1.
   Mframa. Deriv. perhaps *fra*, to mix, to stir up.

3. *Obi ǹkyere abofra onyàmé.* (227)
   No one shows a child the sky.

   Onyàmé. Here the sky, the abode of the Supreme Being. Little children who lie sprawling on their backs looking up to the sky do not need to have it pointed out to them, for they see it better than their elders. There is a rendering of this saying which one might be tempted to read into it, and which it may even possess, but as all the greybeards the writer has questioned do not see it in that light attention is merely directed to it, this is, 'No one shows a child (points out) the Supreme Being, instinct tells him He exists' (but cf. No. 7).

4. *Obi ǹkyere otomfo ba atono ; onim atono a, Onyàmé na okyeree no.* (234)
   No one instructs the son of a smith how to forge ; if he knows how to forge, it is the Supreme Being taught him.

   Otomfo. A smith's anvil and tools are supposed to possess some peculiar power, and a smith's family will take an oath on them, and fowls are also killed and the blood sprinkled on the anvil. For suffix *fo*, see note on No. 78, *kontromfi*.
   Na. See note above on No. 1, *na*.
   Okyeree. Past tense, seen in the lengthening of final vowel.

5. *Onyankŏpoǹ ammǎ asonomjŏa katakyi biribi a, omǎǎ no ahŏdannaǹ.* (2547)
   If the Supreme Being gave the swallow nothing else, He gave it swiftness in turning.

Asonomfõa. Also *asõmfõnã. Katakyi*, a bold or brave person; here a nick-name for the swallow.

Omãã. Past tense. *Ammã* is perfect.

Ahõdannaṅ. Deriv. *hõ*, and *dannaṅ*, reduplication of *daṅ*, lit. self-turning.

6. *Osansa se, 'Ade a Onyàmê aye ṅhĩna ye'.* (2777)
The hawk (poised aloft) says, 'All things that the Supreme Being made are beautiful (good)'.

Aye. Perfect tense.

7. *Me a meda ayannya miṅhũ Onyankõpoṅ, na wo a wubutuw ho!* (2023)
I, who lie on my back looking upwards, do not see the Supreme Being, so what do you expect who are sprawling there on your belly!

Cf. No. 3, but in this case the Supreme Being is distinctly named and meant and not his abode, the sky, as in the other saying.

Ayannya. Deriv. *yam*, the belly, and *agya*, the side opposite, i.e. the back.

8. *Onyankõpoṅ mpe asemmone, nti na okye diṅ mmiakõ-mmiakõ.* (2548)
Because the Supreme Being did not wish any bad words, He gave a name to each thing, one by one.

Asemmone. Asem-bone, the *b* is elided and the consonant doubled. *Nti = eno nti.*

See the myth under note on *kontromfĩ*, No. 78.

9. *Onyàmê ṅkrabea nni kwatibea.* (2538)
The destiny the Supreme Being has assigned to you cannot be avoided.

Nkrabea. Deriv. *okra*, soul, and *bea*, place or manner; hence, destiny. The present writer has not seen it mentioned in the works of any previous writers on the natives of the Gold Coast that these natives, the Ashantis, are just as much believers in Kismet as a Mohammedan. The following seems the idea generally held. Each human being's destiny is preordained and the spirit sets out to enter its mother's womb already knowing its destiny. This has been given it by Onyankõpoṅ, as the legend given later shows, and is known to no one else, though it may perhaps be

ascertained by consulting the fetish priest. ' The word *ǫkra* may
be the same root as *kra*, to bid good-bye to. There is a well-known
saying, *Wokra Onyankǫpǫṅ a, obi nnyina hǫ*, ' When you take leave
of the Supreme Being, no one stands by '. Where exactly this *ǫkra*
or soul comes from, when about to be *reborn* (for the idea of
reincarnation is widely known and believed), is not quite clear.
It would seem, however, to have come from *asamaṅ*, the spirit world,
a replica *below* the earth of the world we now live in (see note
on No. 34 under *ǫsamaṅ*). The reincarnated soul then takes its
way to this world with its destiny already arranged. It is thought
possible, however, for a man's destined hour of death to be cut short
by an accident, which somewhat contradictory idea of the original
Kismet is, however, modified by the prevalent idea that any one who
has thus been taken off before his appointed hour will not be
received back again either into the *asamaṅ*, or underworld, or by
Onyankǫpǫṅ, to whom the *ǫkra* may perhaps first have to pass.
Hence the saying: *Ǫnyàmé ayi no, asamaṅfo ayi no*, 'The Supreme
Being has driven him out, the spirit folk have driven him out '.
This is said of a ghost which is constantly being seen. Such a ghost
will eventually, after its destined time on earth has run, disappear,
having gone to the world of the spirits, and such a ghost is not
quite the same as *ǫsamaṅ-tweṅ-tweṅ* (q. v. No. 34, *ǫsamaṅ*). There
seems a distinct difference between the *ǫkra* and the *ǫsamaṅ*.
The latter can correctly be described by the word ghost or spirit.
As long as a man is alive, his *ǫkra* and how it is regarded is more
or less clearly defined, but what exactly becomes of it after death
according to the native idea cannot be clearly traced. There is
nothing, let it be clearly understood, of spiritual or moral well-
being attached to it. It is rather the bearer of luck, good or bad
(see note on soul washing, No. 147, *nni asumguarede*).

This word *ǫkra* is also a common name for the cat (see note on
No. 122, *agyiṅamoa*) and also means a slave destined to be buried
with his master at death, which word and signification perhaps helps
to throw some light on its meaning.

The legend about destiny referred to above is as follows.
Onyankǫpǫṅ gave a soul which was setting out for earth two
bundles, a large and a slightly smaller one. The soul was told to
hand over one of the parcels, the larger, to another soul which it
would find on reaching the earth. The soul to whom these destiny
parcels were given changed them, taking as its own the one it had

been ordered to give up to another. On coming to the world the soul, now an incarnated one, found its parcel contained only rubbish, whereas the one (the wrong one) it had handed over to the other soul, contained nuggets and gold dust. In other words, the destiny of one was poverty, while the other was born a rich man. Nor does the story end here, for when the person died and returned to *Onyankŏpon* and complained of the fate that had been assigned to it in life, *Onyankŏpon* blamed it for having changed these destinies, its own and that of another entrusted to it. This myth is of value as showing that the *okra* is supposed to come from *Onyankŏpon* before the person is born and returns to him after death.

Nni. Neg. of *wo*.

Kwaribea. *Kwati*, to do without, to avoid, and *bea*.

10. *Asęm a Onyămê adi asie no, ǫteasefo nnaṅ no.* (2855)
The fate (lit. words) that the Supreme Being has beforehand ordained, a human being does not alter.

Adi asie. *Di asęm sie*, is 'to speak words beforehand'. Note this idiomatic use of *sie*, to prepare, to express the idea of a thing being done in readiness or beforehand.

Ǫteasefo. A person, lit. one who lives down, i. e. on earth.

11. *Onyankŏpon ṅkum wo na ǫdasăni (ǫteasefo) kum wo, wuṅwu.* (2546)
If the Supreme Being does not kill you but a human being kills you, you do not die.

The idea underlying this saying is perhaps explained by the belief noted above (No. 9), that should a person meet his death before the time prearranged for him his spirit continues to haunt this world till his allotted span is full, after which it has permission to depart to the spirit world. Again, it may simply mean to exemplify the impossibility of a man avoiding his destiny; and 'but a human being kills you' may mean 'tries to kill you', when he fails to be able to do so, as Onyankŏpon had not yet ordained it.

12. *Onyankŏpon hyę wo nsă kora mă na ǫteasefo kā gu a, ohyia wo so bio.* (2545)
When the Supreme Being fills your gourd cup full of wine and a human being (comes and) pours it away, He will fill it up again for you.

13. *Ǫnyàmé mã wo yare a, omã wo aduru.* (2540)

If the Supreme Being gives you sickness, He (also) gives you medicine.

Aduru. Perhaps from root *dua*, a tree, herb, leaf, medicine good or bad (poison). *Tǒ aduru*, to poison. *Atuduru = atuo-aduru*, i. e. gun medicine, gunpowder.

14. *Ǫnyàmé na ǫwǫ basiṅ fufu mã no.* (2541)

It is the Supreme Being who pounds the *fufu* for the one without arms.

Na. Here emphatic, see note on No. 1.

Ǫwǫ. *Wǫ* or *wǫw*, to pound in a mortar (*ǫwǫaduru*) with a pestle (*ǫwǫmma = ǫwǫ ba*, 'child of the pounding').

Basiṅ. Deriv. *basa*, arm, and *siṅ*, a fragment or part of anything.

Fufu. Deriv. *fu*, white. *Fufu* is the staple food of the Ashantis (the *nsima* of the Mañanja), yam or plantain pounded (first boiled), rolled into balls, and eaten with relish, meat or fish.

Mã. Translated by the preposition ' for ', but really a verb, ' to give '. The language is entirely lacking in prepositions, the place of which are taken by verbs.

15. *Nnipa ñhīnã yę Ǫnyàmé mma, obi nyę asase ba.* (2436)

All men are the children of the Supreme Being, no one is a child of the earth.

16. *Ǫdǒmaṅkǒmã bǫ owu mã owu kum no.* (964)

The Creator created death (only) for death to kill Him.

Ǫdǒmaṅkǒmã. See note on No. 1, *Ǫnyàmé.*

Owu. Death is personified among the Ashantis as a skeleton, a skull with empty eye-sockets *but having ears attached.* (Hence attempts to bluff death as exemplified in Proverbs Nos. 59 and 60.)

This saying illustrates in a wonderfully epigrammatic manner the power of death.

17. *Ǫbosom a onnii guaṅ da, ohũ guaṅ aniwam' mpĕ a, ose, ' Ęyę srade'.* (615)

The fetish that has never had a sheep given to it, when it sees even the matter in the corner of a sheep's eye, says ' It *is* a fat one '.

Ǫbosom. Commonly called a 'fetish ' (Portuguese *feitiço*, French

fétiche, both from Latin *facere*, as already noted, p. 20).
derivation is very doubtful, a possible one being *ǫbo*, a rock
stone, and *som*, to serve.

The word is generally applied by Europeans to the habitation
of the 'fetish' This may be anything from a wooden idol to
a mountain or a river. A 'fetish' is a spirit or 'power' (*tūmi*)
which has its origin from Onyankŏpǫṅ (see note on No. 1, *Ǫnyàmé*).
Fetishes are of various degrees of importance, some of merely local
repute, others e. g. *Tannǫ* (q. v. No. 55) and *Krakye Dente* (see No.
73), widely known. Famous 'fetishes', such as these two named,
may have branch abodes in many villages, the priests of which are
subservient to the high priest at the head-quarters of that particular
cult. A fetish is not necessarily always occupying the abode,
natural or artificial, which it is supposed to favour as its habitation.
It only comes and enters that abode when called by the priest,
by the tinkling of bells and by his gyrations in the ceremonial
dance. When thus summoned it will temporarily occupy the body
prepared and made acceptable for it. It may even come and rest
there of its own accord, but for all intents and purposes a fetish
image, or rock, or tree, is nothing but an image, rock, or tree, till
the priest, who is *en rapport* with the power or spirit which is
known to have adopted one of these places as its abode, calls on
it to come and enter it. Thus a 'fetish' cannot be stolen or die.
An *ǫdum* tree may fall down which was sacred as the known abode
of this power. When that happens all it means is that the spirit
or power will go elsewhere. So in war, if a fetish *body* (abode) is
captured, that does not mean the fetish is captured. It is temporarily lost, no doubt, but its own priests may be able to make an
acceptable home for it once more.

It must be clearly understood that a 'fetish' is not a spirit of
one who has died, and their cult must not be confused with a form
of manes-worship or propitiation which also exists. The writer
only knows of one case where confusion might arise, where the
spirit of a dead man is supposed to have entered a tree. At
Abeane, in Kwau, the spirit of a chief, Mampon Adai, who is said
not to have died, but simply to have disappeared, 'entered a tree'
which for long after had offerings placed near it. In almost every
case, however, where similar offerings are placed at the foot of
a tree, one would be correct in supposing it was for a 'fetish' and
not for a spirit of one departed this life, nor has the writer found

any trace of a preanimistic conception or animatism. } (Spirits of the dead are of course summoned and propitiated; see notes on No. 35, *osaman*, and No. 388, *akonnua*.)

It has been noted that some ' fetishes ', owing to the greater ability of their priests, no doubt, take precedence over others. There would also appear to be a lower grade, with more local, family, or even individual interests, which are known as *suman*. A *suman* may mean anything from a power, having as its abode some image,—undistinguishable often from that occupied by a fetish—to a little charm bound on ankle or wrist to bring luck to the wearer alone. A *suman* would seem to derive its power from the *abosom*, just as the *obosom* in turn gains its own from *Onyanköpon*. Thus we have the whole code of belief of these natives summed up as follows :

1. *Onyàmé*. A Supreme Being (see No. 1).
2. *Abosom*. ' Fetishes ', i. e. spirit, power, *mana* from or of the Supreme Being.
3. *Suman*. Minor deities, deriving their power from the *abosom*.
4. *Suman*. Amulets or charms, a lower grade of the above (3).
5. *Asaman*. A spirit world, inhabited by *asamanfo* spirits (see note on No. 34, *osaman*).
6. *Bayifo*. Witches and wizards, human vampires (see No. 56).
7. *Bonsam*. Monsters, half human, half devil (see note on No. 56, *sasabonsám*).

'Fetishes' are literally, 'in thousands', as witness the common toast or incantation as the Ashanti man pours out a few drops of wine,—*Abosonpem monsá*, ' Thousand fetishes, your wine '.

The writer will only name a few that are served in his own district.

Many are followers of *Tanno* and *Krakye Dente*, *Mpra*, *Apeã*, *Botoku*, *Ateko*, *Tanno-Konkroma* (a conjunction of two fetishes), *Kompi*, *Obofiri*.

The local fetish at Ejura (Edwira, a plant, as the name really should be spelled), besides a branch of *Dente*, is *Tanno Konkroma*.

There is also (at Ejura) a belief that the spirit of a former chief at Ejura entered a large bull elephant which still haunts the neighbourhood, and is known by having within the imprint of one of its feet the imprint also of the foot of a man. This shows that

belief in transmigration is not unknown, though this is the only
case met with by the writer.

Onnii. Neg. of *wọ.* Note form of past tense, made by lengthening of final vowel.

Guaṅ. A generic term, embracing sheep and goats. When either
is especially meant to be designated, then the words *oguanteṅ* and
abirekyi are respectively used.

18. *Ọbosom a ọ'yẹ nnam na odi aboadé.* (616)
The fetish that is sharp (clever at predicting events) is the one
that has offerings vowed to it. ·

Na. Emphatic (see note on No. 1).

Aboade. It is a common practice among these natives to vow
offerings to their particular fetish or tutelary deity in the event of
the requests which they make to it and promises given by it being
fulfilled.

19. *Ọbosom Kye-ẹ́ nantwi, wọmfá mfa abọnteṅ, wọmfa mfa afikyiri, nso
    ẹwọ nes wọdé fá.* (617)
The fetish Kyere's cow is not taken down the street, and is not led
behind the town, nevertheless a way is found to take it.

Wọmfa mfa. The first verb is the auxiliary and the equivalent
of *de* (in a positive sentence), the second *fa* is the finite verb. Note
the *de* in *wọde*, where the sentence is positive.

20. *Ọbosom anim, wọkọ no mperẹnsã.* (618)
One goes before a fetish as often as one likes.

Anim. Cf. *so* in the proverb following. *Anim*, here means to
go before the fetish, *of one's own accord* to consult it; *so*, implies
that the power of the fetish is invoked *on* or *against* the
person.

Wọkọ no. Note the verb *kọ* itself contains the idea of the preposition that has in English to be expressed by, to.

Mperẹnsã. Li . three times, see note on No. 767.

21. *Ọbosom so, yẹṅkọ no mperẹnsã.* (619)
One is not taken before a fetish a great number of times.

So. See note above on *anim*, No. 20.

The meaning is, that the fetish will sooner or later kill the
person who is continually being brought up before it.

22. *Abosom na ɛ̱kyerɛ̱ akomfo̱ ntibahŏ.* (620)

It is the fetishes who show the fetish priests how to turn when dancing.

Na. Emphatic particle, see note on No. 1.

Akomfo̱. *Okomfo̱* plur. *akomfo* ; feminine, *okomfo̱ bā.* More or less synonymous terms are *o̱sofo, o̱bosomfo.*

Okomfo̱ is derived from *kom,* to prophesy, to predict, (also to dance). The *okomfo* is the priest to a ' fetish ', he tends *its abode* and smears it with eggs and blood, to render it acceptable to the spirit, power, or *mana, when it may be called on to come and occupy the receptacle prepared for it.*

The bowl, idol, pot, stone, &c., which the fetish may be called to enter *is an empty nothing* till the fetish priest summons the fetish to enter it. This he does by tinkling a bell, drumming, and, most important of all, by dancing. He will know when the spirit (not that of any man or woman of course) has taken up its abode in the body provided for it by being seized with tremblings and shakings.]

When this happens, he knows that the fetish has come, and is temporarily inhabiting the object which has been prepared for it. The *okomfo* then addresses the spirit and gives its answers to those who have come to consult it. The *akomfo* are very frequently women. A period of training, from two to three years, has to be undergone before a man or woman can become a custodian of a fetish. The office is not by any means a sinecure, and unpleasant results may follow for the priest or priestess should their interpretation of the fetish's words prove false.

In the writer's own district the memory is still fresh of a number of priests who were taken to see a certain chief, (the uncle of the present Sub-chief Kobina Gyimma), Atakora Kwaku, by name, and were asked to predict if he would recover from an illness he had been suffering from. Atakora Kwaku was really dead already when the priests were led in one by one and asked what must be done to cure him. They, in turn, recommended various things, till the turn of a priestess of the fetish *Nkwafea Tannọ* came, who, on being consulted, said nothing could be done as the man was already dead. She thereby acquired great celebrity, while her confrères, who did not escape in time, were all promptly put to death.

Besides tending the fetish and his local habitation and interpreting his words, the fetish priest uses and consults lots (see note on *aka*, No. 55).

Dancing is a marked feature of the cult of all fetishes. The terms *osofo* and *obosomfo*, already referred to, appear to have a slightly different signification. While the *okomfo* not only tends the bodily and spiritual welfare of his particular spirit, but also dances, and interprets its utterances, the *osofo* or *obosomfo* would seem to confine himself more to tending the fetish than to dances or prophecies. Fetish men frequently attain great power and influence, and may even come to occupy important stools, e.g. that of Aguna is to-day held by a fetish priest, or priestly king. (For notes on fetishes see No. 55, *Tanno*, and No. 73, *Krakye Dente*.)

Ekyerè. Note the idiomatic use of the third singular neuter pronoun *e* for the third plural personal *wo*.

23. *Obosomaketere hye ohye a, ohye.* (621)
If the fetish lizard (chameleon) is predestined to be burned, it will be burned.

Obosomakstere. Lit. the fetish lizard, the chameleon, why so called cannot be ascertained. It is worthy perhaps of note that in Mananja folk-lore the *tonkwe-tonkwe*, or *nadzekambe*, i. e. chameleon, enters into one of their religious myths, and would also seem among the Ashantis, judging from its name, to have some similar connexion, though why or in what respect the writer has been unable to trace.

The above saying is one of those to show the unalterable decree of destiny. Cf. Nos. 9, 11, 12.

Hye ohye. The first verb is *hye*, to appoint, to fix, (*hye da*); the second is the verb *hye*, to burn.

24. *Obosomfo kā ne nkŏnim, na onkā ne nkŏgu.* (624)
The fetish priest tells of his victories, but not of his defeats.

(That is, boasts of his successful prophecies, but says nothing about the unfulfilled ones.)

Obosomfo. Better in regard to context *okomfo*, q.v. No. 22.
Nkŏnim, . . . nkŏgu. Deriv. *kŏ*, to fight, and *nim*, success; *gu*, to scatter, disperse.

25. *Eto sikyi ō, eto mfuaté ō, yenyā okomfo kum no.* (3285)
Whether the die falls *sikyi* or whether it falls *mfuaté*, we are going to kill the fetish priest.

C

Sikyi, mfuaté. A wooden or bone die used for consulting lots. Two opposite sides are called *sikyi* and *mfuaté*, the other two, *korosā*, marked with three cross lines ▢▢▢▢ , and *korosā anan*, with four cross lines ▢▢▢▢ . *Mfuaté* is marked with a diagonal line ▱ , *sikyi* is plain ▭ . The ends have no name and no mark.

The saying, besides exemplifying the rather precarious nature of an *okǫmfo*'s work (see note on *okǫmfo*, No. 22), is used to denote something to which there is little or no alternative.

26. *Owu de ne pasüa fa ofi mu a, ǫbosomfo aduru dań nsu.* (3482)
When death encamps over against a household, the medicine of the fetish priest turns to water.

Owu. Death personified (see note on No. 16, *owu*).
Aduru. See note on No. 13, *aduru*.
Nsu. Note, *nsu*, water; *osu*, rain; *asu*, a stream or river, or pool.

27. *Ǫkǫmfo nni ńkǫntŏro na wontība ǫbosonsoafo ti.* (1697)
When the fetish priest has given a false prophecy, the fetish carrier's head is not cut off.

Nni. Imperative (?) of *di*; lit. let him lie (?).
Ńkǫntŏro. *A kǫm*, and *atŏro*, lying prophecy.
Ǫbosonsoafo. The fetish carrier is a separate person from the fetish priest. For etymology (according to Ashantis) of suffix *fo*, see note on No. 78, *kontromfī*.

28. *Akǫmfo aduasā fũę ǫyarefo a, wodi atoro.* (1699)
When thirty fetish priests are looking after a sick man, (some of them) are lying.

Aduasā. See note on No. 767.

29. *Sika nti, na ǫkǫmfo mene agyan.* (2949)
For the sake of gold dust, the fetish priest swallows an arrow.

Agyan. Bows and arrows, except as children's toys, are now unknown amoñg the Ashantis, though from various survivals, as this saying for instance, it would seem they were formerly their arms. (See also note on No. 522, *tafoni.*)
A variation of the above runs, *Sika . . . de ne ti pem dań*, i. e. 'knocks his head against a house'. These sayings show that the *akǫmfo* also combine with their other duties the art of jugglery and self-inflicted punishment. Cf. the Indian fakir.

30. *Obi ṅkyerẹ ọkọmfo ba akọm.* (229)

No one shows the child of a fetish priest how to dance.

Kọm. The connexion between certain ceremonial dances and religion is here clearly seen; the word for 'to prophesy' and 'to dance' (only in connexion with a fetish ceremony, the word on an ordinary occasion being *saw*), being synonymous. Cf. the Mananja question to the stranger whose totem class one wishes to ascertain, *Wo bvina nji ?* What do you dance ?'

31. *Akoko wọ ṅkwa adurŭ a, aṅkā yẹde no tŭba abosom soọ ?* (1661)

If a fowl possessed life-giving medicine, would it be taken and sacrificed over fetishes ?

Yẹde = Wọde.

Tŭba abosəm soọ. Fowls are commonly sacrificed over the images, &c., &c., in which the fetishes are, as occasion requires, summoned to come and take their temporary abode.

32. *Adurŭ a ẹfĭ kọmfo nsam' ṅhĭnā yẹ aduru-pa.* (1044)

All the medicine (charms) that come from the hands of the fetish priest are good (real) charms.

Aduru. Here perhaps rather used as *suman* (q.v. No. 17).

Pa. Lit. good, but also used commonly in the sense of real as opposed to imitation or worthless.

33. *Obi mfa ntŭahŏ nsisi kọmfo.* (169)

No one deceives a fetish priest by dancing.

Mfa, nsisi. Note this, at first sight, confusing and peculiar idiom. The literal translation would be ' One does not by dancing not deceive ', a double negative, but this does not in Ashanti make a positive, the reason being that whereas in the English idiom we have two clauses, a principal and a subordinate, generally in copulative co-ordination, or a principal clause and a subordinate adverbial phrase, in Ashanti the construction really is two or more totally independent principal clauses, the subject of the first in order of speaking being understood with each of the clauses following:

e. g. No one deceives by dancing, English idiom.

One does not dance, one does not deceive, Ashanti idiom.

No one tells a man to strike and kill another. . . English idiom.

In Ashanti the construction would be : One does not tell a man, one does not strike, one does not kill another.

This has no doubt been the original full construction and is

quite in accordance with the simple rules for syntax and grammar of
the language of a primitive race; in time the apparent clumsiness
of the construction or the wish for abbreviation led to the dropping
of the common subject, except of course with the first verb; thus
the negative verbs all came to stand alone in clauses which seem
subordinate (though really principal or independent short sentences)
to the opening, or first clause.

Kǫmfo. (See note on No. 22.) Dancing enters largely into the
training and duties of a fetish priest, and no one not a priest is
likely to be ' half as expert '.

34. *Ǫteasefo na ǫmā ǫsamaṅ kǫṅ dǫ ǫtǫ́.* (3215)
It is the living man who causes the denizen of the spirit world to
long for the mashed yam.

Ǫteasefo. Lit. one who lives down, i. e. on earth.

Na. Emphatic (see note on No. 1).

Ǫsamaṅ. *Ǫsamaṅ*, plu. *nsamaṅfo.* A spirit or ghost of one
who has died. *Asamaṅ* is the spirit world below, not in the sky,
which is the abode of *Onyankǫ̆pǫṅ* and the other class of minor
deities or powers commonly known as 'fetishes' (see note on
No. 17, *ǫbosom*, and No. 1, *Ǫnyǎmē*). The *ǫsamaṅ* is not a soul,
which is rather *ǫkra*, and this latter is in a man during his life on
earth, though it may temporarily leave him during sleep, and even
leave the body of a dying man *before* death (see note on *ǫkra*,
No. 9, under *ṅkrabea*). The *samaṅ* or ghost does not appear to
have an *ǫkra*, but this is not quite clear. A *samaṅ* is in the form
and shape of the mortal body and has all its senses, or some at any
rate, and feels hunger and thirst. It generally inhabits a spirit
world *asamaṅ*, which is much the same as the world the native now
lives in (see note on funeral and burial customs, No. 467).

Nsamaṅfo, ghosts, are supposed to be of three kinds :

1. *Ǫsamaṅ-pa*, a good spirit.

2. *Ǫsamaṅ-tweṅ-tweṅ.* Lit. ' a wait-about, wait-about spirit '.

3. *Ǫtǫfǫ.* The spirit of a man killed, or who met his death by
accident.

Ǫsamaṅ-pa. A man may die in a village, and for long after
the surviving inhabitants may continue all to live without another
death occurring among them, and affairs generally may seem to
prosper, either for the community, or for the family of the deceased.
The spirit is then said to be a good spirit.

Osaman-twen-twen. A spirit or ghost that is seen at intervals by living persons.

To explain this class of ghosts it is necessary to recount a common belief held by the natives. /They think that when a man dies his spirit does not go direct to the world below (_asaman_), but has first, as it were, to report itself (here opinions seem divided), some say to _Onyankopon_, others say to a famous ' fetish ' _Brukum_, which has its earthly habitation somewhere east of the Volta, in Togoland.

In either case the spirit is informed if it is to go to the spirit world below or to haunt the earth temporarily (as in some cases where a man is not supposed to have completed his destiny in this world, in which case he (the spirit), is told to return to its old haunts till that time is complete), or the spirit is forbidden for ever to enter the spirit world and is destined to haunt this earth of living men for ever (why, does not seem clear). Such a spirit then becomes ' a wait-about wait-about spirit' (_osaman-twen-twen_).

It does not seem to have much power for harm, and is shy generally, and confines itself to frightening people. The _saman_ whose stay on earth has been only ordained to last till his destiny has been fulfilled eventually disappears to the world where all the spirits live.

Even when a spirit has gone to the lower world, it is not necessarily considered to have severed all connexion with the world of the living. Hence manes-worship is a distinct branch of the religion which is otherwise chiefly concerned in propitiating the _abosom_, ' fetishes '.

An Ashanti never drinks without pouring a few drops of the wine on the ground for the denizens of the spirit world who may happen to be about (also some for ' fetishes '). Food is constantly placed aside for them. The fetish priests often direct, in cases of illness, and such like, that offerings be made, not to the ' fetish ', but to the departed spirit of a relation to whom they, the priests, with the assistance of the ' fetish ', have traced the cause of illness or misfortune. The departed spirits are regularly summoned from the spirit world on certain ceremonial occasions (see No. 388, note on _akonnua_). Not only men, but animals are supposed to have certain limited powers after death (see note on No. 131, _bommofo_).

The word used for ' to haunt ' is _sēsā_ or _sāsā_. It must be noted

there is absolutely no trace of a belief that spirits ever go to live
in the sky with *Onyankŏpǫ̀n*, but as already noted there is an almost
universal idea that he in some way has power over them to inter-
dict or permit them to enter the spirit world and also to launch
a soul (*ǫkra* rather than *samaṅ*) again into the world of men, reincarnation in fact.

Ghosts are, curiously enough, when visible to the human eye,
reported generally as being white or dressed in white. The near
presence of a spirit (ghost) is supposed to be felt by its peculiar
smell (see No. 38).]

Kǫ̀n dǫ. To long for, lust for, to love. Lit. 'to swell', of the
neck. This expression, with the more euphemistic *pę*, to want,
are the only words in the language to express the sentiment love.
In this idiom we probably get near to the primitive conception of
a word which only refinement and civilization has in time invested
with a higher conception.

It forms one of the numerous examples in this language of
expressions which, having with us a psychological or emotional connexion, are interpreted by the savage in terms purely physiological.
A whole host of such expressions exist, and these idioms, among
other factors, serve to make this language one of great difficulty
for the European to master.

35. *Woyę 'me-ṅkǫ-medi' a, wunyǎ ǫsamaṅ ṅhŭi.* (3571)
If you are an 'eat-by-myself' person, you will often see a spirit.

Wunyǎ . . . nhŭi. Note this idiom, i.e. the auxiliary verb *ṅyǎ*
coupled with the verbal noun (formed by the nasal prefix), giving
the idea of repeated action to the verb, here translated by 'often'.

Ǫsamaṅ. The original text has *asamaṅ*, which is an error.
Ǫsamaṅ is a spirit, *asamaṅ* the spirit world. The spirits are often
supposed to join the living (unseen) when the latter are eating.
Cooked and hot food is supposed to get cold because of the ghostly
fingers touching it.

36. *Ǫsamaṅ-pa hyira ne ba.* (2759)
A good spirit (ghost) looks after its child.

37. *Nsamampǫw mu soduru, wo nǐ wu a, wo abusŭa asǎ.* (2760)
Bent stick in the spirit grove, when your mother is dead that
is the end of your family.

Nsamampǫw. Deriv. *samaṅ*, a spirit, and *ępǫw*, a thicket.

Soduru. A bent or hooked stick which is used for cultivating the soil. Deriv. *aso*, a hoe, and *duru*,=*dua*, stick or tree, shaped thus ⊂══════════▷

Wo nĩ wu a. Lit. when your mother dies, in this case when the parent tree, on which the hooked stick grows, is cut or falls down.

� The saying is allegorical and means that when a child loses its mother it has lost the head of its family. Descent is traced through the mother, and stools, property, &c., pass, not to the son, but to brothers (see note on *abusūa* below).

Nĩ. Mother. The following are the names of various relations, in each case all those persons to whom a particular name applies being also given.

CLASSIFICATORY SYSTEM AMONG THE ASHANTI

Ashanti.	English.	All persons to whom the name may be applied.
A. *Enã* (plu. *enãnom*), *Enĩ, eno,* and *awo.*	Mother.	(1) Own mother. (2) Mother's sister. (3) Own father's various other wives. Also sometimes used as term of respect even when no relationship exists. (See I.)
B. *Agya,* or *ose.*	Father.	(1) Own father. (2) Father's brother. (3) Term of respect not necessarily implying relationship. (See G.)
C. *Onũa,* deriv. *onĩ wa, onĩ ba* (lit. mother's child).	Sister or Brother.	(1) Own sister or brother (*by same mother only*). (2) Own mother's sister's child. (3) Any one of the same *abusūa* family name as your own, see note below on *abusūa.* (See I in table.)
D. *Agya ba* (lit. father's child).	Half-brother or half-sister.	(1) The child of your own father by a mother not your own. (2) Father's brother's child. (See N in table.)
E. *Kunu* (*okunu*).	Husband.	(1) A woman's own husband. (2) Sister's husband. (3) Husband's brother. (4) Half-sister's husband. (See U in table.)

CLASSIFICATORY SYSTEM AMONG THE ASHANTI (*continued*)

Ashanti.	English.	All persons to whom the name may be applied.
F. *Ǫyere* (plu. -*nom*).	Wife.	(1) A man's own wife or wives. (2) Brother's wife. (3) Wife's sister. (4) Half-brother's wife. (See V in table.)
G. *Agya* (lit. father).	Uncle (paternal).	Father's brother. (See B in table.)
H. *Wofa.*	Uncle (maternal).	Mother's brother, who may succeed to stool, property, &c.
I. *Enã.*	Aunt (maternal).	Own mother's sister. (See A and M.)
Ǫsewá.	Aunt (paternal).	Father's sister.
J. *Wǫfasewa.*	Niece.	Sister's child (daughter). Note the feminine suffix *wa*.
K. *Wǫfase.*	Nephew.	Sister's child (son).
L. *Ǫba* (lit. child, son, or daughter).	Child. Niece. Nephew.	Own child, brother's child (daughter or son).
M. *Onŭa.*	Cousin.	Mother's (own) sister's child. (See C and I.)
N. *Agya ne nŭa ba.*	Cousin.	Father's brother's child. (See D in table.)
O. *Nãnã* (*Nãnã-barima, Nãnã-bã*).	Grandparent.	Maternal and paternal grandparents.
P. *Ǫba nãnã.*	Grandchild.	Children of son or daughter.
Q. *Nãnãnkãnsŏ* (lit. 'Grandparent not touch (his) ear ').	Great-grandparent.	Maternal and paternal great-grandparents.
R. *A se.*	Father-in-law.	(1) Wife's father. (2) Husband's father.
S. *Osew.*	Mother-in-law.	(1) Wife's mother. (2) Husband's mother.
T. *Akonta.*	Brother-in-law.	Wife's brother.
U. *Okunu* (lit. husband).	Brother-in-law.	Husband's brother. (See E in table.)
V. *Ǫyere* (*nŭa*) (lit. wife).	Sister-in-law.	Wife's sister. (See F.)
W. *Akŭmmã.*	Sister-in-law.	Husband's sister.

Abusŭa. The following legend is common among the Ashantis to account for the derivation of this word.

They derive it from *Abu* (a proper name), and *sŭa*, to imitate, the reason being given as follows. 'There lived in former times a king of Adanse who had a "linguist" named Abu. This Abu incurred the king's anger and was heavily fined. Now, at that time children used to inherit from their father. Abu asked his children to assist him to pay the fine imposed by the king, but they refused and all went off *to their mother's relatives.* But Abu's sister's children rendered him assistance to pay off his debts, and Abu, therefore, when he died left all his belongings to them. Other people then copied him and willed their property to the sister's children (*Abu-sŭa,* lit. copying Abu).' (The above is a literal translation of the account given by a native.)

This is an excellent example of an aetiological myth. The Ashantis, who now notice that other nations trace descent through the father, have invented this myth to explain the fact that with them descent is traced through the mother, which now strikes them as curious.

It is amusing to notice that the inventor of this myth has not been able to entirely adapt his mental attitude even to the imaginary setting of his tale, for he quite naturally pictures the children, *under* the supposed former *father right,* running off *to the mother's relatives.* (As a matter of fact no case is known of a change from patrilineal to matrilineal descent.)

The law of succession (to stools and property and clan name) among this people is as follows:

The direct heir is (1) the eldest brother by the same mother. (2) Failing such (and he may be passed over for various reasons—incompetency, bodily blemish, &c.), the next in the direct line of succession is the eldest son of the eldest sister, (3) the grandson through the female line, (4) another branch of the same family or clan (*abusŭa*), (5) a slave.

One commonly hears Europeans who have a smattering of native customary law lay it down as a hard and fast rule that the nephew, that is class (2) as above, always succeeds.

This, however, is not the case. There is even a well-known proverb to that effect—*Nīwamma nsae a, wofase nni ade,* 'When (one's) mother's children are not finished, (one's) nephew does not inherit.'

Many of these proverbs illustrate in a remarkable manner the force and strength and unity of relationship on and through the female side, and the almost total disregard or recognition of any kinship tie on the father's side.   See proverbs Nos. 37, 483, 486, 487, 488, 491, 492.

Abusüa means a family or clan name, it is always inherited through the mother.   Each clan is exogamous.   The classificatory system here given, which is incomplete (the writer hopes to go fully into this subject in a future work), might seem to point to a past in which a group of brothers married a group of sisters.   The most important of these clans or families are as follows :

Oyoko.
Asona.
Abrade.
Agona.
Biretuo.
Asene.
Asakyinfo.

Some of these names are those of plants or animals.   *Oyoko* would seem to mean red earth.   Each and all may necessitate the observance of certain taboos (though perhaps another factor determines this). An example of only one will be given here.   A man of the Nyado *nton* will not kill a leopard.   Should he accidentally trap and kill one it will be carried to his village, laid on a mat, bathed by the women folk smeared with white clay, in fact all the funeral rites usually observed on the death of a human being are held over it.   They also beg its pardon.   It is then carried in a hammock (*apa*) and buried.

The python is sometimes treated in a similar way, as also the crocodile.   Even when a man whose *nton*, say, does not prevent his killing a leopard, does so, and another man whose *nton* makes the leopard sacred happens to be near, the latter person will beg permission to take away the body and treat it as described.

The word *nton* has been mentioned.   It does not seem that the animal specially regarded has strictly a connexion with a man's *abusüa*, i.e. the clan name he inherits from his mother, but that this special regard for an animal depends on a person's *nton* which is also hereditary but traced through the male line, and is not exogamous, that is, two persons of the same *nton* may marry, always provided the *abusüa* is not the same.   The *nton* rather than the *abusua* seems to determine the taboo. Each *nton* class has its own special form of greeting (in answering a salutation).

Each taboos certain things, each necessitates a certain day for 'soul washing', and certain forms of sacrifice to accompany that ceremony. (The writer hopes to go into the whole question of totemism among these people in a future work.)

38. *Osamane aũoofŭam ne nunúm.* (2762)

The smell of a ghost is the smell of the ' *nunúm* ' shrub.

Osamane. As *osaman* (q.v. No. 35), but in *Akyem* dialect.

Nunúm. A shrub with aromatic scented leaves.

39. *Osaman tĕɛ ne nsa kyia wo a, wopono wo de mu.* (2763)

When a ghost puts forth its hand to greet you, you draw your's back.

Wopono. Pono, lit. to bend. Hand shaking as a salutation appears to have been a native custom before the advent of Europeans. When shaking hands with a number of assembled persons the person will always commence with the one standing on his right and pass on from right to left.

40. *Osaman ntŭen teasefo ansã-na wadidi.* (2764)

A ghost does not wait for the living to begin to eat before it begins to partake.

Teasefo. See note on No. 34.

41. *Asaman nai biribi a, ewo nhyehye-wo-ákyi.* (2765)

If the spirit world possesses nothing else, it has at least the power of its name.

Asaman. The underworld of ghost people (see note on *osaman,* No. 35).

Nhyehye-wo-ákyi. This saying is difficult to render literally. *Hyehye-wo-ákyi,* boast of your back, i.e. of whom or what is behind you, as for instance where a man would claim to be the subject of some powerful chief to prevent a lesser chief, into whose hands he had fallen from killing him. So here, where applied to the spirit world, about which people do not know much, but which is held in dread, as spirits can come and haunt living men and cause them sickness and even death. So this saying is quoted of a person who makes vague allusions as to what he will do and who will avenge him if he is interfered with.

42. *Asaman, woṅko nsaṅ mma.* (2767)

The spirit world is not a place one can visit and return from again (as a living man).

Woṅko, nsaṅ mma. For the negative see note on No. 33, *mfa, nsisi.* *Mma,* neg. of *ba.*

43. *Asaman, wommǎnǎ.* (2768)

Things cannot be sent to the spirit world (?). (Meaning obscure.)

44. *A samantawa se enim pae a, eẹ sẹ atawa pa.* (2769)

When the 'spirit' *tawa* tree declares it knows how to pop, at best it can hope to do so (only) like the real *tawa* tree (if as well even as that).

Asamantawa. The *tawa,* or *atǎ,* is a tree with large bean-like pods which when ripe burst with a bang. Three varieties are known as *tawa-pa,* the 'real' *tawa,* see note on No. 483, *papǎpa tawa,* an inferior kind, and *samantawa,* a species of the same tree inferior to that again, not fit for human consumption (the seeds of the *tawa-pa* are eaten), but the inferior species are good enough for the denizens of the spirit world. The same idea is seen in the word *samaṅ-sika,* spirit's money, which is applied to metal filings (cf. Chinese imitation paper money).

45. *Onipa wu (wọ) samampọw mu a, wọmfá no mma ofie bio.* (2416)

When a man dies in the spirit grove (cemetery), he is not brought back to the home again.

Wọ. This verb often takes the place of the preposition 'in' or 'at' in English (cf. *mǎ,* see note on No. 14).

Wọmfá, mma. Translate by the passive. For note on the negative see No. 33, *mfa, nsisi.*

46. *Wunni samaṅ aduaṅ a, womfa wo nsa nto mu.* (914)

If you are not going to partake of the spirits' food, do not put your hand in it.

Samaṅ aduaṅ. Food set aside for the spirits.

47. *Wubu wó sumáṅ asumammá a, ekita wo.* (655)

If you call your amulet a trifling thing, it will seize hold of you (kill you).

Sumáṅ. See note on No. 35, *ọsamaṅ.*

Asumammá. Diminutive of *sumaṅ* (see No. 35, *ọsamaṅ*).

48. *Opanyiṅ aʀo seṅ sumaṅ.* (2610)

The advice (lit. mouth) of a man of ripe experience is more potent than (your) little guardian deity.

Opanyiṅ. See note on *panyiṅ*, No. 1.

49. *Sumaṅ kafirmā nyɛ biribi a, na ɛyɛ amĩade.* (3114)

If the little *kafirma* charm is good for nothing else, it is at any rate an adornment.

Amĩade. *Mĩa*, to dress, adorn, and *ade*, thing.

50. *Enni bābiæra a wotrā ẘe yisa hinam sumaṅ so a, enyɛ nnam.* (2306)

There is no special place where one should sit and chew guinea pepper and blow it out over one's tutelary deity, to make it a sharp (clever) little amulet.

Hinam. To blow out in a spray from the mouth, a common form of propitiation. (This is also done in the case of a ' soul washing ', see No. 147.)

The writer has noticed a similar custom among the Maṅanjas of Central Africa, who when propitiating the spirits of their dead also squirt water out of the mouth in this way.

Yisa, nnam. An example of sympathetic magic—' like causes like '—the sharp biting pepper to cause the *sumaṅ* to be sharp.

51. *Obi mfa nɛa wawu sumaṅ ṅkā sɛ, ' Mā me ṅkwā nè akwāhōsaṅ '.* (162)

No one takes the amulet of one who has died (and whom therefore it has failed) and addresses it, saying, 'Give me life and health '.

52. *Wo kra nyɛ a, na wunyā asafo nsam' amanne.* (1760)

If your soul is not a lucky one, you fall into the hands of a ' company '.

Asafo. A union or company of men banded together under a leader, chosen from among their number by popular vote, to compel the recognition of a real or imaginary grievance or to further some plan, good or perhaps bad, upon which all are of one mind ; or perhaps again, merely for the purpose of joining together to work in turns for each other, say at cultivating or clearing a plantation.

These companies or confederations adopt a leader, as already

stated, and assume an emblem or flag, and the confederation is
given a name, generally one explaining the *raison d'être* for the
amalgamation.   The following are a few examples of ' company'
names.

Kyiriamim, ' We hate greediness '.
Apesɛmaka, ' We wish to present our grievance'.
Apagya, ' Strike a light ' (with flint and steel).

Asafo, of course is also a war company (see No. 306, note on
dǫm).

The saying quoted above means, that with an individual, whom
one may run foul of, one may have a chance, but when a whole
community are against you and determined one and all on your
destruction, there is little chance for you.

Kra.   See note on No. 9, *nkrabea.*

Amanne=Ǫman-ade. Ǫman, see note on No. 474.

53. *Nkrabea nhĩnā nsɛ̣.*   (1762)
All destinies are not alike.

Nkrabea.   See note on No. 9, *nkrabea.*

54. *Wode wo kra kaw, na woantua no a, ǫfa wo abufuw.*   (776)
If you are in debt to your soul, and have not paid it, (your soul)
      gets angry with you.

Wode . . . kaw.   Lit. owe a debt to, i. e. (in present context)
fail to fulfil some vow you have made, e. g. a promise to sacrifice
a fowl.   *Kaw*, (Ashanti, *ka*) deriv. perhaps *ka,* to remain.   Note
the following, *de kaw*, to hold or have a debt; *dan kaw*, to sue
for recovery of a debt ; *tua kaw*, to pay a debt.

Woantua.   Perfect tense.

Abufuw.   Lit. swelling of the chest, cf. *kǫn dǫ*, q.v. No. 34.

55. *Obi nkwati Tannǫ nkǫ aka ase.*   (222)
No one consults the lots without calling on (his) fetish (lit. *Tannǫ*).

Tannǫ.   Perhaps the most famous fetish in Ashanti and the
Gold Coast.   Called after the river Tannǫ in which it has its abode.
The fetishes Tannǫ and Bea (also a river), are supposed by some
of the natives to be the children of the Supreme Being Ǫnyàmé
(q.v. No. 1), Tannǫ being the first in importance.   The following
is a popular myth with regard to them.   When the Supreme
Being was premeditating as to where he should set down the
abodes of his children on earth, the goat heard of it and being

a great friend of Bea ran and told him that when his father sent
for Tanno and him, he should rise up and go very quickly so that
he should arrive there before his brother. So when the children
were called before their father, Bea came first and his father, as
a reward, set his abode down in the coolness and shade of the
forest country, whereas Tanno was given a home in the more open
grass lands. In consequence, to this day the followers of Tanno,
'turn their back on ', or ' hate ', i. e. taboo the flesh of the goat.

There are many minor fetishes all owing their power to Tanno
whose name is added to their own, e. g. *Tanno Yao, Tanno Akwasi,
Tanno Konkroma.* The water of the Tanno is brought from long
distances to found a temple or shrine for the spirit in villages far
from the river. The fish in the Tanno are never eaten, nor its
water drunk, and the fish are fed on various ceremonial occasions.

The Tanno fetish is so famous, that its name is sometimes used
almost as a generic term for all fetishes, as in the saying here
quoted.

Ǹkwati, ɛ̀ko. For note on the negative see No. 33, *mfa,
nsisi.*

Aka. Lots, of various kinds, strings with different articles
attached to the ends, *akamatwě* (see No. 412), and dice (see note
on No. 25, *ɛikyi*), a pot of water with models of hoes, axes, and
sometimes a stone celt, in it. These are fished out with a wooden
spoon and the omens read from what turns up. This last is called
nsuoyā. The consulting of lots is part of the duty of the fetish
priest, *okomjo,* (q. v. No. 22), but there is another class of medicine
men, *dunsifo,* lit. 'root folk', i.e. persons who dig for roots for
medicines, who also combine with this occupation that of diviner or
oracle man.

56. *Sasabonsám kọ ayi a, ọsoɛ ọbayifo fi.* (2782)
     When a *sasabonsám* (devil) goes to attend a funeral, he lodges at
     a witch's house.

Sasabonsảm. Deriv. *bonsam,* a devil, or evil spirit (*not* the
disembodied soul of any particular person, just as the fetish is not
a human spirit).

Its power is purely for evil and witchcraft. The *ọbayifo* is perhaps
its servant, as the terms are sometimes synonymous. *Sāsă* or *sĕsă*
is the word used for a person being possessed of a spirit or devil
(*ọyɛ no sāsă*).

The *asasabonsam* is a monster of human shape, living far in the depths of the forest, and only occasionally met by hunters.

It sits on tree-tops and its legs dangle down to the ground and have hooks for feet which pick up any one who comes within reach. It has iron teeth. There are female, male, and little *sasabonsam*. A large fungus growth very like a big cabbage in appearance often found growing on trees is called *sasabonsam kyew*. i. e. devil's hat.

Ayi. Burial, funeral. Deriv. *yi*, to take away, to remove. (For custom of burying slaves, wives, &c., with a dead master, see note on No. 467.) The grave is a deep trench from 6 to 8 feet deep in one side of which a cavity is again dug, forming as it were a room, with three walls. (Cf. the Chinyanja *mudzi*, ' village ' or last home.) The body is placed in this case, which is then fenced or screened off. Chiefs and men of importance are buried in the house in which they die, which then becomes their tomb.

Obayifo. Deriv. *bayi*, sorcery (synonymous term *ayen*), a wizard, or more generally witch. A kind of human vampire whose chief delight is to suck the blood of children whereby the latter pine and die.

Men and women possessed of this black magic are credited with volitant powers, being able to quit their bodies and travel great distances in the night. Besides sucking the blood of victims, they are supposed to be able to extract the sap and juices of crops. (Cases of coco blight are ascribed to the work of the *obayifo*.) These witches are supposed to be very common and a man never knows but that his friend or even his wife may be one. When prowling at night they are supposed to emit a phosphorescent light from the armpits and anus. An *obayifo* in everyday life is supposed to be known by having sharp shifty eyes, that are never at rest, also by showing an undue interest in food, and always talking about it, especially meat, and hanging about when cooking is going on, all of which habits are therefore purposely avoided. A man will seldom deny another, even a stranger, a morsel of what he may be eating, or a hunter a little bit of raw meat to any one asking it, hoping thereby to avoid the displeasure of one who, for all he can tell, is a witch or wizard. (See No. 76.)

The *obayifo* can also enter into animals, &c., e. g. buffalo, elephant, snakes, and cause them to kill people. The *obayifo* is discovered by a process analogous to the ' smelling out ' of witches among the

Zulu, i. e. the 'carrying of a corpse', see note on No. 77. Witches and wizards are guarded against by a *suman* (q. v. No. 17, *ǫbosom*). and a little raw meat or other food is frequently placed at the entrance to a village for them to partake of. This offering also frequently takes the form of a bunch of palm nuts pinned down to the ground with a stick.

57. *Sasabonsám té ase, wose ǫyę ǫbayifo, na menne sę osi odum atifĩna*
  odum nso sow mmoatia. (2783)

When a *sasabonsám* devil is down on the ground he is called a wizard, how much more when he is perched on top of an *odum* tree, and the *odum* tree is also bearing a crop of tailless monkeys as its fruit.

Menne. Lit. I do not mention ; neg. of *de.*

Odum. The *odum* tree (*Chlorophora excelsa*).

The *odum* tree is universally considered among the Ashantis as a potential abode of a fetish and one may constantly see offerings placed at their base. An *ǫbayifo*, too, may alight on them, and also, as mentioned here, the *sasabonsam.*

The tree, like all earthly abodes of spirits, is nothing in itself, but only by virtue of its being the body in which the fetish or spirit may dwell. An *odum* tree that may have been universally revered, on falling down, then becomes merely a tree, for the fetish which invested it with awe will have gone to seek a new abode. *Odum* trees are never cut down for firewood, nor used for making stools.

Sawyers who cut them down for Europeans, for timber, are supposed sooner or later to go mad or die.

The following legend about the *odum* and the supposed etymology of the word *dunsin*, a stump, is curious and interesting. (Cf. supposed origin of suffix *fo*, see No. 78, *kontromfi*). When all the trees were given names the *odum* tree asked all the others to add its name to theirs, but this they would not agree to. Later on, however, as the trees found themselves cut down for firewood, building, &c., &c., while the *odum* still stood untouched and even reverenced, it seems that they, when too late, took its name, i.e. *dunsin* = *odum*, the *odum* tree, and *sin*, a piece or fragment.

It is interesting to note that rubber trees were for long regarded as the abode of little children fetishes because 'they wept when cut'.

1696   D

Big prices for rubber, however, soon caused this idea to be set aside, though the priests first tried to prevent tapping.

Mmoatia. A half-mythical man monkey, supposed to be exceeding swift and used by devils and wizards as messengers.

58. *Sɛ odum osi hɔ a, ose ɔyɛ Ɔtannɔ, na ɔbonsam abesi so . . . . !*

When an *odum* tree stands *there*, it declares it is Tannɔ, but when a devil comes and perches on it . . . . !

Odum. See note above, No. 57.

Ɔtannɔ. See note on No. 55, *Tannɔ.*

Ɔbonsam. See note on No. 56, *sasabonsám.*

59. *Owu a akum wo nã nɛ wo agya wɔ hɔ a, wunnye diṅ sɛ, 'Aka me ṅkõ'.* (3477)

When Death which has killed your mother and your father is there (with you again), you do not say to him, 'I alone remain'.

Owu. See note on No. 16, *owu.* Death, personified, is blind but can hear. When he hears 'you alone remain', he will immediately want to complete his work of destruction.

Nã, agya. For Ashanti classificatory system, see note on *nĩ,* No. 37.

Wunnye diṅ. Wunnye, neg. of *gye,* lit. you do not receive the name of. . .

60. *Owu bekum wo se nɛ wo nĩ a, nsũ sɛ, 'Me se nɛ me nĩ awu', na sũ sɛ, 'Me nɛ m'agya nɛ me nã bɛkɔ'.* (3479)

If Death has come and killed your father and your mother, do not weep, saying, 'My father and my mother are dead', but weep and say, 'I and my father and my mother will go (with you)'.

61. *Owu bekum wo na wofrɛ no agya a, obekum wo, wofrɛ no ɛnã a, obekum wo.* (3480)

If Death comes to kill you and you supplicate it, calling it 'Father', it will kill you, and if you supplicate it, calling it 'Mother', it will kill you.

62. *Owu adare nnɔw fãkõ.* (3481)

Death's sickle does not reap one place alone.

63. *Owu ṅhĩnã yɛ owu.* (3483)

All the different forms Death takes are just the one Death.

64. *Owu na wannyā bābi anko a, na oko asāman.* (3484)
When Death has no particular place to go to, then it goes off to the world of spirits.

Asaman. See note on No. 35, *osaman.*

65. *Owu nè wo ase hyɛ wo adiuma-yɛ a, owu de na woko kan.* (2485)
If both your father-in-law and Death appoint a day for you to do some work, it is Death's you will go about first.

66. *Owu to wo a, wunse no sɛ, ' Fie aberewa !'* (3486)
When Death overtakes you, you do not say to it, 'Look, there is an 'old woman (take her) !'

Sɛ. This word has lost its association with its original root *se*, to say, and become exactly the equivalent of the English 'that'. Were it treated as a verb it would have to be negative, see note on No. 33, *mfa, nsisi.*

Aberewa. An old woman, not a disrespectful term, sometimes used for mother.

67. *Owu wo okyɛkyɛfo adaka ano safɛ.* (3487)
Death has the key to open the miser's chest.

68. *Owu nyɛ pia na woadi mu ahyemfiri.* (3493)
Death is not a sleeping-room that can be entered and come out of again.

Ahyemfiri. Deriv. *hyen*, to enter, and *firi*, to come out.

69. *' Mirewu kyɛna, mirewu ne', na yɛde yɛ ayie ?* (3494)
'I am going to die to-morrow, I am going to die to-day,' do they begin the funeral custom (because of such words)?

70. *Wurewu a, wunse sɛ, ' Mirewu ō ! mirewu ō !'* (3495)
When you are (really) dying, you do not say, 'Oh, I am dying! Oh, I am dying'!

71. *Obi nim nea owu wo a, ankā onsi ho ara da.* (263)
If one could know where Death resided, one would never stop there.

72. *Nea wahintiw awu no, wontutu 'mirika nko n'ayi ase.* (2170)
When a man has met his death through having stumbled (fallen), one does not run to attend the funeral of such an one.

Awu. Subjunctive mood.

Wontutu, ṅkọ.   For negative, see note on No. 33, *mfa, nsisi.*
Ayi.   See note on No. 56, *ayi.*

73. *Ọkom nye Krakye Dente nye.*
    Hunger is not good (good, in sense of, ' to be lightly thought of '),
      neither is *Krakye Dente.*

    Krakye Dente. Probably after Tannọ (see No. 55, *Tannọ*),
the most famous fetish on the Gold Coast.   The present abode of
its chief fetish priest is a cave, situated about thirty feet high on
a rocky hill-side at Kete Krakye on the Volta river, in what was
once German Togoland.
    The spot, which the writer once visited, is situated in a grove
with a broad path leading to it.   At the entrance to the grove
stands the symbol of this fetish, a tall, conical mound about seven
feet high with the apex hollowed in the form of a bowl to receive
the sacrifices made to it.   The path and open space at the foot of
the face of the cliff, where the cave is situated, are kept clean
and swept; the grove itself contains a large circular clearing.
Climbing up the face of the cliff, one comes to the mouth of the
cave, which has been roughly built up, rags hang in front of this
opening.   The entrance is higher up through a narrow passage
which leads into the cave, which again by another passage leads
into a second chamber which opens on to the grove by the walled
up front mentioned.   One has to wait quite a considerable time
before entering the inner cave to allow thousands of bats to fly out.
The floor of the cave where one enters is ankle deep in a fine powder
caused by their droppings.   Piled high against one side of the cave
are hundreds of gin bottles, offerings to the *ọkọmfo*, who sits in
the cave and gives utterance to those who come to consult the fetish,
addressing them in the grove below, from behind the partially
built up face of the rock.   The symbol of Dente, the conical
mound, may be seen in almost every village in Ashanti, and there
would seem some uniformity in this particular design, even among
other fetishes having no connexion with Dente, for their abode is
often a piled up mass of clay, feathers, blood, somewhat in the form
of a cone.   (Cf. the Delphic oracle.)   The following is a tradition
of the supposed origin of the name Dente.   The original name of
this fetish was Koṅkom, and its chief priest resided some hundreds
of years ago at Date (in Akuapem).
    The fetish priest lived in a cave there.   His sanctuary was

violated by a man, who, when the priest was stretching forth
a hand to receive an offering, dragged him out, disclosing a man
covered with sores. After this the priest left Date and went, first
to Agogo, and thence to Kratchi (Krakye), and there took up his
abode in the cave described. Not knowing the Krakye language,
he could not make himself understood, and to inquiries as to his
name, &c., could only reply he came from 'Date', which in the
local language is Dente. For fuller account of 'fetish' worship,
see note on No. 17, *obosom*.

74. *Ọbayifo ba ẉu a, ẹyẹ no yaw.* (59)
When a witch's child dies, it makes her sad.

    Ọbayifo. See note on No. 56, *ọbayifo.*

75. *Ọbayifo ọrekọ ē ! ọbayifo ọrekọ ē ! na wonyẹ ọbayifo a, wuntĩba wo*
    ani. (60)
A witch is passing ! a witch is passing ! (some one cries), but if you
are not a witch you do not turn your eyes to look.

76. *Ọbayifo kum wádi-wammã-mẽ, na oñkúm wámã-me-na-esũa.* (61)
The sorcerer kills (by magic) the one who eats and gives him
    nothing, but he does not kill him who eats and gives him
    (even) a little piece.

    See note on *ọbayifo,* No. 56.

77. *Efunu a ebẹi nnim sũdẹw.* (1163)
The corpse which is coming to knock against (some one) cares
    nothing for cries of sorrow.

The custom of 'carrying the corpse' (*afunsoa*) when the cause
of death is supposed to be witchcraft is briefly as follows. An
open stretcher is made of palm branches, and on this the corpse is
laid, being surrounded by *damãram* leaves (the vivid crimson leaf
one sees so frequently in Ashanti and along the line from Seccondee
to Coomassie) and *emẽ* (mint ?) and *onunum* leaves (q. v. No. 38).
The stretcher is then placed on the heads of two men, who carry it out
into the street. The whole people assemble. The chief, or head
man of the village, advances cutlass in hand, and addresses the
corpse, saying, 'If I were the one who killed you by magic, advance
on me and knock (*si*) me'. And so on each in turn comes up till
the guilty one's turn comes, when the corpse will urge the carriers
forward to butt against him with the litter. A person so accused
can appeal for a change of carriers.

CHAPTER II

78. *Kontromfï se, ' Qberan wu nê kôko '.* (1717)

The monkey says, 'The brave man dies because of his brave heart'.

Kontromfï. Other names for various species of monkeys are *oduahyen* ('the white tail'), *adú,* (the dog-faced baboon), *efo,* (Ashanti, *efoo,* the black colobus monkey).

There are many myths and stories about monkeys, and one at least is worthy of notice, proving as it does that the savages possess even their rude philologists, and showing that they have that innate curiosity which compels them to ask and find a reason for many things (which inquiring state of mind some would deny to them altogether), however childish and unsatisfying to our minds the answers they are contented to accept may be. They say that when *Onyanköpon* created and named all things, He went about accompanied by the *efo* (colobus monkey), and when he had done this work, the *efo* requested that his services and assistance might be rewarded in some suitable manner, and suggested having his name perpetuated for all time by having it suffixed to the names of all peoples, nations, and occupations. To this the Creator agreed. Hence we have the suffix *fo=efo* in all such words, e. g. *Asantefo; Mampon-fo; adïruma-fo,* &c., &c.! The singular suffix, corresponding to *fo* (which is plural) is *ni,* and this is, the natives state (correctly no doubt), derived from *onipa,* a man.

Monkeys are supposed to have got their tails in the following way :

The Creator (*Odomankoma,* see No. 1) made men, monkeys, and tails, &c., &c. (the tails apart from monkeys). The monkeys, after the habit of their kind, would pick up the various things lying about that *Odomankoma* had made, among other things they kept playing with were the tails. One monkey, picking one up, stuck it on behind him, when all the rest copied him. When they tried to take them off again, they found they had grown on, and they were compelled to wear them for ever after.

79. *Kontromfi se, ' Afei ne ampa'.* (1718)

The monkey says, ' Well now I shall *really* speak the truth '.

80. *Kontromfi se, ' Me suman ne m' aniwa'.* (1721)

The monkey says, ' My talisman (against surprise and enemies) is my little eyes '.

Suman. See note on No. 17, *ọbosom.*

Ne. See note on No. 1, *ne.*

Aniwa. Wa is the diminutive suffix (sometimes also feminine), and as *ani* is sometimes used for eyes, can be here translated by 'little eyes '. *Ani* perhaps, however, more literally means face, front, or surface of a thing. *Anim*, lit. in the front, is the word used for face. *Nsu ani*, the face, or surface of the water.

81. *Kontromfi se, ohia ayi akyeafo adi.* (1719)

The monkey says that there is nothing like poverty for taking the conceit out of a man.

Ayi . . . adi. Adi=adiwo, an open space.

Akyeafo. For suffix *fo*, see note on No. 78.

82. *Kontromfi se, ' Wohye m'afonom' a, na meyi asempa makã makyere wo'.* (1720)

The monkey says, ' If you fill up my cheeks (with food), then I shall reveal the truth and tell you'.

Makã, makyere. Subjunctive mood.

83. *Yenim se kontromfi kọn wọ họ, na yede hãmã to n'asenmu.* (2343)

We know the monkey has a neck, but we nevertheless take a string and attach it to its waist.

Hãmã. Lit. a creeper, hence used for rope or string.

N'asenmu. Asen, the waist. Note the following words, all spelt alike (save for the prefix vowel which is generally omitted) and distinguished from each other only by accent or change in vowel sound :

1. (*N*)*sen*, a court herald (*e* as in fed).
2. (*O*)*sẹn*, a pot (*ẹ* broad).
3. (*O*)*sẽn*, from *sẽn*, to surpass (*ẽ* nasal).
4. (*A*)*sen*, the waist (*e* between *i* and *e*).

It is this variety of vowel sounds which (in words otherwise spelt the same) alters the entire meaning, that makes the Twi language one of exceptional difficulty for the European to master.

84. *Obi nhyę kontromfĭ mmă onni soṅ.* (195)

No one compels a monkey to eat the tamarind (?) fruit. (The *ǫsǫṅ*, tamarind (?), is the favourite food of monkeys).

N̄hyę . . . mmă, onni. Note the negatives running throughout ; see note on No. 33, *mfa, nsisi.*

85. *Oduahyęṅ se, ' Nea ęwǫ m'afonom' nyę me dea, nea akǫ me yam' na ęyę me dea '.* (1026)

The white-tailed one (the black colobus monkey) says, ' What is in my cheek is not mine, but what has gone into my belly that is my very own '.

Oduahyęṅ. *Dua,* a tail (lit. stick), and *hyęṅ,* bright or white.

Me dea. *Dea,* as, *me de.* This suffix *de* is used to form the possessive pronouns. This *de* is probably the word *ade,* a thing, and the construction is really the possessive adjective qualifying the noun *ade; me de,* mine (lit. my thing). *Ade,* thing, is again a noun formed from the root *de,* to hold, to possess; *ade,* something held, a possession, a thing. The writer knows no language in which it is possible to get down to roots and root meanings in words more often than in Ashanti or Twi. There are few words of more than two syllables which cannot be broken up into their component parts, and the student of the language who will devote attention to the mastery of roots and basic stems will find his future studies much simplified, and render the acquisition of a vocabulary a much more pleasant task than had he merely endeavoured to learn dissyllabic and polysyllabic words without knowing the roots from which they are built up.

86. *Kontromfĭ akwakorā na ǫware kontromfĭ aberewa.* (1715)

It is Mr. Old-man-monkey who marries Mrs. Old-woman-monkey.

87. *Kontromfĭ kyĕa sęnea akyĕafo kyĕa, nso ne to kǫ.* (1716)

The monkey struts about just as a conceited person does, but its bottom is red nevertheless.

Ne to kǫ. There is a kind of monkey which the natives declare speaks these words, ' *Wo to kǫ, wo to kǫ* ' (lit. You red bottom, you red bottom '), and certainly the sound this monkey makes seems, once one has heard the interpretation given, to be exactly these words. The black colobus monkey with the white tail ' says ', ' *Wahu, wahu ?* ' (Have you seen, have you seen ?). The sounds made by many birds and animals are put in words by the natives, and once one has heard these sounds interpreted into words, it is easy to imagine that the sound produced represents the exact words ascribed. The native does not think it so very extraordinary, and is quite ready to ascribe a limited knowledge of his language to birds and beasts while recognizing that he cannot of course always understand what they say.

88. *Mahũ kontrꝫmfĩ a ne yerĕ awu na wasiw atimum, na wo wansaṅ de, ꬲfa wo hõ dꬲṅ ?* (1445)

I have seen a monkey whose wife has died and he has let his hair grow long in consequence, but as far as you are concerned, Bush-buck, how does it concern you ?

It is the bush-buck (male), with its long horns like plaited hair, to which the allusion is made. The saying is quoted in the sense that one man's troubles are no concern of any but his own family.

Yerĕ. Wife (see also note on *nĩ*, No. 37, table of terms of relationship or classificatory system F). The derivation is possibly from the same root that is seen in *yère*, to be stretched out on, spread out, strained upon.

89. *ꬲsóno akyi ꬲni aboa.* (3029) Cf. No. 90, following.

After the elephant there is no other animal (to compare with it in size and strength).

ꬲsóno. Lit. 'the big one', deriv. *so*, big, and *no*, the pronoun, he ; *ꬲ* the noun prefix. Cf. *susono*, the hippo, lit. 'the big one of the water '.

Akyi. The back of anything, hence behind, used of place and of time. The same root is probably found in *kyi*, to dislike, hate, of a person or thing. In the latter sense it is the word used for taboo, the idea in both these words probably being, to turn the back on. (See also note on No. 132, *wokyi*.)

Nni. Neg. of *wo*, to be.

Aboa. An animal, anything having life, a creature ; used of and applied to animals, birds, fishes, insects, reptiles, and even man, but in this last case generally, though not always, in an abusive sense, 'You beast'.

The word is often used in apposition with the name of the animal, insect, &c., specified, e. g. see Proverbs Nos. 172, 175. If you want to insult a man very much, you call him, '*onipa aboa*', 'a man beast'.

90. *Ęsóno akyi aboa ne bǫmmǫfó !* (3028)

After the elephant is a (still greater) animal, the hunter !

Bǫmmǫfó. See note on *bǫmmǫfo,* No. 131.

91. *Ęsóno kuntań na adowa di panyiń.*

The elephant is big and bulky but the (little) duyker has most experience and sense.

Kuntań. Better perhaps *kuntáńń,* anything huge, ponderous, heavy.

Adowa. A species of duyker, in Ashanti stories has a character for pertness and cleverness.

92. *Ęsóno nni wuram' a, ankă ękó ye ǫbopǫń bi.* (3023)

If the elephant were not in the jungle ('bush'), then the buffalo would be one of the greatest of the beasts.

Nni. Neg. of *wǫ.*

Wuram'. *Wura mu,* lit. in the grass (bush). The word is used in the sense of 'the bush', i.e. jungle, forest, as a whole, whereas without the preposition *mu,* the meaning is restricted to some grass or bush in particular. The plural means weeds, i.e. grass or bush growing where it is not wanted. *Ękwae, kwaem'* is particularly thick bush or dense forest.

Ankă. See note on No. 733, *ankănă.*

Ye. See note on No. 1, *ne.*

Ǫbopǫń. *Aboa pǫń, pǫń* a suffix meaning great, large.

93. *Ęsóno tia afiri so a, eńhŭań.* (3031)

When the elephant treads on a trap, it does not spring (on it).

Afiri. Many of the traps in use are extremely ingenious. *Sŭm afiri* is, to set a trap.

94. *Ǫkáka bu sono să.* (1515)

Toothache breaks the elephant's tusk.

Ǫkáka. *Okekaw,* the many one-tusker elephants are supposed by the natives to have lost the second tusk owing to toothache.

Să. Also *abeń, ęsóno-beń* (=*asommeń*).

95. *Nea ęsóno wui n'afikyiri no, ęhǫ ahabań ńhĭnā săe.* (2244)

Where an elephant died, all the leaves in his backyard were spoiled.

(Trampled down by people coming to cut up the meat.)

Wui. Perfect tense.

N'afikyiri. Lit. back of house.

96. *Osekan-tiá biako n̄n̄uá esóno, n̄n̄ua ko, n̄n̄ua odenkyem-mirempon̄, na wasan̄ agua onankã, na wasan̄ atiba wo wura nsa, na won̄hon̄ wo nto ade mu ana ?* (2850)

One little knife which cannot flay an elephant, which cannot flay a buffalo, which cannot flay a big-throated crocodile, and yet
.   you have gone out of your way (lit. turned back) to flay a python, and gone out of your way to cut your master's hand, will you not be plucked from your handle and cast into some place (out of the way)?

N̄n̄ua. Neg. of *gua.*

Agua. Subjunctive mood.

Won̄hon̄ . . . nto. For note on the negatives see No. 33, *mfa, nsisi.*

97. *Esóno di asãwa.* (3022)

An elephant eats the (little) *asãwa* berries.

Asãwa. Not *asawa*, the cotton plant, but a shrub with small berries, distinguished from the former word by the nasal *ã.*

98. *Esóno afon̄ a, wonné mpakam-mã oha.* (3024)

When an elephant is thin, that is not to say its meat will not fill a hundred baskets.

Wonné. Neg. of *de.*

99. *Esóno afon̄ a, won̄n̄ua no berew so.* (3025)

(Even) when an elephant is thin, it is not skinned on a palm leaf.

Won̄n̄ua. Neg. of *gua.*

Berew. The oil-palm leaf.

100. *Esóno hõ na wobo apuruwá.* (3026)

It is from the elephant that big lumps of meat are cut.

Apuruwá. Deriv. perhaps *puruw*, round.

101. *Esóno kàkrã, na adowa na ode ne ha.* (3027)

The elephant is a huge beast, but it is the duyker that is the (real) king of 'the bush' (jungle).

Kàkrã. With the tone rising on the second syllable, and a long final *ã.* *Kakra*, with an even intonation, has exactly the opposite meaning, 'little, small'.

Ha. *Eha*, the jungle, or 'bush', as it is called in West Africa. By metonymy the word is used for hunting, *ye ha, ahayo*, (the last a verbal noun).

102. *Esóno nyă wo a, adowa bo wo mă.* (3030)

When the elephant has got you in his clutches, the (little) duyker
(comes up) and slaps you.

103. *Obi nnyae sóno akyi di ṅkodi aseredoa akyi.* (300)

No one gives up following an elephant to go and follow the little
aseredoa bird.

Another version often heard is, *obi . . . ṅkobo aseredoa bo.* No
one . . . to throw a stone at the *aseredoa* bird.

Nnyae . . . ṅkodi. See note on No. 33, *mfa, nsisi.*

104. *Obi nni sóno akyi mmoro hŭăsú.* (256)

No one (who) is following an elephant has to knock the dew off the
grass.

Nni . . . mmoro. Neg. of *di,* and *boro.*

Hŭăsu. Deriv. *hŭă,* to brush against, and *nsu,* water.

105. *Wudi sóno akyi a, wontŏa.* (893)

When you follow an elephant you do not get entangled (with
creepers). Cf. No. 104, above.

106. *Obiakŏfo na okum sóno, na amansaṅ ṅhĭnā di.* (455)

It is one man who kills an elephant, but many people who eat its
flesh.

Amansaṅ. Deriv. *omaṅ,* people, nation, and *săṅ,* to draw a line.
(Cf. *santeṅ*), a long line of people.

107. *Ebia wobedi sóno na biribi ṅhĭa wo, na wudi apatā a, na dompe
ahĭa wo.* (444)

Perhaps you will eat a whole elephant and nothing will stick in
your throat, and then you eat a (little) fish and lo! a bone
has stuck in your throat.

Ebia. Perhaps the word is really a sentence—*e bi a,* 'there is
something that . . .'

Ṅhĭa. *Hĭa,* to stick in the throat; perhaps the same word as *hĭa,*
to be in trouble, distress, which is generally used impersonally,
ehĭa me.

108. *Wode kokŭrokó na edi amim a, aṅkă esóno beba ofie.* (753)

If mere bulk and size could be used to further greed and violence,
then the elephant would have come to the haunts of men (to
seize what he wanted).

109. *Wode sóno ɩhõma bu kotoku, na wode den ahyem'?* (768)

You may make a bag out of an elephant's hide, but what are you going to find to put in it ?

Bu. The idea is of bending or folding up the skin to form a bag.

110. *Obi nnim nea esóno di yee kese.* (278)

No one knows what the elephant ate to make it big.

111. *Obi nsusu sóno yam' mmu ahaban.* (346)

No one breaks off a leaf in order to measure the size of an elephant's belly with it.

Mmu. Neg. of *bu.* For idiomatic use of the negative see note on No. 33, *mfa, nsisi.*

Ahaban. Deriv. *ha* (q.v. No. 101) and *ban* (?), to lie or be arranged in a row (?).

112. *Enye aduan na esono nyă di kyen adowa nti na oye kese sen no.* (3597)

It is not the greater amount of food that the elephant eats than the duyker that makes it greater in size than he.

113. *Womfá akărā ntow sóno.* (1084)

A wax (bullet) is not used to shoot an elephant.

Ntow. Tow, lit. to throw or cast, as a stone or a spear, hence, when guns were introduced, of firing ; lit. 'throwing' a bullet.

114. *Gyata dǫsǒ ɩ̃iram' a, ankă nnipa nnyă băbi ntrā.* (1260)

If lions were very numerous in ' the bush ', then man would have no place to stay.

Gyata. Often called simply, ' the great beast' (*aboa kese*).

115. *Woborɔ gyata a, wo tiri pā wo.* (611)

If you strike a lion, your own head will pain you (you will not do the lion any harm).

116. *Gyahene hɔ̃ nye den a, onné kankan.* (1257)

Even when a lion is not a strong lion, it is not called a civet cat.

Onné. Neg. of *de.*

Kankan. Civet cat. Deriv. perhaps, *kankan,* stinking.

117. *Ade hĩa osebɔ a, ǫɩ̃e wura.* (800)

When a leopard is hard pressed for food, it chews grass.

Wura. See note on No. 92, *wuram'.*

118. *Kùrotừiamansã nennan sisia ase mã osisia wosow biribiri.* (1852)
The leopard that prowls about under the thicket causes the thicket
to shake greatly.

Nennan. Reduplication of *nam.*

119. *Kùrotừiamansã fa awuru a, odannan no hunu.* (1851)
When a leopard catches a tortoise it turns it over and over in vain.

Awuru. As *akyekyere.*

Odannan. Reduplication of *dan.*

120. *Kùrotừiamansã se, onam ha mu kwa, akyekyere na ode ne ha.*
(1853)
The leopard declares he prowls the bush to no purpose, and that the
tortoise really owns his jungle kingdom.

The following is the story on which the saying is based. A leopard was prowling about the bush in search of prey, and suddenly
seeing a tortoise, sprang on it, exclaiming, '*Manyã wo*', 'I've got you'.
The tortoise, however, replied, 'As for me, I have been watching
you long before you ever saw me'. The saying is quoted in the
sense that, a king may think he knows all about the affairs of his
subjects, whereas in reality they probably know a great deal more
about his.

121. *Aboa kùrotừiamansã hùnũ ato nijã, ankrãna aboa bi nni ừiram'.*
(519)
If the leopard could spring upon its prey to the right hand, then
no animal would be left alive in the bush.

Lions, leopards, and other animals of the cat tribe are all supposed, as it were, to be left-handed, that is to say, they spring to the
left on seizing their prey. A hunter will try to get a left shoulder
shot in preference to another. Native hunters say they know these
animals are left-handed by observing that animals found killed by
leopards, &c., are always, so they say, clawed on the right side, and
by observing spoor which, when turning, goes off to the left.

Nifã. Possible derivation, *enĩ fã; enĩ,* honour, (*di no enĩ*) and
fã, place. There is a scrupulous distinction in many ways between
the left and the right hand. (See note on No. 725.)

Ankrãna. Ankã, ankãna, see note on No. 733.

Wuram'. See note on No. 92.

122. *Aboa a osebo antumi anni no, agyinamoa mfa no afõ.* (497)
The animal which the leopard has been unable to kill and eat, the
cat is not going to eat its carcass.

Antumi aani. Anni, neg. of *di*. For note on the negative see No. 33, *mfa, nsisi*.

Agyinamoa. Deriv. *gyina*, to stand, and *ɛmɔa*, ditch, hollow, hole. There is a phrase, *ɔkɔ gyina ɛmɔa*, he has gone to hide himself (lit. gone to stand in a hole), hence of the cat crouching to spring. Another common name for the cat is *ɔkra* (lit. soul), and an Ashanti literally often calls his cat, ' *me ɔkra* ', my soul. When one of the household is ill and the family cat disappears, hope of recovery is given up. The Ashantis do not eat cats, but the Fantees do. Though not held in any particular veneration they are considered as uncanny and never ruthlessly interfered with.

123. *Obi nkyerɛ ɔsebɔ ba atow.* (233)
No one teaches a leopard's cub how to spring.

An almost similar saying is common in Malaya, where, as Sir Hugh Clifford told the writer, they say, ' No one teaches the tiger's cub how to kill ',—the interpretation in both countries, Malay and Ashanti, being the same, i. e. ' The king's sons do not need to be taught violence '.

124. *Wode sebɔ ɱhɔma sua adɯinni a, na wode aɯie.* (765)
When you use a leopard's skin for practising leather work on, it shows you have mastered your trade. (Cf. No. 373)

Adɯinni. Adɯini, a skilled trade, such as goldsmith, leatherworker, &c.; *adɯinni* (double *n*) = *adɯini di*, to practise a trade. Leopard-skins, used for *omanhene*'s drums, litters, &c., are much rarer than sheep- or goat- skins, and hence would not be used for experimental work unless a man was thoroughly sure of his skill.

125. *Osu fiɯe sebɔ a, ne hɔ na ɛfow, na ne nɯɑ̆rɑ̆n-nɯɑ̆rɑ̆n de, ɛmpopa.* (3054)
When rain beats on a leopard it wets him, but it does not wash out his spots.

Osu. Rain, see note on No. 26, *nsu*.

126. *Ɛko kum Krãnni a, menkɔ no ayi, na Okrãnni kum 'ko a, minni ne nãm.* (1598)
When a buffalo kills an Accra man, I do not go to his funeral, and when an Accra man kills a buffalo, I do not eat its flesh.

Ɛko. The West African buffalo or ' bush-cow ', probably, after the elephant (some might place it first), the most dangerous of all animals when wounded and followed up.

Ayi. See note on No. 56.

Okrănni. Suffix *ni* for *onipa*, an Accra man.

Ṅkraṅ is the Accra of the European.

The saying above quoted is meant to express deep and undying hatred, or two persons or conditions that could never have anything in common or become reconciled to each other.

127. *Otwĕ dua yɛ tiā a, nea ọde pra nehŏ ara neṅ.* (3412)

The duyker's tail may be short, but it brushes its body with it notwithstanding.

Neṅ. *Neṅ = ne no.*

128. *Otwĕ ṅhŏma silane nea eyɛ hare.* (3413)

The duyker's skin (hide) splits where it is thinnest.

Hare. Light, quick, nimble; here thin, fragile.

129. *Otwĕ aṅkọ gua, ne ṅhŏma kọ.* (3414)

The duyker does not go to market, but its skin does.

Antelope hides are used for covering loads to keep the rain off.

Aṅkọ. Lit. has not gone.

130. *Otwĕ nɛ otwĕ kŏ na wohũ gyahene a, na wọkọ afã na woguaṅ.* (3415)

When two duykers are quarrelling, and they see a lion (coming), off they run together (forgetting their quarrel).

131. *Otwĕ ani anseṅ a, na ɛfi bọmmọfo.* (3416)

When the antelope is unhappy, it is the hunter who is the cause.

Bọmmọfo. Also spelled *obọmofo*, and *ọbọfo;* deriv. *bọ* to strike, to hit. Hunters among this people, with a few exceptions, are not as skilful trackers or as close observers of the habits of game as their brothers in East and Central Africa.

They have one accomplishment, however, which, as far as the present writer knows or has seen, is not known to the Anyanja, Angoni, or Chipeta shikari. They can call up the smaller game, bush-buck, duyker, &c., by imitation of the bleat of the doe or kid. (Cf. the calling of moose.)

Hunting among the Ashantis is a recognized profession. It is not every native who would care to take the risks involved, for not by any means the greatest of these risks is the actual danger run by hunting bush-cow or elephant. The Ashanti shikari runs other risks. 'A mad hunter' (*ọbọfo damfo*) is a common expression, a sort of equivalent of our 'as mad as a hatter'. If the hunter does not take great care to propitiate the spirits (*sāsā*) of the larger species of game he may kill by ceremonial dances (*abofosi*), he is supposed in time to become mad. The *otromo* (*bongo*), is an especially dangerous animal in this respect. In a hunter's dance the man goes all over again in realistic mimicry the killing of the animal whose *sāsā* he wishes to avoid entering his body. .

Butchers also are thought to go mad sooner or later for a similar reason.

132. *Otwĕ nyā nantu a, wokyi.* (3417)
When (you see) a duyker which has a (thick) leg, that is something you avoid (make a taboo).

Nyā nantu. Lit. got a calf (on its leg).

Wokyi. The verb *kyi* is used in two senses, to hate, to dislike, of a person or object, and to hate in the sense of refuse to eat an animal or thing owing to some religious (totemic) observance, that is, it is exactly rendered by the word taboo.

The native literally says, 'I hate fish', 'I hate goats' flesh', 'I hate eggs', or whatever may be his particular taboo. The derivation is possibly the root *kyi*, back, to turn one's back on, see note on No. 89, *akyi.*

133. *Otwĕ m'pŏrɔw adu kŭrom' !* (3418)
Let the antelope rot in the hollow of the tree! (A congener of our 'dog in the manger'.)

The following is the story on which the above is founded. A certain man had a hunter whom he used to send to kill game but he never allowed him the smallest portion of any animal he brought in. One day the hunter, having killed an antelope (a duyker), hid it in a tree and went and asked his master saying, 'If I should happen to kill anything to-day, will you give me a piece?' The master said 'No'. The hunter then went off muttering as above, 'Let the antelope. . .'

Adu. For *dua.*

134. *Odɛnkyɛm da nsu mu, nso ɔnom mframa.* (859)
The crocodile lies in the water, but it also drinks (breathes) the air.

Nsu. See note on No. 26.

Ɔnom. Lit. drinks. Cf. Hausa *sha iska*, to drink the air.

135. *Ọdeṅkyẹm ẅereẹ sene ẅere-pá dẹ.* (860)

A crocodile's skin is sweeter than any other skin.

The skins of many animals are used to boil down and make soup of. Some, sheep's, goat's, &c., only in times of want, others, again, as the hippo's and elephant's, are considered a delicacy.

The word *ẅere*, skin, is found in many idiomatic expressions, which curiously remind one of English slang, e.g. to jump out of one's skin; by the skin of one's teeth, save your skin, &c. E.g. *ne ẅere bo*, the price of his skin, the value of a slave; *ne ẅere nsŏ mmã no*, lit. his skin is not big enough for him; that is, of a person jumping about, fidgety; *me ẅere fi*, lit. my skin has come out, I have forgotten; *me ẅere kyekye*, my skin has become tight, I am happy, &c.

Ẅere-pá. See note on No. 483.

136. *Funtumfrafu deṅkyẹm frafu, wọwọ yafunu koro nanso wọnyã biribi a, wọfom, nanso wọn nhĩnara wọ yafunu koro, nanso wodi no amenemutwitwi.*

The 'Two-headed crocodiles' have but one belly for both, yet when either of them get anything they fight among themselves for it, for though they both have only one belly for each of their separate heads, each wants the food to pass down its own throat. (This proverb is not among those in the 'Tshi Proverb' book.)

Funtumfrafu deṅkyẹm frafu. There is a mythical crocodile supposed to have two heads and two necks which merge into a common belly, which again merges into two tails. This emblem is one of the many 'Ashanti weights', most of which are probably symbolical; see note on No. 591.

This clever metaphor clearly states the ideas of a communistic people.

Funtumfrafu. *Funtum*, to collect together, *fra*, to mix, and *fu=afunu*, belly; *funtum-frafu deṅkyẹm frafu*, therefore means literally, 'Bellies mixed up, crocodiles mixed up'.

Wọn nhĩnara. Lit. they all; *nhĩnara=nhĩnã ara.*

Amenemutwitwi. Deriv. *amene*, throat; *mu*, in; *twitwi*, to rub, i.e. of the food rubbing (in its passage down the gullet) the throat.

137. *Wutiẅa asu ẅie a, na wuse ọdeṅkyẹm ano pọw.* (3405)

When you have *quite* crossed the river, you say that the crocodile has a lump on its snout.

Wutẅa . . . wie. Translate, 'When you have finished crossing', 'or quite crossed'. The English idiom 'to finish doing anything', which is expressed by a finite verb and a participle, is in Ashanti, and all other native languages known to the writer, expressed by two finite verbs. E.g. 'he has finished doing' is translated by two finite verbs in two principal clauses, he has done, he has finished. *Wa* is understood before *wie.*

138. *Ọkọ́tọ́ a ọda siká hõ po tẅẹ̀re abẹ́.* (1739)
Even the crab, that lives where the gold dust is, eats palm nuts. (Palm nuts are supposed to be the food of poor people.)

Ọkọ́tọ́. Either the land or sea crab. Crab claws are tied on the hair of a child whose brothers and sisters have all died (such a child is called *begyinaba*, lit. 'it will stand (remain) child'). See also note on No. 486, *kobuobi*, for prefix 'ko added to names of such children by way of cheating Death into supposing the child is really a slave, and also No. 574 note.

Hõ. Here a locative complement of the verb *da.*
Tẅẹ́re. To skin with the teeth.

139. *Ọkọ́tọ́ ṅwo ɛnõmä.* (1740)
A crab does not give birth to a bird.

140. *Ọkọ́tọ́ bẹne asuo 'ti na onim asuo kasä.* (1741)
Because the crab lives near the river he knows the language of the river.

Bẹne. Perhaps past tense.
'Ti. For *nti.*
Kasä. Speech, language; deriv. *kã asem* (?).

141. *Ọkọ́tọ́ bọ pẹmmo a, ọsaṅ n'akyi.* (1742)
When a crab falls down plump on its bottom, it turns back. (To fall so is considered a bad omen.)

142. *Ọkọ́tọ́ foforó aperẹw mu nni nãm.* (1743)
A young crab has no meat in its claws.

Foforó. Lit. new, here 'young'.
Nni. Neg. of *wo.*

143. *Ọkọ́tọ́ guaṅ a, oguaṅ kọ pom'.* (1744)
When a crab runs away it is towards the sea it flees.

Pom = *ẹpo mu.*

144. *Okɔtɔ na onim sika dabere.* (1745)

It is the crab that knows where the gold dust is to be found.

Dabere. Lit. 'the sleeping-place of'.

145. *Okɔtɔ annyã adayé nti na ɔda amõa mu.* (1746)

Because the crab has no good place to sleep in, it lives in a hole.

Adayé. Da, to lie, to sleep, and *ye,* good.

146. *Okɔtɔ po di sukɔm, na menne ɔkwaku a ɔda ɔsoro.* (1747)

Even the crab gets thirsty, not to speak of the monkey that sleeps up above.

Sukɔm. Lit. water hunger, *nsu ɔkɔm.*

Menne. Neg. of *de.*

147. *Aboa dompó nni asumguarede nti na ɔnam asu hõ bɔ akɔtɔ.* (505)

Because the otter (?) has made no preparation for the washing of its soul, that is why it walks about digging for crabs (to offer to the soul).

Nni asumguarede. Di asumguarede (asu-mu-guare-ade). The following is an account of 'a soul washing' (*ɔkra-guare-ade; ɔkra-guarede*). Perhaps once a year an Ashanti fixes on a day on which to wash his *ɔkra* (soul or spirit). See note on No. 9, *ṅkrabea.* The relatives are informed, and as many pure white fowls collected as the person can afford.

On the appointed day the fowls are carried down to the water in an *aibowa* (brass or metal bowl). *Adibira*[1] (a small plant) and *ṅsome* leaves which have been collected are then dipped in the water and the fowls are sprinkled over. The person who is washing his soul then addresses it, asking it to prosper him and bring him luck. (This part of the ceremony may also be performed at home). On returning to the house the fowls are killed and the blood sprinkled about the corners of the house compound. Yams or plantains are mashed and cooked (no oil being used in order that they may be white). These and the fowls are eaten by the assembled friends. There is for that day a complete cessation of all work; no one can demand payment of a debt or swear the king's oath (see note on No. 496, *wokã*) on the person on that day. The idea of a good or perhaps rather, lucky *ɔkra* being white is a strong belief; *ɔkra biṅ,* black soul, is said of an extremely unlucky man; there is no connexion with morality or purity of soul in our sense of the word.

[1] The town of Ejura (which should rightly be spelled EDWIRA) is so called after the plant.

148. *Kotǫkǫ rekǫ kotǫkǫ a, ǫmfa adidide.* (1750)

When the porcupine is going to visit the porcupine, he does not take any food with him.

Kotǫkǫ. The Ashantis call themselves *Asante Kotǫkǫ*, the Ashanti Porcupines. The saying above means, when an Ashanti man goes on a visit to an Ashanti man he will rely on the hospitality of his host. The idea in the name *Asante Kotǫkǫ*, is '*nemo me impune lacessit*'.

Adidide. Adidi (reduplication of *di*, and *ade*).

149. *Aboa akyekyereę nni ntama, nsoso awǫw nne no da.* (522)

The tortoise has no cloth, hair, or wool, nevertheless it does not ever feel the cold.

Nni. Neg. of *wǫ.*

Nsoso. Reduplication of *nso.*

Nne. Neg. of *de.*

150. *Mmoadǒmǎ ṅhǐnǎ foro bo, akyekyere ṅ' kǫforo bi, wapǫṅ afǐwe.*

All animals (can) climb stones, but let the tortoise try to, and he tumbles down. (Said of an unlucky person.)

Ṅ'kǫforo. Imperative mood, with the auxiliary *kǫ.* Lit. let him go and climb.

Wapǫṅ. Perfect tense, 'he has fallen down'. See note on No. 757.

151. *Akyekyere nni nufu, nso ǫwo a, onim nea oyę yeṅ ne ba.* (1924)

The tortoise has not any milk, but when it gives birth, it knows how to rear its child.

Nufu. By metonymy for *nufusu (nufu nsu),* lit. breast water.

152. *Akyekyere kǫ serew serew na oguaṅ ara neṅ.* (1925)

The tortoise goes off in a laughable manner, but he can escape all the same.

Neṅ = ne no.

153. *Akyekyere na okyerę ne bǫberę na wǫbǫ no.* (1926)

It is the tortoise itself that exposes its vulnerable spot (the head) and has it struck.

When the natives want to kill and eat a tortoise (the flesh of which is much relished), they scratch the tortoise on the back, which makes it show its head.

154. *Akyekyere dę ne yere amanne, ose, ' Wǫw m' akyi mmęsǎ (wǫw mmęsǎ gu m' ǐtiko), nǎ meṅkǫfǐwę agoru'.* (1928)

When the tortoise seeks a quarrel with his wife he says, 'Plait the tress of hair falling down my back and let me be off in search of some fun'.

155. *Akyekyere se, 'Obarima mfẹre aguaṅ'.* (1929)
The tortoise says, 'A man need not be ashamed to run away'.

Mfẹre. *Fẹre* has a great variety of meanings, the idea of embarrassment or shyness seeming to be at the root of all. It is used of the respectful fear a child should have for a parent, and also for the strictness with which a parent treats his child. (See No. 378.) The word is used in a religious (religious in the wide sense, as in Tylor's famous 'minimum definition') signification, e.g. *fẹre Onyankŏpọṅ*, sometimes in the place of *kyi* (q.v. No. 132), to shun, to make taboo; and as in the sense used above, fear of ridicule. Cf. No. 718.

156. *Akyekyere se, 'Ntẹm ye, na ọjŏm ye'.* (1931)
The tortoise says, 'Haste is a good thing and deliberation is also a good thing'.

157. *Ṅhwĩ nyẹ-nā a, aṅkā akyekyere nni bi?* (1467)
If hair was not difficult to grow, would not the tortoise have some?

Nyẹ-nā. *Nā* is suffixed to certain verbs and gives the verb the idea of difficulty in the performing of the action implied in the verb. Thus *yẹ-nā*, difficult to be done; *tow-nā*, difficult to throw, &c.

158. *Wokọ awuru kŭrom' na odi dọte a, wudi bi.* (1584)
When you go to the village of the tortoise and it eats earth, you eat some oo. (Cf. No. 297.)

Awuru. Another name for the tortoise, *akyekyere*.

159. *Awuru reẁea (na) ne ba reẁea, (na) hena na obegye wọṅ tātā?* (3504)
The tortoise crawls, and his child crawls, and which will take the other and teach him how to walk upright?

Reẁea. Present continued action, expressed by *re*.

Obegye wọṅ tātā. *Gye tātā*, to teach an infant how to walk. *Tātā*, lit. baby language, spoken to the child to encourage it to try and stand and walk towards the person who is holding out the hands to receive (*gye*) it.

160. *Ọkétéw a ọtare pọdọ hŏ bo yẹ tow-nă.* (1542)
It is difficult to throw a stone at a lizard which is clinging to a pot (without breaking the pot).

Ǫtare. *Tare* has the idea in it of anything adhering to or lying close up against a thing; hence, to plaster with mud (the wall of a house). Here of the lizard lying close up against the pot.

Hŏ. A complement of the verb *tare.*

Tow-nă. See note above, No. 157, *nyę-nă.*

Ǫkétéw nè ketebǫ sę diṅ na wǫnsę̌ hŏnam. (1545)

The lizard (*ǫkétéw*) and the antelope (*ketebǫ*) have names which are similar, but their appearance is not the same.

Ǫkétéw nim sę ayanikaw bęba nti na obutuw siei. (1546)

Because the lizard knows its belly will become painful, it lies down on it (before the pain comes).

Any one who has watched lizards will have noticed them pressing their bellies against the ground, raising themselves up again on their two fore feet, then laying themselves flat again, for all the world like one of Sandow's exercises, where you raise and lower yourself with your arms, while lying face down on the ground.

The chameleon's belly is supposed to burst and the animal to die on its giving birth.

The natives consider lying on the stomach a cure for belly-ache. The saying above is the Ashanti congener of our 'prevention is better than cure'.

Siei. See note on No. 10, *adi asie.*

Ǫkétéw wǫ yam aduru a, aṅkă yam ansi no adurade. (1547)

Had the lizard medicine against eczema, then its body would not be clothed with eczema.

Yam. A skin disease (eczema?). The rough mottled bodies of some lizards give them the exact appearance of having some skin disease.

Adurade. A shirt or burnous.

Ǫkétéw ṅwe mako na fifiri mfi atiberǫrǫ. (1548)

The lizard does not eat pepper and sweat break out on the frog. (A man bears the brunt of his own actions.)

Atiberǫrǫ. A small frog. The common word for frog is *apotǫrǫ.* Both words are onomatopoetic, *rǫ rǫ* suggesting the croaking of frogs.

Ṅwaw de nehŏ sie a, na wǫfa no tope. (3427)

If the snail takes care of itself, when it is taken, it will be taken as a big snail.

Snails are collected and strung on sticks; they fetch a big price and are considered a great delicacy.

Tope. A full-grown snail.

166. *Ṅwaw wu ṅkwaṅ mu a, empŏrǫw.* (3430)
When a snail dies in the soup, it does not rot.

167. *Ǫwǫ de ahŏyerew na ǫka.* (3446)
It is owing to being disturbed that a snake bites.

168. *Ǫwǫ aduru, wǫtew no ahŏǫhare.* (3447)
The herbs to apply to a snake bite are quickly plucked.

169. *Ǫwǫ ṅka onipa kwa.* (3448)
A snake does not bite a man without a cause.

170. *Ǫwǫ ṅkesua ṅkŏ na ebesuw wuram' a, aṅkã biribiara nseee e.* (3449)
If it were only snakes' eggs that were addled in ' the bush ', that would not have mattered at all.

Nseee e. Lit. nothing would have been spoiled at all. The final particle *e*, makes the statement very emphatic.

171. *Ǫwǫ te se hãmã, na wǫmfa ṅkyekyere ade.* (3451)
A snake is like rope, but it is not (for that reason) taken to bind a thing with.

172. *Aboa naṅkã nim adekyĕe a, aṅkã ǫda ṅẃia-da ?* (524)
If the python knew when it was dawn, would it sleep in the day-time ?

Ṅẃia-da. Lit. ' day sleep '.

173. *Woṅhũ ǫwǫ ti a, wǫmmǫ no abã.* (1450)
Unless you see a snake's head, you do not strike at it (any other part of the body).

Woṅhũ . . . wǫmmǫ. 3rd pers. plural, can be translated by passive, or ' you ', indefinite pronoun.

174. *Onankanini da ase anyã ǫṅwãm.*
The python lies on the ground and has got a toucan.

This proverb is represented among the Ashanti weights. (Cf. No. 136).

See note on No. 591.

The saying is used meaning that a man need never despair of getting anything, however impossible it may seem at the time.

CHAPTER III

INSECTS: THE SPIDER, FLY, ANTS.

175. *Aboa ananse nam na oso ne dan.* (525)
The spider walks and carries his house (web).

Aboa. See note on No. 89, *aboa.*

Ananse. The spider in Ashanti folk-lore comes easily first as the hero in most of their animal tales. To such an extent has this been so, that the very word for a story in this language, be the spider one of the dramatis personæ or not, is *anansesem,* i. e. *ananse asem,* lit. words about a spider. That these stories probably had a religious or totemic origin seems possible, for to this day a sobriquet for the Supreme Being is *Ananse kokroko,* the Great Spider '. The spider is credited with being very wise, but in Hausa folk-lore he is rather of the lovable rogue order. The following little story, out of the scores current, is given, being a literal translation taken down from the lips of a native.

' The Spider collected all the wisdom of the world and shut it up in a gourd, and was climbing up a tree to deposit it on the top. He got into difficulties, however, before he reached half-way up, as he had tied the gourd on to his belly, and it hindered him from climbing properly. His son, *Ntikuma,* who was watching him, said, " Father, if you had really all the wisdom of the world with you, you would have had sense enough to tie the gourd to your back ! " His father, seeing the truth of this, threw down the gourd in a temper. It broke, and the wisdom it contained became scattered, and men came and picked up what each could carry away.'

The wife of the spider is known as *Konori* or *Konoro*

176. *Ananse a onpe anwene bi anwene, na onwene tempon mu.* (2098)
A spider which does not really wish to spin spins its web on a much frequented road (where the people passing soon break it).

Anwene. *Nwene,* to weave or plait. This word is also used for the moulding of a pot, in which use we probably have a survival showing that pots were once made by first making a basketwork frame on to which the clay was daubed. A further relic of this method of manufacture may be seen in the criss-cross designs which are sometimes used to ornament pots.

177. *Ananse se asantrofi se, ' Se wobefue ase so a, fue ase so, se nso wobedi ńkorowa hene a, fue ńkorowa hene so di'.* (2099)

The spider says to the night-jar (?) 'If you are going to look after the beans, look after the beans, but if you are going to be leader in the *ńkorowa* dance, then confine your energies to that' (lit. be leader in the *ńkorowa* dance).

The following is the story on which the above saying is based. The night-jar (?) had a plantation of beans which he had reason to suppose the spider used to come and steal from. Now, both he and the spider were very fond of dancing the *ńkorowa* dance, and the spider used to take advantage of this, and steal off to the bean farm whenever he saw the night-jar at the dance. One day the *asantrofi* hit on the following plan to circumvent the spider. Plucking out some of his feathers, he stuck them in a clay model and set it up in his bean garden and then returned to the dance. The spider, seeing him thus engaged, managed to slip away and went off to steal the beans. Much to his surprise he found what he thought to be the *asantrofi* bird there, and so again returned to join the dancers. Lo, and behold, there was the *asantrofi* among the revellers ! Off he slipped to the beans once more, but again there was the night-jar. Returning once more and finding the night-jar (back, as he thought), at the dance, he addressed him in the words of the saying quoted above. The saying is meant to imply that there is often some ulterior motive underlying what looks like merely friendly advice.

178. *Ananse antoń kasa.* (2100)

The spider has not sold words.

He has given them freely. The allusion is to the great number of spider stories current among the Ashantis, among whom in fact every story is known as *anansesem*, lit. ' words about the spider ', whether the spider appears or is alluded to in the story at all. See note on No. 175, on *ananse*.)

Antoń. Perfect tense.

179. *Agya Ananse adi asemmone na 'yepam no, na wannyã bãbi ańkoro na oseń padee ani.* (1240)

Father Spider did wrong and we drove him away, and as he had no place to go he hangs from the crossbeams of the roof.

For the story on which this saying is founded see note on No. 175.

Asemmore = Asem bone.

Aṅkoro. Akan dialect for *kọ.* For note on the negative see No. 33, *mfɛ, nsisi.*

180. *Agya Ananse ṅwoo ne ba Ntikūmā na ọwọ nea ọso ne bọtọ.* (1241)
Before Father Spider begot his son *Ntikūmā* he had some one to carry his bag.

This saying is quoted in the sense of 'you are not indispensable, and can go if you want to, I can get some one to take your place', or, 'I managed quite well before I had you'.

Ṅwoo. Past tense, formed by lengthening of final vowel.

Ntikūmā. See note on No. 175.

181. *Ẹfere nti na agya Ananse de ọtwĕ kyew hyẹ adọw.* (1112)
Because of shame Father Spider takes an antelope skin hat when he goes to ask people to come and assist him at his hoeing.

Hyẹ adọw. Cf. *hyẹ da*, to appoint a day for doing anything. The meaning is somewhat obscure. The following interpretation may be given. Antelope skin hats (not now seen anywhere) were worn thirty or forty years ago by some 'elders'. The allusion may be to the markings on the bodies of some spiders not unlike a spotted bush-buck's skin. The spider is supposed to have put on this hat to cover some blemish on his head.

182. *Mireguare suọhyew na ananse reguare ne mma, na meguare suoṅ-ŵini ẹ ?* (1237)
I bathe in hot water, and the spider keeps washing his children in it, so I shall wash in cold water and what can he do then ?

When water bubbles and 'sings' on being boiled, these natives say 'There is Father Spider washing his children'. The saying is quoted in the sense of 'I'll get the better of him somehow'.

183. *Obi ntó anansesẹm ṅkyerẹ Ntikūmā.* (359)
No one tells stories to *Ntikūmā.*

Ntó . . . ṅkyerẹ. For the double negative see note on No. 33.

Anansesẹm. Lit. 'words about the spider', but this is the term used for any story whatever, even one in which the spider does not appear in any way.

Ntikŭmă. The spider's child. As the spider is the fount and origin of all stories, the son, *Ntikŭmă,* would be supposed to know every story in the world, having heard them from his father. The saying is used in the sense of ' I know all about that, tell me something I do not know '. (See note on No. 175, *ananse).*

184. *Ṅwansana de ne nsa gu n'akyi a, ose, ' Nea aka akyiri na ẹdǫsö'.* (2570)

When the fly stretches his legs (lit. hands) behind him, he says, ' There still remains a lot to come ' (lit. what is behind is much).

If one watches a fly closely it will sometimes be seen to stretch its feet backward over its body. This proverb is used in the sense of ' I have done a great deal for you, but you can still hope for future signs of favour.'

185. *Ṅwansana ampa funu hŏ a, wǫde no sie.* (2571)

When a fly does not get up off a dead body, he is buried with it.

Funu. Ẹfunu. Deriv. *funu,* useless, rotten, hence a carcass, dead body.

Ampa. The *hŏ* is probably the reflexive pronoun, and *pa hŏ,* to take itself off. It might, however, be taken as complement of *funu.*

186. *Ṅwansana pobi, onni ano, na ǫtŭẹre bebuṅ.* (2572)

The bluebottle fly (?) has no mouth, but it can strip the green palm nuts.

Onni. Neg. of *wo.*

Bebuṅ. Deriv. *abẹ,* and *buṅ,* green, unripe.

187. *Ṅwansana pobi si abeyā mu a, wotaforo mu.* (2573)

Though the bluebottle fly sits on the dish, you lick inside it.

Abeyā. Akyem dialect, in Ashanti *aẁowa.*

188. *Ṅwansana yẹ sisi a, onsi gya mu.* (2575)

Wherever else a fly is going to alight, it does not alight on fire.

Yẹ sisi. Here *yẹ* is an auxiliary verb having the meaning of ' about to ', ' be prepared to '.

189. *Ohurii di bem, ṅwansana na ǫyẹ me sẹ.* (1463)

Now surely the tsetse had good reason to bite me (as every one knows it is a biting fly), for here is the common house fly doing the same (and it is not supposed to bite at all).

This saying is quoted in the sense of 'I prefer, if I must be badly treated, to be badly treated by a superior and not by my equal or inferior', or, again, it was a saying often put in the mouths of slaves who, when their old master had died and left them to his nephews, on being badly treated by them, would say that after all they could not blame their former master for any bad treatment, here were his nephews doing the same.

190. *Ohurii nni gyamfo.* (1464)
The biting fly has no one to come to his aid in trouble. (Cf. No. 192, below.)

Gyamfo. For note on suffix *fo* see No. 78, *kontromfi.*

191. *Ohurii si akyekyere akyi kwa.* (1465)
The biting fly gets nothing by alighting on the back of the tortoise.

192. ' *Meka nnipa nhĩnã,' nti na ohurii annyã ogyamfo.* (1480)
'I shall bite all men,' because of that the tsetse has no one to come to his aid in trouble.

193. *Mfotế pãm ansã-na woaye yã.* (1146)
Ants have to unite (in great numbers) before they (can) make a noise.

Yã. A hissing sound.

Pãm. Nasal *ã. Pam*, probably the same root, means to join, to mend by placing together.

Woaye. Lit. have made. Perfect tense.

194. *Mfotee te se dibie, nanso o nè no nse.* (1147)
A white ant is like a louse, and yet they are not really the same.

Dibie Also *dibiw.*

195. *Mfote a wuwu a wobedi wo nãm no, na wote ho a, wobe wo tam.* (1149)
The white ants that will, when you die, devour your flesh, when you are alive eat your clothes.

A . . . a. The first *a* is the relative pronoun, the second the adverb, introducing the adverbial clause of time.

196. *Obi nkotoa chãhini wo nè bón anò ná onse se, ' Wo ho bon'.* (215)
No one tracks a black ant to the mouth of its hole and then says, 'You stink'.

Ṅkọtoa . . . onse. For note on the second negative see No. 33, *mfa, nsisi.*

Ọhāhíni. The large black ant, which has a most offensive smell; not the large biting ant, which is *ṅkráṅ.*

197. *Obi nnyina ṅkráṅ mù ntutú ṅkráṅ* (313)
No one stands among black ants and picks off black ants.

198. *Ṅkesua tọ ṅkraṅ mu a, mā ẹnna mu, na wọnam hŏ kwa.* (1539)
When an egg falls among black ants, let it lie there, for they will walk over it without being able to do it any harm.

CHAPTER IV

BIRDS: THE HEN AND COCK, VULTURE, HAWK, PARROT, BIRDS IN GENERAL.

199. *Obi nton ne kokobere kwà.* (363)

No one sells his (laying) hen without a good reason.

Kokobere. *Koko, akoko,* a fowl; *bere,* feminine suffix; *akokonini.* a cock. An onomatopoetic word, cf. Chinyanja, *nkuku,* and Hausa, *kaza.*

200. *A koko nom nsu a, ode kyere Onyankŏpoṅ.* (1653)

When a fowl drinks water, it (first) takes it and shows it to the Supreme Being.

This pretty idea is of course derived from noticing the habit a fowl has of throwing its head back when it is drinking.

Onyaṅkŏpoṅ. See note on No. 1 on *Onyàmé.*

201. *A koko di wo yoṅkŏ aŵi a, pam no, na dabi obedi wo de.* (1644)

When a fowl is eating your friend's grain, drive it away, for some day it will eat yours.

202. *Akoko ani sã bùrofua.* (1652)

The fowl's eye is keen to see the single grain of corn.

203. *Akoko se, 'Ade ansã a, aṅkã memĕe?'* (1655)

The fowl says, 'If it had not got dark, should I have had my fill?'

Ade ansã. Lit. *ade asã,* thing(s) are finished, i.e. it is dark. Cf. *ade kye,* lit. thing(s) appear, i.e. it is dawn.

Aṅkã. See note on No. 733.

Memĕe. Past tense formed by lengthening of final vowel.

204. *Akoko naṅ ṅkum ba.* (1648)

The hen's foot does not kill (her) chicken.

Naṅ. Sometimes *nantam'* (i.e. 'in the space between the feet') is given instead of *naṅ,* in this saying.

205. *Akoko hyeṅ kye ofie a, obere.* (1646)

When a white fowl remains a long time in a house, it gets red (with earth and dust).

206. *Akoko ntakăra na ęmă akoko yę kęse.* (1658)

It is the feathers on a fowl that make it big.

Na. See note on No. 1, *na.*

(This saying has been heard in the sense that, it is the number of subjects whom a chief has who make him important.)

207. *Akoko ntakăra nyiṅ a, etuatua ne hŏnam mu.* (1659)

When the feathers of a fowl grow, they still remain attached to its body.

Cf. No. 206, above. The feathers are here again likened to the subjects of a chief who even when they increase in wealth or importance should still be subject to their chief.

208. *Wo kyere akokotaṅ a, wo tase ne mma kwa.* (1956)

When you have caught the mother hen, you pick up the chickens without difficulty.

Akokotaṅ. The suffix *taṅ*, applied equally to animals and persons, denotes a state of parentage.

209. *Obi ntŭa akoko ano mmă akyĕ.* (385)

No one says 'Good morning' before the cock has done so.

Ntŭa ano. Lit. to cut the mouth, i.e. forestall in speaking. The day ends roughly when a man retires to rest. A child born at, say, 10 p.m. on a Monday is called *Kwabena*, i.e. Tuesday's child.

210. *Akokobere nim adekyĕe, na ofŭę onini ano.* (1664)

The hen knows when the dawn comes, but she nevertheless looks to the cock (to make it known).

211. *Akokonini bow nsă na ne ŭerę afi akŏrŏmă.* (1669)

When the cock is drunk he forgets about the hawk.

Ŭerę afi. See note on No. 135.

212. *Akokonini se, 'To tamfo ṅkŏ a, aṅkă maboṅ anadŭo na woakum me'.* (1673)

The cock says, 'Had I nothing but enemies left, then when I have crowed in the night I should have been killed'.

A cock crowing at midnight or long before dawn is immediately killed, as it is considered unlucky. Cf. custom in Scotland of rubbing a cock's feet with salt which crowed before the usual time.

213. *Okokonini, gyae wohŏ kyere, na wo nã ne kesua hóno.* (1671)

O cock, leave off being puffed up with pride ; after all, your mother was only an egg-shell.

Hóno. Used of the outer covering of things, husk, bark, shell.

214. *Obi mfa akoko nañase ade, mfa nkoto akokofiberew nañase.* (151)

No one takes the string of beads off a fowl's leg and goes and puts it on the leg of a partridge.

(The owner often identifies a fowl by a bit of cloth, string, or beads round its leg.)

Nañase ade. Lit. the thing at the bottom of a foot or leg.

Mfa, nkoto. Note the negative verbs following the first negative *mfa.* See No. 33, *mfa, nsisi.*

215. *Akoko nni asŏ nanso ónnyã ne sŏtore a, wode bo no ara.* (1651)

A fowl has no ears, so does not get them boxed, but it gets its beating all the same.

Sŏtore. Deriv. *asŏ,* ear, and *tore,* to fall on (?).

216. *Akoko-pa na owo asense, asense (se), 'Me nkŏ mifi hĕ ?'* (1654)

An ordinary fowl hatches out an *asense* chicken, and the *asense* one (asks in wonder) saying, 'I alone, where did I come from ?'

Asense. A fowl with curled ruffled feathers.

217. *Akoko se, 'Kyere akyekyere tutu no', na ono akyekyere se, 'Na wo de, woabĕre'.* (1656)

The fowl says, 'Catch the tortoise and pluck it,' but he (the tortoise) replies, 'As for you, you will (lit. have tired) tire of trying that'.

Akyekyere. Also called *awuru.*

218. *Akoko ti si ahĕ na worebo mu fe ?* (1660)

How big is a fowl's head that they should be striking at it ?

Si ahĕ. Lit. it stands how much, i.e. it is not large enough to warrant one hitting it if one does not want to kill the fowl altogether.

219. *Okokonini, gyae akuntun-akuntun, na yen nhĩnā ye kesua mma.* (1670)

Cock, desist from self-glorification, for we are all the children of eggs.

Akuntun. Lit. to bend, hence to walk with an affected gait, to swagger.

220. *Akokǫ a wo nè no da no, wompę no ntęm.* (1641)

The fowl which sleeps in the same hut as yourself, you are not in a hurry to go and search for (you know it will come back to roost, and you will be able to catch it then).

221. *Akokǫ da ntęm a onyi kaw mmä ne wura.* (1642)

When a fowl comes soon to roost, it does not get its master into debt.

222. *Akokǫ nè krakum kŏ.* (1650)

The fowl and the turkey quarrel.

Krakum. Dutch, *kalkoen.*

223. *Merebekum akokǫ, makum obereku na mafŭę sę adekyĕe beyę dęn ?* (1815)

I am going to kill (my) fowl, (and) I have (already) killed the clock bird (?), in order to see what the dawn will do.

(The coming of dawn is not what causes the cock to crow or the *obereku* to give forth its liquid notes, but rather these are the cause of the dawn breaking, in the native mind.)

Na mafŭe. Subjunctive mood.

Adekyĕe. See note on No. 203, *ade ansä.*

224. *Wunim nyansa bebrebe a, womä akokǫ akyä.* (2331)

If you are too wise a man (said in a sarcastic sense), you say ' Good morning' to a fowl (i.e. you will find yourself led into committing some supreme folly).

225. *Wokǫ obi kŭrom na okum akokǫ mä wo di a, ęnyę ne de no na woadi, na wo de a ǫwǫ fie no na woadi.* (1568)

When you go to some one's town and he kills a fowl for you to eat, it is not his fowl you have eaten, but your own which is at home.

226. *Aboa kŏkosakyi kasa kyerę obonúkyĕręfo a, ote.* (513)

When the vulture gives the hyena advice, he heeds it.

Kŏkosakyi. Also *opete* and *akrampä,* the vulture.

Obonúkyĕręfo. Also called *pataku,* the hyena.

The saying is based on the following story. The mother of the hyena died and all his friends assembled to take part in the funeral custom. Day after day passed, and still the body remained unburied, and the mourners began to feel the pangs of hunger.

The hyena alone seemed to remain plump and fat and in no hurry to bring the obsequies to an end by allowing the body of his mother to be buried. Now the reason was that he was all the time visiting the spot where the corpse was *and eating some of it.*

The vulture, which had been attracted by the smell, had seen all the hyena was doing, and on the mourners again pressing the hyena to bury the body, and on his again refusing to do so, drew him aside and told him he had seen all that was going on, whereupon the hyena, fearing disclosure, quickly agreed to bury the body.

The saying means that two persons of similar natures and tastes soon mutually understand each other.

227. *Aboa kòkosakyi nni tuo, na oṭọṅ asommeṅ.* (514)
The vulture has not a gun, but he sells elephants' tusks.

> *Nni.* Neg. of *wọ.*
> *Asommeṅ.* See note on No. 94, *sĕ.*

Dead elephants, and other game are often located by vultures wheeling aloft above the carcass.

228. *Aboa kòkosakyi se akasadi nti na ọka sumăna so.* (516)
The vulture says it is in order to avoid payment (for what he eats) that he remains on the dung-hill.

> *Akasadi.* Deriv. *di kasa,* to fine or make liable for expenses incurred.

229. *Aboa akrampă, wudi bi biṅ na obi nni wo de.* (517)
Vulture, you eat the excrement of every one, but no one eats yours.

230. *Kòkosakyi akrampă, ne diṅ anyẹ dẹ, na ne hŏ anyẹ hŭăm.* (1679)
The vulture has not a good name and its body has not a good smell.

> *Hŭăm.* Of a good smell; *bọṅ* used only of a bad smell.

231. *Kòkosakyi mpẹ ofie aba a, aṅkă onsisi sumănă so.* (1680)
If the vulture did not wish to come into the house, it would not stand about on the dung-hill.

232. *Kòkosakyi ẹe, odompo hŏ bọṅ.* (1681)
The vulture says that the civet cat stinks.

> *Bọṅ.* See note above, No. 230.

233. *Opete takᾰra tᴗa oᴗira ṅkontompo a, otu tᴗene.* (2691)
When a vulture's feather tells its master a lie, he (the vulture) plucks it out and casts it away.

Oᴗira = Owura.

234. *Opete hõ na ẹyẹ ṅkwasea, nanso okyi aguare-anni.* (2687)
A vulture's body is a foolish looking thing, yet even he does not eat without first having had his bath.

Okyi. See note on No. 132, *wokyi.*

Aguare-anni. The following is one interpretation given to the writer of the above, ' A Hausa man, whom every ọne knows stinks, may be *seen bathing his hands* and feet ' (ceremonial ablutions).

235. *Ọsansa fị̃ri ahunum' reba se, 'Mekọkyere nipa madi ', na afei akoᴗia akokọ.* (2775)
The hawk comes swooping down from the sky saying, ' I am going to catch a man and eat him ', and behold ! he makes off with a fowl.

Madi. Subjunct., lit. that I may eat. *Na* is understood.

236. *Ọsansa kọ abuw a, ọde n'akyi gyaw akrõmᾰ.* (2776)
When the hawk goes to sit on her eggs, she leaves the *akrõmᾰ* (another kind of hawk) to keep her watch (in the sky).

237. *Akõ ntakᾰra, sẹ wuhũ ne ṅko a, ntow no bo, na ọfi dodow mu.* (1610)
A parrot's feather, if you see but a single one, do not throw a stone at it, for it comes from where there are a great many more.

238. *Akõ ano yẹ deṅ a, obi ṅkyere no nni.* (1607)
Because the parrot has a loud voice, no onẹ catches hold of it to eat it.

Ano yẹ deṅ. Lit. mouth is hard. This, in connexion with the parrot, might perhaps be given its literal meaning ' mouth (beak) is hard ', but the phrase is generally used in the sense of, loud mouthed, blustering.

Ṅkyere . . . nni. Nni, negative of *di.* For note on the double negative see No. 33, *mfa, nsisi.*

239. *Akõ mpẹ sẹ obi hũ ne ṅkesua nti na ọtow gu duam'.* (1608)
A parrot lays its eggs in the hollow of a tree because it does not wish any one to see them.

240. *Anŏma biaɛŏ wǫ wo nsam' a, eye seṅ nnŏmā du a ɛwǫ ahunum'.*
(2480)

Cne bird in your hand is better than ten birds in the sky.

Wǫ. Here the verb takes the place of the preposition in English. *Wǫ* has here its original meaning of ' to stick to (a person, place, or thing) ', from which is derived its subsidiary meaning of ' to be ', ' to exist in '.

Eye. The verb *ye*, to be good ; not to be confused with *yɛ*, to be, to make, to do.

Seṅ. See note on No. 261, *nnam kyeṅ.*

241. *Anŏma biara wu wǫ soro a, ɛye deṅ ara a, ne ntakara ba gu fam'.*
(2481)

When any bird dies in the sky, whatever happens (lit. whatever it does), its feathers come falling to the earth. (Cf. No. 754.)

242. *Anŏma bonɛ na ǫsee ne berebuw.* (2482)

The bad bird fouls its own nest.

Na. Emphatic particle, translated here by the definite article.

Ǫsee. Perhaps past tense, 'fouled'.

Berebuw. Deriv. *bere*, place, and *buw*, to sit on, to squat on, hence ' nest '.

243. *Anŏma de akǫ-nè-aba na eṅwene berebuw.* (2483)

The bird makes (lit. weaves) its nest by going and coming.

244. *Anŏma kese antu a, obua da.* (2484)

When a big (full-grown) bird does not trouble to fly (in search of food), it goes to sleep hungry.

Obua da. To fast ; lit. to cover up (the food) (and) sleep.

245. *Anŏma koro di aẁi a, otiatia so.* (2487)

When one bird alone eats the grain, it treads it under foot (there being more than it can eat).

Aẁi. Guinea corn.

246. *Anŏma kyɛ dua so a, ogye bo.* (2488)

When a bird remains too long on a tree, it has a stone thrown at it.

Ogye bo. Lit. it receives a stone.

247. *Anŏma nǎm ṅkǫsŏ kyɛ.* (2489)

There is not enough meat in a bird to divide up (among a number of persons).

Nkǫsŏ. Sŏ, to reach.

248. *Anõma ne nua ne nea ǫ nè no da.* (2490)

It is one of its own family that a bird roosts with.

Nua. Here in its wide sense of any one who has traced descent through the mother's side. See note on No. 37, *abusũa.*

249. *Anõma ano ware a, ǫde didi asuogya na ǫmfá ntwa asu.* (2492)

When a bird has a long bill, it uses it for eating on its own side of the river and not for stretching across the water (to eat on the opposite bank).

This saying is often heard quoted in cases of land disputes.

CHAPTER V

DOMESTIC ANIMALS: THE DOG, CAT, SHEEP AND GOATS,
CATTLE AND HORSES.

250. *Ǫkrǎmǎṅ a ǫkǫ ahayǫ waṅhũ, na agyinamoa na ǫbeye deṅ ?* (1765)
The dog which has gone a hunting has not had any luck, so what
can the cat (hope to) do?

Ahayǫ. *Yɛ ha,* to hunt. See No. 101, *ha.*
Agyinamoa. See note on No. 122, *agyinamoa.*

251. *Wo krǎmǎṅ se ǫbɛkyere sóno amǎ wo a, ǫdǎdǎ wo.* (1769)
When your dog says he will catch an elephant for you, he is
deceiving you.

Sóno. See note on No. 89, *esóno.*
Amǎ. Subjunct. mood. The verb here takes the place of the
English preposition, for.
Ǫdǎdǎ. Also *sisi* and *gyige,* with similar meaning.

252. *Ǫkrǎmǎṅ se ǫremfa ǫyere da, na ǫfa ǫyere no, ǫfa n' agya yere.* (1770)
The dog says he will never commit adultery, but when he does so,
he commits it with his own father's wife.

Ǫremfa ǫyere. *Fa ǫyere,* lit. to take (another's) wife, euphemistic
for 'to commit adultery'. For note on *ǫyere* see No. 88.
No. Note that this adverbial particle, like *yi,* does not only intro-
duce a subordinate clause of time in which the event takes place in
the past, but also one in which the verb may be present or future.

253. *Ǫkrǎmǎṅ ne atiremsɛm da ne bo, na ɛnna ne tirim.* (1773)
A dog's thoughts lie in his chest, but not in his head. (That is, he
is always barking (talking) and never keeps anything to himself.)

Ɛnna. Negative of *da.*

254. *Obi se wo sɛ, 'Ǫkrǎmǎṅ ani yɛ anaṅ' a, ǫboa, abieṅ yɛ ṅhwĩ.* (416)
If any one says, 'A dog has four eyes', he is lying, two are (tufts
of) hair.

Ǫboa. *Boa,* to lie or to be mistaken; also like its compound,
boǎpa, to pretend, see No. 361.

255. *Wo nè krämäṅ bǫ abusũa a, nisu mpa wo ani ase da.*

If you take a dog (i.e. a quarrelsome, noisy person) as a relation, tears will never dry in your eyes.

Abusũa. See note on No. 37, *abusũa.*

256. *Ǫkrämäṅ anom yę no dę a, ǫṅwe ne kǫṅmu nnawa.* (1768)

Even when a dog's mouth is watering, he does not gnaw at the bells round his neck.

Anom ye no dę. Lit. 'in the mouth is sweet'.

Nnawa. Dā or *dawa* (same root probably as *da* in *dade,* iron), a bell, often hung round dogs' and cows' necks.

257. *Ǫkrämäṅ fa kesua a, ębębǫ wǫ n' anom'.* (1766)

When a dog picks up an egg, it will break in his mouth.

Wǫ. Translate by ' in ', but really a verb, *wǫ,* to be. See note on No. 240, *wǫ.*

258. *Ǫkrämäṅ na obu bę sę, ' A de kęse nyera'.* (1767)

The dog has a proverb which runs, 'A big thing does not get lost'.

Obu bę. Bu, probably same word as *bu* in *bu fǫ, bu bem,* to utter, to pronounce; *bę = ębę,* a saying, proverb, riddle.

259. *Ǫkrämäṅ si pata so na ęnyę ǫno na ǫforee a, na obi na ǫmãã no so sii hǫ.* (1772)

When a dog is (found) up on top of the store rack, and could not have climbed up himself, then some one must have lifted and put him there.

Pata. A rack or ceiling, often above the dwelling room where odds and ends, pots, calabashes, and yams and plantains are kept.

Ǫforee, ǫmãã, sii. Past tense, formed by lengthening of final vowel.

260. *Ǫkrämäṅ se, ǫpę 'mirika-húnu atú, na menne sę n'ase guaṅ atew ayera.* (1771)

The dog says he likes to run about without any particular reason; how much faster will he run when he hears his mother-in-law's sheep has broken loose and is lost.

Atú. Subjunct. after verb *pę,* see note on No. 2, *wǫpę.*

Menne. Neg. of *de,* to mention; lit. I do not mention, that is, not to speak of. . .

261. *Agyinamoa no pĩafo a, aṅkā oye nnam kyeṅ krāmāṅ.* (1285)
Had the cat only some one to help it, it would be sharper even
than the dog.

Agyinamoa. See note on No. 122. The idea is that the cat
' walks by itself '.

Pĩafo. *Pĩa* as *sũm akyiri, sũm atiko,* to help, encourage, egg
on—as a man his dog when hunting.

Aṅkā. See note on No. 733.

Nnam kyeṅ. The comparative degree is expressed by using the
verb *kyeṅ* or *seṅ,* to surpass. Hence in pidgin English, ' he good
pass ', ' he bad pass ', &c.

262. *Agyinamoa nam fie sẽ ne kotoku a, anadẁoboa mfa ne nsa ntom'.*
(1283)
When the cat walks about the house carrying his bag, the night
animal (the mouse) does not put his hand inside.

Fie. Deriv. perhaps *fĩ,* to come out ; *ofie,* the place a person
comes out from, his house.

Sẽ. To carry slung over the shoulder, to hang up.

Mfa, ntom'. See note on No. 33, *mfa, nsisi.*

263. *Agyinamoa wu a, ṅkura yam'.* (1286)
When the cat dies, the mice rejoice.

Yam. Lit. the belly. Here the words *eye woṅ,* are probably
understood before *yam. Eye me yam* is equivalent to *eye me de.*
The common phrase is *me bo ato me yam,* I am happy. Lit. my
chest has fallen into my stomach. See note on No. 34, *kōn do.*

264. *Agyinamoa akoa ne botokura.* (1284)
The cat's slave is the mouse.

Botokura. The field-mouse.

Ne. See note on *ne,* No. 1.

265. *Obi ṅkyere agyinamoa akrommo.* (228)
No one teaches a cat how to steal.

Akrommo = Bo nkroṅ.

266. *Obi ṅkyere agyinamoa apákyi mù fĩẽ.* (228)
No one teaches a cat how to look into a calabash.

267. *Aboa agyinamoa nni biribi, nanso owo ahōohare.* (506)
If the cat has nothing else, it has agility.

Ahŏǫharę. The original gives *ahŏęhę́rę*, perhaps some unusual dialectal form or perhaps an error; *ahŏǫharę* is derived from *hŏ* and *ǫharę*, lit. lightness of body.

268. *Aboa agyinamoa nim sę ntŭĕmu yę dę a, añkä ǫtŭĕ ne mu du Abŭrokyiri.* (507)

If the cat really thought stretching itself (after a sleep) was a delightful sensation, it would go on stretching and stretching till it reached to Europe.

Abŭrokyiri. Europe. Lit. 'White man's far away' or 'White man's back', i.e. what lies behind where the white man comes from.

269. *Oguanteñ ñwo aberekyi.* (1233)

A sheep does not give birth to a goat.

Oguanteñ. Oguañ (q.v. No. 17, *guañ*) and *teñ*, long; here, long-legged.

270. *Nea oguañ gyinae na ne ba gyinae.* (2165)

Where the sheep stands its kid stands.

Gyinae. Lit. stood, past tense.

271. *Obi mfa aberekyi nto guanteñ hŏ.*

No one compares a goat with a sheep.

272. *Oguañ bewu, na onnyä ñwui a, wǫmfrę no guañfunu.* (1227)

When a sheep is going to die, but is not yet dead, it is not called a dead sheep.

273. *Oguañ ano kä ñkyene a, onnyae ĭe.* (1230)

When a sheep's mouth touches salt, it does not stop eating it.

274. *Oguañ funu mpaw ǫsekañ.* (1228)

A dead sheep does not choose the knife (it is to be cut up with).

275. *Oguañ wuda yę ǫdesäni wuda.* (1231)

The day on which a sheep dies is also the day on which a man dies.

276. *Oguanteñ se, 'Mefŭbę ǫsebǫ na mawo no so'.* (1232)

The sheep says, 'I shall look on a leopard that I may give birth to one like it'.

The idea is common among the Ashantis that a child is influenced in its mother's womb by what the mother has seen or been impressed by during pregnancy.

The saying is taken as meaning, one should not be guided by

appearances. In this case the ewe, seeing only the leopard's beautiful skin, does not inquire as to its ferocious nature.

Na mawo. Subjunctive mood.

277. *Odwennini ye asisi a, efiri ne kŏma emfiri ne mmeṅ.* (1060)
When a ram is brave, (its courage) comes from its heart and not from its horns.

278. *Aberekyi se ọbẹdaṅ guanteṅ a, tuntum mpa mu da.* (94)
Though the goat determines to turn into a sheep, there will always be a patch of black somewhere.

Mpa. Pa, generally in its reduplicated form of *popa,* means 'to rub out, blot out'; lit. 'black will never be rubbed out'.

279. *Aberekyi se, obi nnamtew ṅkowu.* (95)
The goat says no one will (willingly) walk to his death.

The Ashantis say that, whereas a cow or sheep will walk to the slaughtering place, the goat, which in the ordinary way will follow like a dog, has often to be carried.

Nnamtew ṅkowu. For note on the negatives see No. 33, *mfa, nsisi.*

280. *Aberekyi se, nea abogyabum wọ no, ẹhọ na adidi wọ.* (97)
The goat says that where there is much blood, there is food.

Abogyabum. Deriv. *mogya* or *bogya,* blood, and *bum,* to cover, to spread (?).

281. *Aberekyi se, ' Wọatọ me nă, na wọanto me'.* (98)
The goat says, 'They have bought my mother, but they have not bought me'.

282. *Aboa aberekyi na obu ne bẹ se, 'Ade pa na wọkata so'.* (498)
The goat has a saying which goes, 'A good thing is (sure to be) covered over'.

283. *Nantwi mmeṅ ani awo, nso ase ye mono.* (2109)
The outer surface of a cow's horns is hard, but underneath is soft.

Mmeṅ. Sing. *abeṅ.*

284. *Obi ntọ nantwi nammọṅ.* (354)
No one buys a cow's footprint.

Nammọṅ. Deriv. *ẹnăṅ,* foot, and *bone,* hollow or hole.

285. *Ẹnye nantwi nkŏ na ọfiri Sàraha baa Kumase.* (3612)
It is not only cattle that come from Salaga to Coomassie.

Sàraha. Salaga, a large Hausa and caravan centre in the
Northern Territories of the Gold Coast, once a famous centre of
the slave trade, to which the above saying alludes.

Kumase. Now officially spelled Coomassie. The derivation is
from *kum*, to kill, and *ase*, under, beneath, i.e. 'under the kill
(tree)', from a large tree under which executions used to take
place, when the town was the head-quarters of the Ashanti paramount chief.

286. *Opoṅko mmaṅ kwa.* (2707)
A horse does not turn to the side without a cause. (That is, it is
  answering to the rein.)

287. *Opoṅko agyimi a, nea ote no so nnyimii e.* (2708)
Though the horse is a fool, it does not follow at all that the rider is
  a fool.

E. Emphatic with negative.

288. *Opoṅko aṅko osa a, ne dua ko.* (2709)
If the horse does not go to war, its tail does.

Osa. See note on No. 317, *osa*.

Ne dua ko. A horse's tail is considered as a charm to bring
victory to an army, and is always taken on a campaign by a general
and his captains. It is often called *obodua, aboa dua,* i.e. animal's
tail. Horses, of course, do not live long in Ashanti owing to 'fly'.

289. *Opoṅko wo dua, esóno wo dua, na opoṅko de kyeṅ sóno de kākrā.*
  (2710)
A horse has a tail and an elephant has a tail, but that of the horse
  is a little larger than that of the elephant.

Dua. Lit. stick, hence tail.

Esóno. See note on No. 89, *esóno*.

Kākrā. See note on No. 101, *kākrā*.

CHAPTER VI

290. *Akura te sẹ nantʋi a, na agyinamoa akoa ara neṅ.* (1837)
Even if the mouse were the size of a cow, he would be the cat's
slave nevertheless.

Agyinamoa. See note on No. 122, *agyinamoa.*
Neṅ = Nẹ no.

291. *Akura se, ' Nea okum me nyẹ me yaw sẹ nea ọde me fʋe fam'.* (1836)
The mouse says, ' He who kills me does not hurt me as much as the
one who throws me on the ground' (after I am dead).

292. *Ṅkura dódew bọre tũ a, ẹnno.* (1838)
When a great number of mice dig a hole, it does not become deep.

Ẹnno. Neg. of *dọ.*

293. *Aboa kisi nyã fufũ a, obedi, na ọwọma na ẹṅkọ ne boṅ mu.* (511)
When the rat gets *fufũ* (pounded yam, cassava, &c.), he will eat it,
but the pestle (used for pounding it) does not go into his hole.

Aboa. See note on No. 89.
Fufũ. See note on No. 14.
Ọwọma. A wooden pestle used for pounding grain in a wooden
mortar (*ọwọaduru*). The derivation is *ọwọ ba,* i.e. the pounding
child, or child of the mortar.

294. *Okisi kọfa adʋe na Ọnyàmé bọ-ayeremu a, ọdaṅ atʋene.* (1553)
When the rat goes to eat palm nuts and the Supreme Being flashes
the lightning, he throws them away.

Ọnyàmé. See note on No. 1, *Ọnyàmé.* Lit. when the Supreme
Being strikes (the darkness) clear.

295. *Okisi apo adʋe.* (1555)
The rat is tired of palm nuts.

Apo. Pọ, to refuse, to decline. The chief food of the rat is
supposed to be palm nuts. The saying is taken to mean, a man
tires of what he has too much of.

296. *Okisinini aṅhũ adʋe-bọ, na ọbére bọ a, ọʋe bi.* (1557)
When Mr. Rat does not know how to crack a palm-nut kernel, but
Mrs. Rat does, he eats some (of her's).

297. *Wokǫ okisi kŭrom' na ǫẁe ǹṅẁeā a, woẁe bi.* (1572)

When you go to the rat's town and he eats palm-nut kernels, you eat some too. (Cf. No. 158.)

Ǹṅẁeā. Plu. of *adẁe.*

298. *Obi mfi aboa no anim mmǫ hama.* (171)

No one begins to twist creepers into a rope in front of an animal (he hopes to catch).

Mmǫ. Neg. of *bǫ.*

299. *Aboa a ǫbęba nnim waw.* (495)

The animal that is coming (towards the hunter) knows nothing about the man lying in wait for it.

Waw. To prop up, hence of the screen of palm leaves or branches which the hunter sets up and behind which he crouches at the water-hole. See note on *kǫtew dua,* No. 327.

300. *Aboa a ne hŏ wǫ ṅhwi fi fifiri a, woṅhŭ.* (496)

When an animal with a hairy skin sweats, it is not (so easily) noticed. (Cf. No. 305.)

Fifiri. Root *fi,* to come out from.

301. *Aboa bi reṅka wo a, ǫṅṅwěṅ ne sě ṅkyerę wo.* (500)

When an animal is not going to bite you, it does not show its teeth at you.

Ǫṅṅwěṅ, ṅkyerę. For the negative see No. 33, *mfa, nsisi.*

302. *Aboa ne nea ǫẁe wura wǫ wuram'.* (526)

It is the animal that eats grass that lives (is to be found) in the grass.

303. *Aboa no ṅhintaw nnyaw ne dua.* (528)

That animal does not hide and leave its tail sticking out.

304. *Aboa no kaw nea n' ano sŏ.* (529)

That animal bites wherever its mouth reaches to.

305. *Mmoadŏmǎ ṅhĭnǎ fi fifiri, na ṅhwĩ na ęmmǎ yeṅhŭ.* (541)

All animals sweat, but the hair on them causes us not to notice it. (Cf. No. 300.)

The saying is used in the sense that a rich or powerful man can bear losses or troubles better than a poor one, though both may equally have their worries.

CHAPTER VII

WAR, FIGHTING, HUNTING, GUNS, AND WEAPONS.

306. *Dọm gu a, wọnhyeǹ no abeǹ.* (956)

When an army suffers defeat a horn is not blown in its honour.

Dọm. Deriv. perhaps *dọ* and *mu.* An Ashanti army is divided up into main body, flankers, rear and advance guard, and possibly both tactics and formation were modelled on our own, though this they themselves deny.

The main body is called *adọnteǹ (dọm teǹ)* and also contains the special bodyguard of the ancestral stools which are carried to war. This bodyguard is known as *ankọbea* (lit. do not go anywhere else). The right flank is *nifā* (lit. right hand), the left flank is *beǹkum* (left hand). A body of men are thrown outside these flanks again, called *nawase*, whose duty it is to prevent a flanking movement on the part of the enemy. The *nawase* do not disclose their position unless attacked. The advance guard are known as *twafo* (cutters), as the name implies, to clear a way through the dense bush. These are preceded again by the scouts, some four to six men called *akwanserafo.* The rearguard is known as *kyidọm* (lit. behind the army).

The whole force is under a general, *ọsahene* (see note on *ọsa,* No. 317), and under him again are the various *safohene,* or company (*dọm fakuw*) commanders. Each *safohene* has his own drums and horns (No. 507, *bọmma*). Strategy is not unknown, and the following story is authentic. A general on camping for the night lit fires all round an imaginary camp, and cutting hundreds of plantain leaves spread them on the ground with the white or light coloured side uppermost to represent sleeping men. He then retired with his force. The enemy attacked the supposed camp from all sides, and mistaking the fire of their own men for that of their opponents, inflicted heavy casualties on themselves. The Ashanti, however, rarely fight at night, darkness no doubt holding many terrors other than fear of the enemy. Horse's tails are considered a war charm (see No. 288), and the wounded are switched with

them to make them rise. The use of stockades they say they have
learned from Europeans. They are known as *apia* or *apampim*.

The camp followers are called *asansafo* (*nsansa*, a camp).

When the battle is going against an army, the chief will stand upon
his stool (an unheard of insult on ordinary occasions), perhaps really
with the idea of insulting the manes of his ancestors into assisting
the hard-pressed army when prayers and entreaties have failed.
Skulls of fallen enemies are put round war drums, the jaws on the
horns. Only a general and company commanders take their women
folk with them.

Bows and arrows and shields were undoubtedly formerly the
weapons of the Ashanti, but so many hundred years ago that all
tradition and remembrance has been lost and forgotten. (See note
on *tafoni*, No. 522.)

307. *Dom ṅṅui a, woṅkaṅ atofo.* (957)
The slain are not counted before the (hostile) army has been
    routed.

Ṅṅui. Neg. perfect tense of *gu.*

Woṅkaṅ. Translated by the passive voice.

Atofo. Deriv. *to*, to fall ; *fo*, personal suffix, see note on No. 34,
osamaṅ. *Otofo*, any one who has been killed in war or accidentally
met his death.

308. *Dom, wokŏ no abooduru, na wonkŏ no ahĭ-dodow.* (958)
An army is driven back by courage and not by insults, however
    many.

Abooduru. Deriv. *abo*, chest, and *duru*, strong.

309. *Dom kum ano-sese-ade, na dom ṅkum dommarima.* (959)
The (victorious) army slays him who shouts out challenges and
    insults, but it spares the brave man.

Ano-sese-ade. Lit. the mouth that keeps on saying things, i.e.
insults.

Dommarima. *Dom obarima*, a man of war, a warrior.

310. *Dom nnim dom akyi.* (960)
An army does not know what is at the rear of an army.

311. *Obarima, woye no dom āno, na wonyé no fie.* (50)
A man is made in the forefront of battle and not (by remaining)
    at home.

312. *Ǫkŏ aba a, na nsise aba.* (1600)

When war has come, rumours have come.

Nsise. Deriv. *se*, to say, reduplicated, lit. 'say, say', i.e. reports.

313. *Ǫkŏ ba a, na nsise bǫ kŭrow.* (1601)

When war comes, it is rumours that cause the fall of the town.

314. *Wokŏ, kǫ wo anim a, na wuyi dǫm.* (1589)

When you fight and press on to your front, then you will conquer.

315. *Wokŏ ṅkrăṅ na eṅkǫ a, wontŭbene abe ṅṅu mu.* (1590)

When you are fighting black ants and they will not go away, you
    do not peel palm nuts and put amongst them.

Ṅkrăṅ. The large and fierce black ants that may be seen at
times marching in an irresistible column and quickly putting to
flight the entire household in any habitation that may lie on their
line of march. A form of torture among the Ashantis was to peg
a person down in the path of a drive of these insects.

The saying above quoted means that war is war and not to be
waged in kid gloves.

Enkǫ. Note the use of the 3rd person neuter sing. for the 3rd
person plural.

Wontŭbere . . . ṅṅu. For the negatives see note on No. 33,
mfa, nsisi ; ṅṅu, neg of *gu*.

316. *Wokŏ na wunyi dǫm a, womfá nnommúm.* (1591)

When you fight and do not win, you do not lead away captives.

317. *Ǫsa, wokǫ ao ṅkatae dodo.* (2730)

Many gun-lock covers go to war.

Ǫsa. War. Possibly the word has this meaning only by
metonymy, the original meaning being a narrow path (cf. 'war
path'), leading through the dense 'bush' or forest.

Wokǫ ne. Note the absence of any preposition in Ashanti, in
fact there are none, their place being taken by verbs. See note on
No. 240, *wǫ*; and No. 14, *mă*.

Ṅkatae. A cover of antelope, or often wart-hog skin, to slip over
the lock of a flint gun to keep the powder dry. *Ṅkatae,* a noun
formed from the verb *kata,* to cover. Every gun used by the
Ashantis has such a cover attached to the barrel which readily slips
round under or over the pan, as desired. (See No. 329.)

318. *Ǫsa, wǫkǫ no wǫṅ agya mma.* (2731)

When one goes to war, it is against one's father's children (i.e.
brothers by one father but by different mothers).

Agya mma. Half-brothers (or sisters) by the same father but
different mothers. Descent is matrilineal; hence the ' father's child '
is not reckoned a kinsman at all, and in the event of a dispute the
children half-brothers might find themselves ranged on different
sides. (See note on No. 37, *abusйa.*)

E.g. *abusйa yε dǫm*, one's own relations, i.e. on mother's side,
are an army.

319. *Obi nturu yarefo ṅkǫ 'sá.* (377)

No one carries a sick man on his back when going to war.

Nturu. . . . ṅkǫ. See note on No. 33, *mfa, nsisi.*

320. *Obǫfó à wókodi nǒ yaw na otuo apae akǎ ne nsa yi, na wo de, woso
brǫde bεdεw rekǫ hě?* (549)

The hunter to whom you serve as attendant has been wounded in
the hand by the bursting of his gun, so, as for you, where are
you setting off to with the bundle of plantains?

Wókodi . . . yaw. *Di ǫbǫfó yaw*, means to accompany a hunter
to the bush, as a kind of attendant, carrying food and water and
assisting him to cut up and carry home anything shot.

Brǫde. Plantain, not indigenous. Deriv. *boro ǫde*, lit. European
yam.

Bεdεw. A rough basket plaited out of palm leaves.

321. *Obǫfó aboa a wafǒm no bíara nyε ketewa da.* (550)

No animal that a hunter has ever missed is small. (Cf. No. 323.)

Wafǒm. *Fǒm*, to make a mistake, generally used with *so*, hence
to miss with gun, arrow, &c.

Another common saying to express exaggeration is as follows:
Ɛnnε me tow owansaṅ kεse bi tuo me fǒm no so, To-day I fired at
a very big bush-buck but missed it.

322. *Obǫmofo, a woakum pete (a wonn ine nǎm), woasεε wo atuduru.*
(600)

Hunter, who have killed a vulture (the flesh of which cannot be
eaten), you have wasted your powder.

Atuduru. See note on No. 13.

323. *Ọbọmọfo aboa a ọkọ na osŏ.* (601)

To the hunter the animal that gets off is (always) the big one. (Cf.
No. 321, above.)

324. *Ọbọmọfo diṅ bata sŏnnam hŏ.* (602)

The hunter's name clings to the elephant's meat.

Bata. To lie close against, hence as here, to be mentioned in
connexion with.

Sŏnnam. *Ẹ sŏnɔ nam.* (See No. 89, *ẹsóno.*)

325. *Ọbọmọfo fi wuram ba na okura mmerẹ a, wommisa ahayọ mu
asẹm.* (603)

When the hunter comes from the bush carrying mushrooms, he is
not asked for news of his hunting.

Wuram. See note on No. 92.

326. *Ọbọmọfo kọ wuram' mã osu tọ afibe no, mã ntummoa keka ne hŏ,
mã awọw ade no, mã ofiberem' awọ no, ne ṅhĩnana yẹ due na
mede memãe.* (604)

When a hunter goes to the bush and is beaten by the rain, and
bitten by flies, and suffers from the cold, and is pricked by
thorns, all these hardships are included, when I tell him
I am sorry for him.

Ntummoa. Deriv. *tum,* black; and *mmoa,* insects.

327. *Ọbọmọfo kọtẹw dua na aboa amma a, ọsaṅ ba ofie.* (605)

When the hunter crouches behind a tree, but the game for which
he is lying in wait does not come, he returns home.

Kọtẹw dua. Lit. to fix a stick in the ground, hence used of
cover taken by a hunter when waiting for game, perhaps at a water-
hole, where he may have made an artificial screen of branches.
(Cf. *waw,* No. 299.)

328. *Ọbọmọfo nnim aboa yarefo.* (606)

The hunter does not spare (lit. know) the sick animal.

329. *Osu tọ na ọbọmọfo bekum aboa a, ẹfi ne katae.* (3062)

If the rain falls and the hunter kills an animal, that is thanks to
the skin cover of his gun lock.

Katae. See note on No. 317, *nkatae.*

330. *'Gye akyekyere kọmã agya,' nso yẹ ahayọ ?* (1262)

Here take the tortoise and go and give it to father,' would you
also call that hunting?

331. *Ẹnyẹ obi nè bọmọfo na ẹkọọ wuram'.* (3589)

No one went with the hunter to the bush (i.e. there is no one to contradict you, for you were alone when it happened).

332. *Otuo nyã otiafo a, na odi abaninsẹm.* (3388)

It is (only) when a gun has a man to cock it, that it performs war-like deeds. (Cf. No. 339.)

Otiafo. Tia otuo, to pull back the striker of a flint-lock gun, to cock.

Abaninsẹm. Abaniṅ, a male, and *asẹm.*

333. *Otuo paé kã ọbọmofo a, wommisa nea odi ọbọfo nam.* (3389)

When the gun bursts and wounds the hunter, the man who happens to eat venison is not blamed for the accident. (Lit. is not asked about it.)

334. *Otuo mpae Abŭrokyiri mmẹkã onipa wọ Abibirim'.* (3390)

A gun does not burst in Europe and wound a man in Africa.

Abŭrokyiri. See note on No. 268.

Mpae . . . mmẹkã. For the negative see No. 33, *mfa, nsisi.*

335. *Wo atuo sŭa a, na wo asẹm sŭa.* (3391)

When your guns are few, your words are few.

336. *Otuo tã hŭaṅ a, na ẹ nè poma sẹ pẹ.* (3392)

When the lock of a gun is out of order, it (the gun) and a stick are just alike.

Otuo tã. The lock of a flint-lock gun; *hŭaṅ,* lit. springs back, that is, will not catch or cock.

337. *Otuo ntow aboa bi nnyae ṅkọhyehye aboa bi ŭere mu.* (3394)

A gun-(shot) does not wound one animal and cause pain to another animal. (Lit. the skin of another.)

338. *Otuo yera nĩfã mu nà ẹkofi adọnteṅ mu a, na ẹṅkọọ bãbi ẹ.* (3395)

When a gun (a soldier) is missing from the right flank of the battle and appears in the forefront of the fight, it did not go amiss.

Nĩfã . . . adọnteṅ. See note on No. 306, *dọm.*

339. *Tŭẹrebo nti na otuo di abaninsẹm.* (3422)

Thanks to the flint-stone the gun performs warlike deeds. (Cf. No. 332.)

Tŭẹrebo. Tŭẹre, to strike, and *ọbo,* a stone.

CHAPTER VIII

340. *Ǫba a ǫbeyę yiye, woꞥyęꞥ no kętę-pa so ꞥkǒ.* (6)
  The child which is to turn out any good is not reared entirely
  on (even) a beautiful mat.

  Ǫba. Deriv. possibly *ba*, to come, to come forth, something
  produced, also used of the young of animals.

  Note *ǫbā*, is a girl, the long *ā* being the feminine and diminutive
  suffix *wa*.

  Woꞥyęꞥ. *Yęꞥ*, to rear, nurture, or bring up. Also used of
  rearing animals and chickens.

  Kętę. A mat woven of grass.

341. *Ǫba sę ǫse, nanso ǫwǫ abusǔa.* (7)
  A child (may be) like his father, but he belongs to the mother's
  side from which he takes his name.

  Abusǔa. Referring to the matrilineal descent. See note on
  No 37, *abusǔa*. For *ǫse* see note on No 37, *nī̃*.

342. *Ǫba nsǔ a, wǫmmā no nǔfu ?* (8)
  Is it only when a child cries that he is given the breast ?

  Nǔfu. See note on No 151, *nufu*.

343. *Wo ba nȇ to gu wo sȋrę so a, wode baha na eyi, na womfá ǫsekaꞥ
  ntȋba.* (10)
  When your child's excrement falls on your lap, you wipe it off
  with dry plantain fibres, but you do not take a knife and cut
  (the place) off.

344. *Wo ba saw asa-bone a, sę no sę, ' Wo asaw nyę fę ', na nsę no sę,
  ' Okra, tete gu mu '.* (11)
  When your child dances badly, tell him, saying, ' Your dancing is
  not good ', and do not say to him, ' (Little) soul, just dance as
  you want to '.

  Okra. See note on No 9, *ꞥkrabea*. Here used as term of
  endearment.

  Tete. Deriv. *tetew*, to tear up, to spoil.

345. *Wo ba sisi wo kora ba a, enyé, nanso wo kora ba sisi wo ba a, enye.* (12)

When your own child cheats your fellow wife's child, that is not right, and when your fellow wife's child cheats your own child, that is not right either.

Kora. When a man has two or more wives each is called the ' *kora* ' of the other; *kora* means ' jealous '. An exactly similar idiom is found in Hausa where one wife is called by another *kishia.*

346. *Oba-bone nnim kasakyere.* (13)

A bad child does not take advice.

Nnim. Lit. does not know.

347. *Nea abofra pe ototo.* (2124)

What a child wants he buys.

(Said of a foolish person who must have everything he sees and fancies.)

348. *Abofra bo nwaw na ommo akye yere.* (557)

A child breaks a snail, but he does not break a tortoise. (Cf. No. 368.)

Nwaw. See note on No 165.

Ommo. Neg. of *bo.*

Akyekyere. Also called *awuru.*

349. *Osekan-fua na egye nehŏ abofra nsam'.* (2846)

It is the knife-blade without the handle that frees itself from the hands of a child (by cutting him).

350. *Abofra nsam' ade nye hye-nã.* (573)

It is not difficult to fill a child's hand.

Hye-nã. See note on No. 157, *nye-nã.*

351. *Woye abofra a, nserew akwatia.* (3564)

When you are a child, do not laugh at a short man.

Akwatia. Akoa-tia, short fellow.

352. *Abofra nte ne nã nè n' agya asem a, eye mmusu (. . . odi aduañ a ñkyene nnim').* (581)

When a child does not hear the words of its father and mother, there is misfortune in that (. . . he partakes of food in which is no salt).

Na. See note on No. 37, *nĭ.*
N'agya. See note on No. 37, *nĭ.*
Ǹkyene. See note on No. 577.
Nnim'. Neg. of *wǫ.*

353. *Abofra hŭ ne nsa hohoro a, na ǫ ne mpanyiǹfo didi.* (564)

When a child knows how to wash his hands thoroughly, he and
(his) elders (can) partake of food together.

Hohoro. Reduplication of *horo.* Note the distinction in meaning between the following words, *hoho,* to wash the hands or face,
horo to wash things, pots, clothes, &c., *guare,* to bathe the whole
body, hence used for ' to swim '.

354. *Abofra tŏa fufŭ a, otŏa nea ebekǫ n'anom'.* (583)

When a child cuts off a piece (of boiled) yam, he cuts off what will
go into his mouth.

Fufŭ. See note on No. 14.

355. *Abofra kā na enkǫ ǫpanyiǹ nsa, na n' aduaǹ de ekǫ panyiǹ anom.*
(566)

A child's ring does not go on an elder's finger, but as for his (the
child's) food it goes into the elder's mouth.

Nsa. Names of the fingers are, *kokorobeti,* thumb; *akyere-
kyerekwan,* first finger, lit. point out the way ; *nsateahenę,*
middle finger, lit. king of the fingers ; *ahene akyiri,* third finger, lit.
finger after the king; *kokobeto,* little finger, lit. is the hen going
to lay ?

356. *Obi nsoma abofra ǹfŏę n'ani akyi.* (343)

No one sends a child on an errand and looks to see if he is pleased
or not.

Nsoma . . . ǹfŏę. For note on the negatives see No. 33.

N'ani akyi. Lit. behind his eyes, used for ' eyebrows '. *Fŏę
n'ani akyi,* means ' to look to see if a person is pleased or otherwise
by his expression '.

357. *Wokǫ kŭrow bi mu, na dŏom a mmofra to no na mpanyimfo na
ęto gyaw woǹ.* (1577)

When you go into some village, the songs which the children sing,
the old folk once sang and left behind to them (that is,
tradition is handed down).

358. *Abofra sũ a, wommo no duam'.* (578)

When a child cries, he is not bound to a log.

Wommo. Neg. of *bo.*

359. *Abofra ye nea wonye a, ohũ nea woṅhũ.* (587)

When a child does what is not (usually) done, he perceives what is not (usually) perceived. (Cf. 360 below.)

Wonye . . . woṅhũ. Lit. they do (or, one does) not do . . . do not perceive, (impersonal verbs here translated by the passive).

360. *Abofra ye nea opanyiṅ ye a, ohũ nea opanyiṅ hũ.* (586)

When a child does what a grown up person does, he sees what a grown up person sees. (Meaning, he is punished as a grown person is punished.) Cf. 359 above.

361. *Abofra boápa wù a, woboápa sié nò.* (558)

When a child pretends to be dying, (the best thing to do) is to pretend to bury him.

Boápa. See note on No. 254, *oboa.*

362. *Abofra a oko asu na obo ahina.* (554)

The child who goes for water is the one who breaks the pot.

Na. Here emphatic, *the* one, or, it is the, &c. (See No. 1, *na.*)

363. *Abofra bo mmusu akroṅ a, ofa mu anum.* (555)

Out of nine mischievous tricks a child thinks to play on others, he suffers for five of them himself.

Akroṅ . . . anum. For notes on numbers see No. 772, *aduonum.*

364. *Abofra koda gya na opere hõ a, ne ntama hyew.* (559)

When a child goes to lie by the fire and is fidgety, his cloth catches fire.

365. *Abofra ṅfwe okwanseṅ ase kwa.* (563)

A child does not look into the soup pot for nothing (he expects to be given some).

Okwanseṅ. Deriv. *ōseṅ,* a cooking pot, and *ṅkwaṅ,* soup.

366. *Abofra ketewa bi te fi kese bim' a, mã no due, na wahũ amanne* (567)

When a small child lives (alone) in a great big house, pity him, for he has seen misfortune (that is, he has responsibility beyond his years).

Te. To sit, to live, (*tena*, to sit, i.e. be seated). The translation of this word literally by the native interpreter has given rise to one of the commonest of the hideous pidgin English expressions which are so common in West Africa, 'he live for', the verb 'live' being used in the place of the English verb 'to be'. Most pidgin English can be traced to some idiom peculiar to the vernacular, which has been followed by the native interpreter when putting the words into English.

Fi. See note on No. 262, *fie.*

Bim' = *Bi mu.*

Amanne = *Oman ade.*

367. *Abofra kotow panyiṅ ṅkyeṅ.* (568)
The child squats beside the elder.

Kotow. To squat, also used of 'to kneel down'. The Ashantis do not (now) seem to squat down on their thighs like so many African tribes (the *Mananja* and *Angoni*, for instance, who invariably adopt this position when resting, eating, &c.) This may be a result of European influence and the almost universal use of stools. Whether their remoter ancestors adopted a squatting position could no doubt be proved by an examination of an ancient male skeleton (*tibia*), (the female, for obvious reasons, even among tribes who habitually squat, never adopting this position). Professor Thomson, of Oxford, has shown that this squatting position in course of time has an effect on the external portion of the upper tibial articular surface.

Panyiṅ. See note on No. 1.

368. *Abofra ano ye deṅ a, ode hyeṅ abeṅ, na omfa ṅhyeṅ woadúru.* (571)
Even when a child has a strong mouth, he blows a horn with it and not a mortar. (Cf. No. 348.)

Ano ye deṅ. Lit. a strong mouth, i.e. quarrelsome, loud voiced. (See No. 238.)

Omfa ṅhyeṅ. Note the double negative. (See note on No. 33, *ṅsisi.*)

Woadúru. See note on No. 14, *owo.* The grain mortar with its wide mouth is likened to some huge musical instrument.

369. *Abofra se okoforo dunsiṅ a mã omforo, na okosõ anim asaṅ aba.* (574 and 403)
When a child says he is going to climb the stump of a tree, let

him climb (it), for when he has gone up it (a little way) he will turn back again.

Dunsiṅ. *Dua*, a tree, and *siṅ*, a piece, a fragment of anything. For etymology (according to Ashantis) see No. 57, *odum.*

Anim. See note on No. 80, *aniwa.*

Asaṅ aba. The literal translation is ... he goes up it that he may turn back ; *asaṅ* and *aba* are subjunctive mood.

370. *Abofra se obeso gya mu, mã onso mu, na ẹhye no a ọbẹdaṅ akyene.* (575)

When a child says he will catch hold of fire, let him catch hold of it, for when it burns him he will (soon) throw it away.

371. *Abofra se ọbẹyẹ mpanyinne a, mã ọnyẹ, na ebia obenyã ọpanyiṅ a, obi nnim.* (576)

When a child says he wants to act as if he were already a chief, let him do so ; as to whether he will ever become one, that no one knows.

Mpanyinne. *Mpanyiṅ-ade.*

372. *Abofra sika te sẹ anyaṅkõma gya, wotĩba so a, na adum.* (577)

A child's gold dust is like a firebrand of the *anyaṅkoma* tree ; when it is broken up it soon burns out.

Sika. See note on No. 591.

373. *Abofra sũa adĩbini-di a, ẹnye ọsebo ṅhõma na ọde sũa.* (579)

When a child is learning his trade as a leather worker, he does not practise on a leopard's skin. (Cf. No. 124.)

Ọsebọ ṅhõma. Leopard skins being rare in comparison with sheep and goats' skins will not be used for experimental work.

374. *Mmofra hũ kọre a osu atọ aboro no a, wose ọyẹ opete.* (591)

When children see an eagle draggled by the rain, they say it is a vulture.

Osu. See note on No. 26, *nsu.*

375. *Mmofra ṅ'kotu a, woaṅhũ tu ; mpanyiṅ ṅ'kotu a, wotiatia so.* (592)

When children go to pluck them (the *mpempema* mushroom), they do not do so skilfully ; when grown-ups go to do so, they trample on them.

The mushrooms to which this saying refers are known as the *mpempema*, i.e. 'thousands and thousands'. They are very small and grow close together. The saying refers to anything that is almost impossible to do.

376. *Obi nsoma abofra osoro na onhūann' ase antiberi.* (341)
No one sends a child up aloft and then knocks away the ladder from beneath him.

> *Nsoma. . . . onhūan.* See note on No 33, *mfa, nsisi.*
> *Antiberi.* Deriv. *tiberi,* to lean against.

377. *Obi nsoma abofra na ommefa no so abufuw.* (342)
No one sends a child on (a difficult) errand and gets angry (if he does not perform it well).

> *No so.* Lit. on, about.
> *Abufuw.* Lit. *ebo,* chest, and *fuw,* to swell. See No. 34, *koṅ do.*

378. *Opanyiṅ fere ne mma a, na ne mma suro no.* (2602)
When an elder (a parent) is strict with his children, then his children fear him.

> *Fere.* See note on No. 155, *mfere.*

379. *Opanyiṅ se ná wanyé à, mmofra nsuro no.* (2613)
When the grown-up threatens to punish, (lit. says) but does not carry out his threat (lit. but does not act), the children do not fear him.

380. *Opanyiṅ kye a, edibo.* (2606)
When an elder portions out the dish, it becomes cool. (A wise (old) man knows how to settle disputes).

381. *Opanyiṅ nyiṅ wo ne batibew.* (2611)
An elder grows at the elbow (i. e. becomes rich).

> *Nyiṅ wo ne batibew.* 'To grow at the elbow' is a phrase meaning 'to have amassed riches, to have put aside money'.

382. *Obi ntutu anõmã ṅkokyere opanyiṅ.* (382)
No one plucks a bird and goes and shows it to an elder (to inquire its name). Cf. No. 719.

383. *Opanyiṅ di nsem ṅhĩnã akyi a, oman bo.* (2597)
If an elder were to follow up every (little) offence (in order to inflict punishment), a people (nation) would (soon) go to ruin.

> *Oman.* See note on No. 474.

384. *Opanyiṅ nni abaṅsosem akyi.* (2598)
An elder gives no heed to idle rumours.

Nni. Neg. of *di,* lit. does not follow.

Abaṅsosẹm. Lit. ' words over the wall '.

385. *Ǫpanyiṅ a wanyiṅ nĕ nea wakǫ Asante aba, ne nea wakǫ Abŭrokyiri aba, atorofo a ẹwǫ ǫmaṅ mu neṅ.* (2596)

The elder who has grown very old is the one (who says) he has gone to Ashanti and returned; (who declares) he has been to Europe and back, a liar among the people is he.

Asante. This is the correct spelling. The *h* which has been introduced comes from the pronunciation (wrong) of the word by the *Ga* or *Accra* people, and became adopted from them by Europeans. This proverb is evidently one from the Coast regions, where Ashanti was looked on as some unknown land from which no man returned alive, and as inaccessible as Europe. The saying means ' an old man's tale '.

Abŭrokyiri. See note on No. 268.

Atorofo. See note on No. 604, *ǫtŏrofo.*

Neṅ = Ne no.

386. *Ǫpanyiṅ didi adibone a, oyi n'asaṅka.* (2600)

If an elder eats greedily, (he finds) he has to remove his own dish.

Adibone. *Adi,* to eat, and *bone,* bad.

N'asaṅka. A flat dish made of baked clay.

387. *Ǫpanyiṅ due, ' Mante, mante '.* (2601)

An elder evades responsibility by saying, ' I have not heard, I have not heard '.

Mante. The saying is also sometimes taken to mean, an ' elder should turn a deaf ear to a good deal of the tittle-tattle he hears '. *Mante* is also the name of a charm supposed to act as the name implies.

388. *Ǫpanyiṅ begye me nsam' akoṅṅua a, onnyĕ asase a mete so.* (2603)

Though an elder may take from my hand the stool I sit on, he cannot take from me the ground I sit on.

Begye. Lit. come and take.

Akoṅṅua. A stool, often showing in its carving a high degree of aesthetic art. The stool is the symbol of chieftainship. The paramount chief of all the Ashantis sat on the so-called ' golden stool ', the stool of next importance being the ' silver stool ' of the *Omanhene* of Mampoṅ. Each chief has his own stool, and when he dies his stool is blackened all over, a concoction of sooty spiders' webs and white of eggs being used. The stool is then set in the 'stool house', (*ṅkoṅṅua fie*), along with other stools of departed chiefs. Every twenty days (*adai*) a sheep is killed and the blood smeared on the stools, each being taken in turn, while at the same time the chief or *ọkyeame* (q.v. No. 481, note on *ọmămpăm*) mentions the name and deeds of its departed owner. The meat is shared among the people and there is singing and dancing. The above all takes place on 'Wednesday *adai*'. On 'Sunday *adai*' all the stools are taken out from the 'stool house' and carried in procession to the burial ground ; the chief at present occupying the stool leading, carrying a gun, as a mark of servitude to the departed spirits. As the procession goes along the crowds follow, and any one who wishes may make requests to any of the stools (which are now supposed to be tenanted, for the time being, by the spirits of their departed owners). A deafening clamour results as the crowds pour out their petitions. The burial ground reached, only the 'Queen mother', stool carriers and *ọkyeame* and *baṅmofo*, undertaker, are allowed to enter. Here another sheep is killed. On the return to the 'stool house' the chief distributes presents, drink, and food.

The bells (one at each end) on a stool are for tinkling to summon the spirit from the *asamaṅ*, spirit world. The stool carriers, on the occasions mentioned above, may be seen swaying from side to side, 'the spirits are pushing them '.

An Ashanti, when rising from his stool, will generally tilt it up against the wall or lay it on its side lest a departed spirit wandering round should sit on it, when the next one to sit down 'would contract pains in his waist '.

The cowries seen fastened under many stools are 'earnest-pennies' representing various transactions, which are then, by the taking and giving of such a pledge, considered as definitely clinched bargains.

389. *Ọpanyiṅ mĩ nsọno.* (2607)

An elder can satisfy his hunger with his intestines. (That is, he has other resources to fall back on when needs be, when hunger (used metaphorically for trouble) overtakes him.)

Nsọno. Note the words *nsọno*, intestines ; *ẹsono*, an elephant ; and *sono*, to be different.

390. *Ọpanyiṅ nẹ̀ mmofra hũ nantew a. wọsoa ne bọtọ.* (2608)

When the elder and the children know how to adapt their steps to one another's, they (the children) carry his bag.

Hũ. To see, to perceive how a thing is done or its appearance, hence to know. *Fĩẹ* means to look at a thing, regard it, that one may perceive (*hũ*) its nature or application.

391. *Ọpanyiṅ anim asẹm ye ọkã-nã.* (2609)

It is not an easy matter to speak face to face with an elder.

Ọkã-nã. See note on No. 157, *nyẹ-nã.*

392. *Ọpanyiṅ ano seṅ sumaṅ.* (2610)

(The words from) the mouth of an old man are better than any amulet.

Sumaṅ. See note on No. 17, *ọbosom.*

393. *Ọpanyiṅ tirim na wọ́họ̀ṅ akũmã́.* (2613)

It is on the elder's head that the axe-head is knocked off (the shaft).

Wọ́họ̀ṅ. Translated by the passive. *Họṅ* is used of pulling or knocking out something embedded in something else, as a stick out of the ground, a hoe from its handle, &c., probably an onomatopoetic word.

Akũmã́. An axe, also called *abonua*, deriv. *ọbo dua*, stone stick (?), stone axe. There are abundant evidences of a long forgotten stone age in Ashanti. The present writer made a large collection of over a hundred celts or neolithic stone axes (now in the Pitt Rivers Museum at Oxford), see a paper on ' A Collection of Ancient Stone Implements from EJURA, Ashanti ', by Prof. H. Balfour in Vol. XII, No. xlv, Oct. 1912, of the *Journal of the African Society.* There is no recollection or tradition of a stone age among these natives, and the celts are known by them under the name of *ọnyàmé akũmã́*, i. e. God's axes; the etymology of the word *abonua*, if correct, *ọbo*, stone, and *nua* (*dua*), a stick, which is the native word for axe, being the only clue that these celts were used by the remote ancestors of the Ashantis and not, as some persons are inclined to believe, by a different race and civilization once inhabiting this region. The wearing away of an axe on a stone is also mentioned among the drum messages, see note on *tĩ͗a*, No. 507.

The interpretation given to the above saying is, that an elder, or man of weight and experience, can bear the brunt of troubles which may assail the youthful and inexperienced members of his family.

394. *Opanyiǹ to asã a, na ewo mmofra de mu.* (2617)
When the old man's bottom is flat, its fatness has gone to the children.

To asã. Lit. has come to an end, decreased, diminished ; hence, has got thin.

Ewo . . . mu. Lit. it is in.

395. *Opanyiǹ ntǒ bo-hyew nto abofra nsam'.* (2618)
An elder does not roast a hot stone and place it in the hand of a child.

Ntǒ . . . nto. For note on the negatives see No. 33, *nsisi.* Note how the vowel sound alters the meaning of a word, *tǒ* (nasal), to roast ; *to,* close *o* sound, to place.

396. *Opanyiǹ ntrã ofie na asadua mfow.* (2619)
The elder does not sit in the house and (allow) the loom to get wet.

Asadua. Asawa, cotton, and *dua,* a stick, i. e. loom.

397. *Opanyiǹ wo ǹkwã a, onni mfensã.* (2620).
Even when an old man is strong and hearty, he will not live for ever.

Onni. Neg. of *di.*

Mfensã. Mfe abiesã, lit. three years, but used for an indefinite period of time (see note on No. 767).

398. *Mpanyimfo na ebu be se, ' Gya me naǹ ', na wonse se, ' Gya me ti '.* (2622)
Experienced men have a saying, ' Leave my legs alone ', but you will not hear them saying, ' Leave my head alone '.

Ebu be. See note on No. 258.

The following is the explanation given by the Ashantis of this saying. Long ago, when wild animals, lions, hyenas, and leopards, were even more numerous than now, a man, when he lay down to sleep, always took care that his feet and not his head were nearest to the doorway. Thus, if a wild animal got into the hut, it would most probably seize the man's legs, who would then shout ' Leave my legs alone'; whereas had his head been nearest the door, and been seized hold of, he would have been unable to shout 'Leave my head alone'. The proverb means, a man of experience will not put himself in a position from which he cannot extricate himself.

399. *Mpanyimfo se, 'Maye se wo peň'.* 2623)
The elder (lit. elders) says, 'I have done as you (are doing now) once upon a time (or, I was as you are)'.

400. *Se mpanyimfo pe wo atŏtŏ aɯe a, wuňhuruw ntra ogya.* (2624)
If the old people want to roast and eat you, you do not jump over a fire.

Atŏtŏ aɯe. Note the construction in the subordinate noun clause after the verb *pe.* (See note on No. 2, *wope.*)

401. *Mpanyimfo ye wo guaňñuaň, na se wuguaň a, akyiň no woserew wo.* (2625)
When the grown-ups (frighten you to) make you run off, and you do so, afterwards they laugh at you.
Guaňñuaň. Reduplication of *guaň.*

402. *Akwakorā te ho ansāna wowoo panyiň.* (1877)
An old man was in the world before a chief was born.
Te. Lit. lived, see note on No. 366.
Wowoo. Past tense, note lengthening of final vowel.
Panyiň. Here in the sense of one in authority, see note on No. 1.

403. *Aberewa a onni sẽ no n'atadɯe gu ne kotokum'.* (100)
The old woman with no teeth has 'tiger' nuts in her bag. (She may have some reason unknown to you for keeping them.)
Sẽ. The names for the teeth are: *obomofo sẽ* (lit. hunter's teeth), canine teeth; *nyepi,* molars; *adonteň sẽ* (lit. main body teeth, from military term), incisor teeth. Human teeth are valued as *sumaňs.*

404. *Aberewa fɯe akoko, na akoko fɯe aberewa.* (101)
The old woman looks after (her) hens and the hens look after the old woman (by laying eggs and hatching out chickens for her).
Akoko. See note on No. 199.

405. *Aberewa ko asu a, obeba, na ne ntem na yérepé.* (102)
When an old woman goes to fetch water (we know) she will come

back, but it is how long she will be about it that we want (to know).

Ne ntẹm. Here *ntẹm* would seem really a noun instead of an adverb; lit. her quickness (in returning).

The saying means that if old persons do things that younger people do, they must not expect any consideration on account of their age. (Cf. following.)

406. *Aberewa nim ade a, ónnye ne bañ.* (103)
If an old woman (says) she knows (every)thing, let her put up her
    own fence. (Cf. No. 405 above.)

Ade. See note on No. 85, *me dea.*

Ónnye. Imperative of *gye.*

407. ' *Makyĕ, makyĕ,*' *kum aberewa.* (1992)
'Good morning, good morning,' (eventually) kills an old woman.

Makyĕ. Me mã wo akyĕ, I give you morning. The old woman, who sitting by the house all day, and having nothing to do but return salutations, is said to be killed eventually by them.

CHAPTER IX

408. *Ọhem-mone nni bābi, na ọsafohene-bone na ọwọ bābi.* (1300)
There is no such thing anywhere as 'a bad king', though 'a bad vassal chief' may be found.

Ọhem-mone = *Ọhene-bone.*

Nni. Neg. of *wọ.*

Ọsafohene. A sub- (or, vassal) chief, also in a military sense, a captain of a war company. *Omań-hene,* i.e. chief of a nation, king, is the highest title. *Ọhene* is somewhat vaguely applied either to the supreme chief or king, or even to some quite small chief of a town or village, though this latter is more correctly *ọdekuro,* lit. holder of the village.

409. *Ọhene a obekum wo mmae a, na wokań ahene dodow a woasõm ?* (1301)
When the chief who will kill you has not yet come (on the stool), can you count how many chiefs you have served under ?

410. *Ọhene bi bere so wohũ, na obi bere so wọáyére.* (1303)
In one chief's reign skins are treated by having the hairs singed off, in that of another the skins are spread in the sun. (Times and manners change.)

Bere. Lit. time.

Wọáyére. Lit. they have spread (them) out. Translated by the passive.

411. *Ọhene bedi wo kasa a, efi mamfo.* (1304)
When a chief is going to compel you to do something, he does so by the authority of the people.

Bedi . . . kasa. Di kasa, to compel a person to pay for some wrong he has done.

Mamfo. For note on suffix *fo* see No. 78, *kontromfĩ. Mamfo = ọmań-fo.*

412. *Qhene bekum wo a, ennim ahamatĭŏĕ.* (1305)

When a chief is going to kill you, it is useless consulting the lots.

Ennim. Neg. of *wọ mu.*

Ahamatĭĕ. Lit. draw or pull the strings, see note on No. 55, *aka.*

413. *Qhene nè uɵ kã a, na okum wo.* (1307)

When a chief and you are on (too) intimate terms, (some day) he will kill you. (Cf. 421.)

Kã. Mɛ nè no kã = he and I are friends.

414. *Qhene anim na wọṅkã, na n'akyi de, woose.* (1308)

One does not speak out one's mind in the presence of a chief, but behind his back one does.

Anim. See note on No. 80, *aniwa.*

N'akyi. See note on No. 89, *akyi.*

415. *Qhene nufu dọsŏ a, amansãn na enŭm.* (1309)

When a chief has plenty of milk, then all people drink of him.

Nufu. Lit. breasts, but by metonymy milk.

Enŭm. Note this idiomatic use of the 3rd person sing. neuter pronoun for the 3rd person plural masc. or fem.

416. *Qhene nyã ahŏtrãfo pa a, na ne bere so dŭo.* (1310)

When a king has good councillors, then his reign is peaceful.

Ahŏtrãfɵ. Deriv. *hŏ* and *tĕna*, lit. one who sits beside.

Ne bere so. Lit. in his time.

Dŭo. Lit. cool.

417. *Qhene nnyã wo a, na wouse, ' Q nè me kã '.* (1311)

As long as a chief leaves you alone, you say, ' He and I are good friends '.

Nnyã wɔ. Lit. does not get (hold of) you.

418. *Qhene asŏ te sɛ 'sono asŏ.* (1312)

The ears of a chief are as the ears of the elephant (i.e. he hears all that is going on).

'Sono. See note on No. 89, *ɛsóno.*

419. *Qhene asŏ te sɛ sọñē; emu akwaṅ boro apem.* (1313)

The ears of a chief are like a strainer; there are more than a thousand ways to them.

Sọñē. An openwork basket for straining palm oil.

420. *Ọhene ntam te sẹ bayérẹ amóa, obi ntọ mu mfa nehŏ tọ́trọtọ̌ mfi adi da.* (1314)

A chief's oath is like the hole a yam is planted in, no one falls into it and gets out again unhurt.

Ntam. See note on No. 496, *wokā.*

Bayérẹ. One of the many species of yam (*ọde*).

Ntọ, mfa, . . . *mfî.* Note the negative throughout, see note on No. 33, *mfa, nsisi.*

421. *Ọhene tamfo ne nea ọ nè no fî mmofraase.* (1315)

The enemy of a chief is he who has grown up with him from childhood. (Cf. No. 413.)

Tamfo. Tañ, to hate.

Mmofraase. Deriv. *mmofra, ase.*

422. *Ọhene te sẹ odum, onni anim nni akyiri.* (1317)

A chief is like an *odum* tree, he has no front and no back.

Odum. See note on No. 57, *odum.*

423. *Ọhene ba ntutu 'mirika ṅkọfwẹ tiri.* (1321)

A chief's child does not run to look at a head (that has been cut off).

The heads of persons executed are brought to the chief's house.

Ntutu . . . *nkọfwẹ.* Note the two negatives, see note on No. 33, *nsisi.*

424. *Aheṅkwā di adwẹne na wadwẹṅ asẹm.* (1322)

A chief's servant eats fish and gets ideas.

There is a play on the words *adwẹne,* a fish, and *dwẹṅ,* to think, the noun from which is *adwẹne,* thought. (Cf. No. 446.)

Aheṅkwā = Ọhene-akoa.

425. *Aheṅkwā na ọmã ọhene hŏ yẹ hŭ.* (1324)

It is the chief's servant that causes the person of the chief to excite fear.

426. *Ọsafohene nsua na wakŏ.* (2756)

A war captain does not take the oath before going to fight. (Lit. in order that he may, &c.)

Ọsafohene. See note on No. 306, *dọm.*

Nsua. Sua, to take an oath before going to fight.

The *safohene* has already taken the oath and is not required to do so again before going to war. The oath is taken as follows:

The man stands before the chief, sword in hand, the left hand being placed on the heart, pointing his sword at the chief, he swears ' *Me kă ntam kese se mekŏ mamă me wura ne me sase nea mede meye obi akoa no, mekŏ mato. Me soma korabo na wanko a, mede me ti me sane hŏ. Se nea me kăe yi manye a, me kă ntam kese*'.

Translation—' I swear the great oath that I will fight for my king and my country rather than become any one's slave, I will fight and fall. If I fire a bullet and it will not pass (in front), I myself and my own head will go forward. If I do not do these things I swear, I take the great oath.'

427. *Ade a ohene pe na woye mă no.* (783)
Whatever a chief wishes is done for him.

Ade. See note on No. 85, *me dea.*

Mă. Really a verb, here translated by the preposition ' for ', see note on No. 240, *wo.*

428. *Nnipa nhīnă pe ohene aye, na (woanyă?) woannyă na wose, mpo ahenni ye yaw.* (2432)
All men would like to be chief(s), but when they cannot get what they want they declare that even to rule as a chief has its worries.

Woannyă. The original gives this verb in the positive, but this is probably an error.

Ahenni. Deriv. *ohene di*, to rule as chief.

429. *Ade hīa ohene nana a, okita tuo, na onsoá akete.* (798)
When a chief's grandson is poor, he holds a gun but he does not carry a mat.

Nana. More often *nănă, oba* is understood, see 37, *nĩ.*

Akete. To carry one's own sleeping-mat is considered very degrading.

430. *Ade hīa odehye a, ehīa no kàkrā.* (797)
When a free man lacks something, it is something very big he lacks.

Odehye. Plu. *adeyhye*, a free man, as opposed to a slave (*odonko*); also used in the sense of one of good family, a nobleman.

Kàkrā. See note on No. 101, *kàkrā.*

431. *Odehye bo dam a, wofre no asăbow.* (834)
When a man of noble family is mad, people say he is only the worse for wine.

Odehye. See note above, No. 430.

Wofre. Lit. they say.

Asabow. Deriv. *bow nsă.*

432. *Odehye diṅ nyera da.* (835)
A free man's name is never lost.

433. *Odehye, wodi no apată, na wonni no sono.* (836)
Nobility should be borne as one eats fish (humbly) and not as one
partakes of elephant flesh (proudly, and boasting about it).

Apată. Fish, dried, is a common food all over Ashanti. Elephant's
meat is naturally rather a luxury, and people will give much even
for a small piece just to be able to say they have eaten it.

434. *Odehye ṅhyehye, na sika na ehyehye.* (838)
Fame of being noble born does not spread abroad, it is the fame of
riches that spreads.

Sika. See note on No. 591.

435. *Odehye ankŏ a, akoa guaṅ.* (839)
When the free man does not fight, the slave runs away.

436. *Odehye mu nni abofra.* (840)
Among royalty no one is a child.

437. *Odehye, wonnŏa wonni, na sika ne asem.* (841)
An ancient name cannot be cooked and eaten ; after all, money is the
thing.

Wonni. Neg. of *di.*

438. *Odehye, wompae.* (842)
A man of royal blood does not need to have his name proclaimed.

Wompae. Pae, used of the proclamations of the *osen,* herald.

439. *Odehye nsore, wosi no mfensă.* (843)
The offering on the grave of one of the royal house is placed there
for many years.

Nsore. A burial grove. Deriv. probably *n,* not, and *sore,* to rise
up; but also by metonymy, the offering placed on the grave.

Mfensă. Lit. three years, but used for indefinite number; see
note on No. 767.

This proverb is quoted by a person who is reprimanded or re-
proached for not having performed some action, and is equivalent
to answering, 'Oh, I have plenty of time yet in which to do that,
there is no hurry'.

440. *Odehye te họ a, akoa nni ade.* (844)

When the free man is there, the slave does not take command.

Nni ade. Di ade, to take possession, inherit, take command. This saying is not strictly accurate as there have been cases where the legitimate heirs have been passed over and the stool given to a slave. See proverb following.

441. *Odehye wu a, akoa di ade.* (845)

When a free man dies, a slave succeeds. (See No. 440, note.)

442. *Odehye nye abofra na woabọ ne diń abọ owu diń.* (846)

One of royal rank is not a common fellow that he should have his name coupled with the name of Death.

Abofra. Child, boy or girl, but also used in the sense of servant, fellow.

Owu. Death personified for description, see note on No. 16, *owu.* Note, among the Ashantis it is bad etiquette, if not actually criminal, to mention the word 'death' in connexion with the name of a chief. There are many euphemisms to express 'he is dead'; e.g. *wakā ńżyens gu*, lit. he has cast away salt; *okọ asamań*, he has gone to the spirit world; *ọka bābi*, he remains elsewhere. *Wayẹ Onyankǒpọ̀ǹ de*, he has become the property of Onyankọpǒǹ.

443. *Akoa mpaw wura.* (1625)

A slave does not choose (his) master.

Akoa. A servant, slave, but the latter is better *ọdọnko. Akoa* is also used in the sense of 'that fellow' (*akoa no*). ⸢Slaves were probably quite well treated in Ashanti and had not much to complain of. It is true that they were liable to be sacrificed, or perhaps buried with their master on his death, but such a fate was also possible for free men. Slaves who proved themselves able could, and often did, succeed to their masters' property. Slaves, apart from those born such, might be put in three classes: (1) those who became such by having been bought or captured in war; (2) those pledged or pawned by their relatives or themselves to liquidate debts, or as security for a debt; (3) those who voluntarily placed themselves under a master for protection. To fully understand the proverbs which follow it is necessary to remember that so-called 'slavery' *in Africa*, as practised by *the Africans themselves*, was seldom or never that terrible thing with which later and exotic associations have invested the word.⸣

'An African Slave.' The words have gained much of their

sinister meaning, to our ear, owing to the transplantation of
a more or less necessary and not wholly to be pitied individual,
from his indigenous surroundings (where his status in, and advantage to, the social system were assured and fully recognized),
to a 'civilized' and a 'Christian' community, which had long
forgotten all that thousands of years of experience in dealing with
this class had taught his rude African master. The demand for
slaves in the Christian markets of the world, and all the horrors
that this traffic brought to Africa and to her people are apt to
blind one to the fact that this 'open sore' was much of our own
making. One is prevented from seeing that here, in its original
home, 'slavery' (another word is almost needed to express it) did
and (in a mild form, and shorn of its more glaring abuses) does
much to hold together the communistic savage community till
such time as education and advancement favour greater inde-
pendence and individualism.

444. *Akoa ṅhyẹ nehŏ ntu sa.* (1615)
A slave does not make up his own mind about going to war.

Ṅhyẹ . . . ntu. For use of negatives see No. 33, *mfa, nsisi.*
Sa. See note on No. 317, *ọsa.*

445. *Akoa nim wura.* (1622)
A slave knows (his) master.

446. *Akoa di guaṅ a, ne hŏ guaṅ no.* (1612)
When a slave eats a sheep, he is in trouble.

Guaṅ. Oguaṅ, a sheep, see note on No. 17, *guaṅ.* Besides
perhaps being a play on the words *guaṅ,* sheep, and *guaṅ,* trouble
(cf. No. 424), the proverb means that the slave who eats a sheep,
that is, sacrifices it to a fetish, must be in great trouble, or have
committed some crime unknown to his master, or is making some
promissory offering to his fetish, in any of which circumstances his
master would want to know all about it.

447. *Akoa ampọw a, na ẹfiri ŵira.* (1626)
When a slave is not well behaved, the cause can be traced to (his)
master.

Ampọw. The literal meaning of *pọw* (often reduplicated *popow*)
is to clean, polish, rub up, hence here perhaps used figuratively,
polished, polite, in which sense the word is often used.
Ŵira = Wura; ŵira is in the Akan dialect.

448. *Akoa nni awu na woṅkum owura.* (1619)

When a slave does not commit murder, his master is not killed.

The master was held absolutely responsible for every act of the slave, who was considered as having not only a body which was not his own, but also a mind. Hence any act of a slave was considered as an act of his master.

449. *Akoa nim sŏm a, ofa ne ti ade di.* (1620)

When a slave knows how to serve (his master well), he is permitted to take his own earnings.

Ne ti ade. Lit. his head thing, i.e. the price paid for a person or thing. Cf. *tiri nsã*, the wine placed before the parents of a girl as a legal symbol that the woman has been given in marriage.

450. *Akoa a onim sŏm di ne wura ade.* (1621)

A slave who knows how to serve succeeds to his master's property. (Cf. No. 441.)

451. *Akoa nyã nehŏ a, ofre nehŏ Sonani.* (1623)

When a slave becomes a rich (and free) man, he calls himself one of the *Asona* family (a noble family).

Sonani. For notes on Ashanti totem and family names, see note on No. 37, *abusũa*.

452. *Akoa di fɔ.* (1611)

A slave is (as a matter of course) guilty.

453. *Akoa ṅkyere nnannua.* (1617)

A slave does not point out where good sticks for building are to be found.

Nnannua. Lit. house sticks, *nnaṅ*, plu. of *ọdaṅ*, a house. The usual house is a framework of sticks plastered with mud. The slave on seeing suitable sticks should go and cut them, and not merely come and report, when he will only be asked why he has not brought them.

454. *Akoa nni mpọw kwa.* (1618)

A slave does not eat the second yam crop without good reason.

Nni. Neg. of *di*.

Mpọw. The second crop of yams; the first is called *mmọtọkroma*. This second crop is used exclusively for planting out the following season, and for a slave to eat them would mean he was contemplating flight before then.

455. *Akoa nyansa wo ne wura tirim.* (1624)
A slave's wisdom is in his master's head.

456. *Akoa sare asuko na womã oko a, òguan.* (1627)
When a slave has ceased to go for water and is (again) made to go,
    he runs away.

    Sare asuko. Asuko, the verbal noun from *ko,* to go, and *asu,*
water. *Sare,* to give up doing something one has been in the habit
of doing. Here a slave, who had become so far a privileged person
that he was no longer ' the hewer of wood and drawer of water ',
on being ordered to become so again, would consider himself so
badly treated that he would try and escape and find a new master.
The saying means that a privilege once granted is difficult to
withdraw.

457. *Akoa te se kyekyire, wode nsu kakra gu no so a, na ahono.* (1628)
A slave is like unto corn ground into flour ; when a little water is
    sprinkled on it, it becomes soft. (A slave is easily influenced
    by kind treatment.)

    Kyekyire. Indian corn roasted and ground. (The original,
No. 1628 in ' Tshi Proverbs ', has *kyekyere* for *kyekyire* in error.)

458. *Akoa te se tũerebo ; enni otuo ano a, enye 'ye.* (1629)
A slave is like the flint on the striker of the gun which, if it were
    wanting, would make the gun useless. (He is a necessary
    member of the community.)

    Tũerebo. See No. 339.
    Enni. Neg. of *wo.*
    'Ye = Yiye.

459. *Wo nkoa suro wo anim asem a, wonni nĩm mmã wo.* (1630)
If your slaves fear (to speak) before your face, they will not gain
    victories for you.

    Wonni. Neg. of *di. Di nĩm* or *nkõnĩm,* to win a fight.
    Mmã. See note on No. 727 and No. 14.

460. *Nnonkofo bãnu fũe nantũi a, okom kum no.* (976)
When two slaves look after (your) cow, hunger kills it.

    Nnonkofo. Nnonko, the Ashanti name for the country to the
north of Salaga, now the ' Northern Territory ' of the Gold Coast.
Fo, a personal suffix, see note on No. 78, *kontromfĩ.* As many
of the slaves used to come from here, the word *Nnonkofo,* sing.

ǫdǫṅkoni, came to be synonymous with *akoa*, slave, and used entirely in that sense.

461. '*Ahīa me na fwę mã me,' nti na obi yęę akoa.* (1335)

'I am in want, so look after me,' that is why some men became slaves (lit. one became a slave).

Yęę. Past tense, formed by lengthening of final vowel.

Akoa. See note on No. 443, *akoa.* This comes under class 3.

462. *Owura nè akoa ntam' nni, 'twĕ mã mentwĕ'.* (3501)

Between master and slave there is no 'pull and let me pull' (no striving for the mastery).

463. *Wo wuŗa tan wo a, na ǫfrę wo akoa dehye.* (3503)

When your master hates you, then he calls you a free-born slave.

Akoa dehye. A slave who was originally free-born, but through debt or some other misfortune lost his original status; see note on No. 443, *akoa.* The slave mentioned here comes under class 2.

464. *Obi ntǫ akoa na ǫmmęhyę no so.* (352)

No one buys a slave to act as a restraint on himself.

Ntǫ . . . ommęhyę. Note the double negative, see note on No. 33, *nsisi.* *Mmę*, neg. of auxiliary verb *bĕra.*

Hyę . . . so, to press on; hence, to oppress.

465. *Wunni wuŗa a, obi kyere wo, tǫṅ, di.* (921)

When you have no master, some one catches you and sells you for what you will fetch.

Wunni. Neg. of *wǫ.*

Tǫṅ, di. Lit. sell, eat, i.e. sell and use the proceeds.

466. *Wofęre wo afŭnā a, wudi nnuaṅfĩṅ.* (1115)

When you fear to reprimand your slave girl, you eat stale food.

Wofęre. See note on No. 155, *mfęre.*

Nnuaṅfĩṅ. Nnuaṅ, aduaṅ, and *fĩṅ*, not *fĩ*, bad.

This proverb might almost seem to be spoken by some mistress in Mayfair, worried by the servant problem and fearful lest her cook takes offence and gives notice.

467. *Akoa ǫhantanni, wǫde no sie funu.* (1614)

A proud slave is taken and buried with the corpse (of his master).

It was the custom in Ashanti in the old days, when a chief or any one of importance died, to kill slaves, wives, and attendants, to accompany their master to the spirit world, *asaman* (see No. 35, *osaman*).   As soon as the chief breathed his last, and before the news of his death was publicly announced, two slaves, generally girls, were taken to where the corpse was laid out for washing and killed, either by strangulation or by having their necks broken across a stick; this was known as *yi aguare*, 'to remove from the bathing (place) '.   After the body had been washed and decked in all its finest cloths, another victim was killed at the entrance to the house by having his throat cut (first having the *sepow* knife driven through his tongue and cheeks to prevent him swearing any oath), the blood being allowed to fall on the drums.   Chiefs were often buried sitting on the shoulders of a man who thus standing was entombed alive.   Before burying or killing the different victims they were each assigned their duties in the next world which they had to perform for their dead master.

468. *Obi nhũ bi kwaberaṅ ṅhuruw nsi.*   (187)
No one sees a strong slave belonging to another man and jumps for joy about it.

Nhũ, ṅhuruw, nsi.   For this idiom see note on No. 33, *mfa, nsisi.*

Kwaberaṅ = *Akoa-oberaṅ.*

469. *Obi akoa di péreguaṅ na womã asũãsã to no a, oyi kaw sũã mã wutua.*
When some one's slave who is worth a *péreguaṅ* of gold dust (£8) is sold to you for an *asũãsã*'s worth (about £6), he is pretty sure to go and incur some debt for a *sũã*'s worth (about £2) that you will have to pay.

Péreguaṅ, asũãsã, sũã.   See note on No. 591, *nsenĩa*, for notes on Ashanti weights.

470. *Abusũa ṅhĩnã ye abusũa, na ye fũefũe mmetĕmã so de.*   (683)
All family names are family names (and good enough at that), but we search well between the thorns of the oil palm for the good nuts nevertheless.

Abusũa.   A family or clan name traced through the female line. See note on No. 37, *abusũa.*

Mmetĕmã.   Deriv. *betem*, a cluster, and *mma*, plu. of *oba*, child, lit. cluster of children, i. e. bunch of palm nuts.

471. *Abusũa te sɛ ṅfŏbireṅ, egugu akuw-akuw.* (684)
Family names are like flowers, they blossom in clusters.

472. *Abusũa yɛ ɔom, na wo nã ɔba ne wo nua.* (685)
The family is an army, and your own mother's child is your real
    kinsman (brother or sister).

    See note on *abusũa*, No. 37.
    Nã. See note on No. 37, *nĩ.*
    Nua. See note on No. 37, *nĩ.*

473. *Abusũa dua, wontĭbá.* (686)
The family tree is not cut.

474. *Nea ɔmaṅ bi kã serew na ɔmaṅ bi kã sũ.* (2199)
What one people talk and laugh about, another people talk and cry
    about.

    Ɔmaṅ. A nation, a people. Used, however, also in the sense
of a town, and the people of that town. This probably is its
original meaning, the various towns or villages possibly under
independent chiefs gradually coming under a central authority, the
ɔmaṅ-hene.

475. *Ɔmaṅ rebɛɔo a, efi afi mu.* (1996)
When a nation is about to come to ruin, the cause begins in the
    homes (of its people).

    Ofi. See note on No. 262, *fie.*

476. *Ɔmaṅ bɔ, na menné abobow.* (1998)
A nation is (can be) destroyed, how much more one home (lit.
    a gate).

    Menné. Neg. of *de.*
    Abobow. See note on No. 495.

477. *Ɔmaṅ Akuapem, wokonyã ade a, wose, 'Obusufo!', nso woannyã a,*
    wose 'Okãrabiri!' (1999)
The Akuapem people say, when you get wealthy, 'Mischievous
    fellow!', and when you have nothing, they say 'Unlucky one!'.

    Okãrabiri. Lit. black soul. See note on No. 147.

478. *Ɔmaṅ kum wo a, na ɔhene kum wo.* (2000)
When (the united) people (want to) kill you, then the chief kills
    you.

479. *Ọmaṅ te sẹ adesoa, woṅhũ mu ade dakoro.* (2001)

A people are like unto a load (containing many things), you cannot perceive all the contents in a single day.

Adesoa. Lit. *ade,* a thing, and *soa,* to carry, something carried, a load.

Mu ade. Almost a compound word, lit. 'the in-it things', i.e. contents.

480. *Ọmaṅ từa wo sãmã a, wompopa.* (2002)

When it is the unanimous wish of a people that you dress your hair in a certain way, you are compelled to do so (lit. you do not rub it out).

Sãmã. Various patterns cut on the hair of the head.

481. *Ọmaṅ rebẹbọ a, ọmãmpám na ókừra pồma.* (1997)

When a nation is about to come to ruin, then the salamander holds the staff.

Ọmãmpám. The salamander. The name in Ashanti means literally 'mend nation' (*pam ọmaṅ*), i.e. unite, join together in harmony and peace. The following is the Ashanti story of how it came to get this name.

' The salamander was formerly known as the *Bọamaṅ* (i.e. break-up nations). This name he was given by the *ẹsono,* elephant, who is supposed, according to this story, to have given all the animals their names. The salamander protested against being given this name, but in vain, so he went off and adopted the following plan in order to get it altered. He went alternately to the chiefs of the *Ṅkraṅ* (*Accra*) and *Akuapem* nations, and told each in turn that the other was about to attack him, and these nations were on the point of going to war. It transpired, however, that the salamander was the real cause of all the trouble, and he was caught and asked to give an explanation of his false reports. He freely acknowledged what he had done, but pleaded justification in his name, *Bọamaṅ* (destroy nations). His excuse was accepted, but his name was altered from *Bọamaṅ* to his present one, *Mãmpám* (unite nations).

The salamander is said by the natives to be deaf; in the saying above he is represented as the *ọkyeãme.* The staff held by a chief's *ọkyeãme,* that is, spokesman, is generally bound round with the skin of the salamander (as a kind of 'sympathetic' magic, no doubt).

The word *okyeăme* is universally spoken of and rendered as
'linguist' by the Europeans in this colony. It has of course
nothing to do with linguist (i.e. one skilled in languages). The
okyeăme is a court official who acts as the mouthpiece of the chief;
etiquette neither allowing a chief to speak directly to, or be spoken
to directly by, his subjects. The idea of linguist or interpreter is
entirely foreign to the word. The *okyeăme* need not, and probably
does not, know any language but his own, and if the word is to be
rendered in English at all, it should be by the word, spokesman.

482. '*Agya, gyae na menkă,*' *wokyi.* (1238)
'Father, stop, and let me tell (you what you ought to do)', it is not
 permitted to speak so.

 Agya. See note on No. 37, *nĩ.*
 Menkă. Imperative.
 Wokyi. See notes on No. 89, *akyi,* and No. 132, *wokyi.*

483. *Agya mma nyă a, mepe ; enă mma nyă a, mepe papăpa.* (1239)
 When (my father's children get (anything), I like that; when (my)
 mother's children get (anything), I like that even better.

 Agya mma. Children of your own father but by another
 mother, and therefore, as descent is traced through the female line,
 not considered as your *onũa* (i.e. brother or sister by *your own*
 mother). See note on terms of relationship, No. 37, *abusũa.*
 Enă mma. Children of one's own mother. See note above.
 Papăpa. The word *pa* means good, well; here lit. good, good,
 good, the word being repeated to make a superlative or express
 emphasis. It is also used in the sense of 'real', 'genuine', see
 No. 44 and No. 135.

484. '*M'agya dea, mémfa, me nă dea mémfa',* *na ebere aibi.* (1243)
 'It is my father's, so let me take it; it is my mother's, so let me take
 it', that brings (a child) to stealing.

 Dea. Not to be confused with *dea = nea,* he who. Here *de,*
 with the enclitic *a,* probably giving emphasis, is the possessive.
 See note on No. 85, *me dea.*

485. *Wo agya akoa tìba dua a, wuse,* '*Eye merew*'. (1244)
 When your father's slave cuts down a tree, you say, 'It is soft wood
 (easy to cut)'.

486. *Wo nã ba ne Kobuobi a, añkã wobese sẹ kyene kẹse fata no ana ?* (2060)

Even if your mother's son is ' *Kobuobi* ', would you tell him that the big drum was a fit thing for him to carry ?

Kobuobi. The prefix *ko*, before proper nouns, is a contraction for *ọdọnko*, a slave (q. v. No. 460, *nnọñkọfo*), and is added as a kind of nickname to the name of a person of slave or humble origin, and also to those of children whose brothers or sisters have all died. *Kobuobi*, that is, slave boy *Buobi* may be in duty bound to carry the big drum, but being your own real brother you would not want to taunt him with the fact.

See also note on No. 138. This and many other of the proverbs tend to show how strong is the idea of relationship on the mother's side alone.

487. *Wo nã ọba ne wo nua.* (2061)

Your mother's child is your kinsman (brother or sister).

See note on No. 37, *abusũa*, and above.

488. *Wo nã di hĩa a, wunnyae no ñkọfa obi nyẹ nã.* (2063)

When your mother is poor, you do not leave her and go and make some one else your mother. (Cf. No. 492.)

Nã. See note on No. 37, *nĩ.*

Wunnyae, ñkọfa. Note the negatives, see No. 33, *mfa, nsisi.*

489. *Wo nã añkõ gua a, na womãnã wo nã né kòra.* (2064)

When your own mother does not go to market, then your step-mother is sent.

Wo nã né kora, a step-mother. It must, of course, be remembered that the Ashantis are polygamous, so that a child, besides its own mother, may have anything from one to several hundreds of step-mothers. See note on No. 345, *kora.*

490. *Wo nã wu na wobẹyẹ ayi a, didi ŵie ansã, na ñkọtọ piti na wo ani ñkowu mpanyimfo anim.* (2067)

When your mother has died and you are about to celebrate the funeral custom, finish eating first, lest you go and faint and shame yourself before the elders.

Didi ŵie. See note on *wutũa . . . ŵie*, No. 137.

Ani ñkowu. See note on No. 33, *mfa, nsisi.*

491. *Wo nã awu a, wo abusũa asã.* (2068)

When your mother dies, you have no kindred left.

See note on No. 37, *abusũa.*

492. *Wo nã nye a, na wo nã ara neñ.* (2069)

Even if your mother is not a good woman, she is your mother nevertheless. (Cf. No. 488.)

Neñ = ne no.

493. *Wudi wo agya akyi a, wusũa ne nantew.* (898)

When you follow behind your father, you learn to walk like him.

494. *Wunni nã na woko obi fi agoro a, na otu ne mma fo a, wode tu wohõ bi.* (912)

When you have no mother and you go to some one's house to play, and she (the mother) admonishes her children, you profit by some of that advice yourself.

Agoro. A verbal noun, (for) playing.

495. *Agorũ a ereba wo nã nè wo agya abóbów ãno nó, wompe ntem ñkofwe.* (1211)

The dance which is coming to your mother's and your father's door, you do not go off in haste to look at elsewhere.

Abóbów. The entrance to the square or open courtyard round which the houses of an Ashanti family are built.

Wompe ... ñkofwe. Note the double negative; see note on No. 33, *mfã, nsisi.*

496. *Wokã wo agya a, wokã wo nã bi.* (1489)

When you swear the oath of your father, you should also swear that of your mother.

Wokã. Ntam is understood.

Several kinds of oaths are to be recognized. First, there is the common form of oath taken at ordeals, where a man swears by his particular 'fetish' that he is speaking the truth, and calls on it to punish him if he is in the wrong. This form of oath is too well known to require a detailed description.

The second form is less well known. Like the first it is also a form of legal procedure.

Me kã ntam, 'I swear the oath of so-and-so'. These are the words said by an Ashanti man or woman who has a dispute with another. Let us suppose two people are quarrelling, words run

high, perhaps blows follow, suddenly one of the persons fighting
says to the other, 'I swear the oath of (whoever it may be) that
I am in the right'. There and then the matter ends for the time
being, for by saying these words the quarrel has been removed
from the sphere of a private dispute, with a possibility of a private
settlement, to become a purely public affair to be heard and settled
in the court of the chief whose oath has been sworn. Students
of Roman Private Law will notice the curious resemblance in
this procedure to the LEGIS ACTIO SACRAMENTUM, which was
also a method of removing a dispute from the sphere of private
settlement and securing a trial *in judicio*. Now the meaning
of this oath is as follows. The person who used the oath mentioned some particular day on which local tradition has ascribed
some dire calamity to have happened to the family of the tribal
chief. Each local chief may have such a black day. When
a person mentions such a day, which subject is ordinarily taboo,
it behoves the head of the family, whose unlucky day has been
thus recalled, to investigate the whole matter under dispute, and,
if necessary, punish the person who has wrongly used the power
or dread of this event to prove his case. It has been seen that
one of the litigants 'swears the oath', it is now the duty of the
other party to answer it (*bo ntam so*), lit. 'beat on the oath', that
is, also swear the same oath that he is in the right. Should the
second party fail to do so, the case is simply given against him, no
evidence or witnesses being required, the mere fact that he refuses
to respond to the oath proving him to be in the wrong. Should,
however, the oath be duly answered, then the case will be heard in
open court. Heavy fees attach to these oaths, each party putting
down his 'oath fee'. The fee of the party who wins the case will
be returned to him, that of the other party is forfeited to the chief.
It is thought that, did a chief whose oath has been taken refuse to
investigate the case, a similar calamity would befall his family.
The swearing of an oath constitutes a form of appeal to a higher
court. Not being satisfied with the judgement of one court, a person
can appeal to a higher by swearing the oath of the next most
important chief, the oath in this case being sworn against the
okyeăme or spokesman of the chief who gave judgement and not
against the original party to the suit. In this manner appeals can
be carried right up to the court of the paramount chief by the
swearing of the 'great oath' (*ntam kese*). This is the equivalent

of saying, '*Memeneda Koromante*', i.e. 'Koromante Saturday'. *Koromante* is a place on the Fantee coast where Osai Panyin of Coomassie was defeated and slain by the Fantees. This calamity was considered so terrible that even the name came to be proscribed and became known as simply *ntam kese*, the great oath/

Other important oaths are *Akantamansu*, from the name of a battle near Dodowa, where Osai Yao of Coomassie and many other chiefs were defeated and slain.

Wukuda, Wednesday's oath, is another.

An interesting modern example is *Abanakyi*, lit. after or behind the castle, castle being used as the personification of the English Government; this oath referring to the last rising in 1900 in Ashanti.

Any man who was about to be executed was usually pierced through both cheeks by a skewer-like knife (*sepow*), which prevented him from 'swearing the king's oath', which would have necessitated the delay of an investigation and trial before he could be executed.\

The third form of oath is perhaps more of the nature of a curse. By it a person invokes the death of the king, the words used being the simple formula, '*Obosom nkum ohene*,' 'May a fetish kill the king'. So terrible a crime is this considered that in describing it the custom is to say, 'he blessed (or, sprinkled) the sacred *edwira*' on the king. / When the writer was endeavouring to ascertain the exact curse used, he had great difficulty in getting his native informant to repeat it, and finally only got him to do so accompanied by loud cracking of his (the native's) fingers round the ears.

Now any one who thus 'blessed' the king was without exception and without possibility of pardon, killed. But a curious custom is in vogue. The curser is permitted to name (within reasonable limits) the day and manner of his death, and during this interval is granted absolute licence. He can demand any man's wife, money, and goods, to use and do as he likes with till the day of his death.

In this custom we have one of the most powerful checks on the personal despotism of kings and chiefs; for on one occasion on which a man was driven by the treatment he had received from the chief or king to 'bless' him, with the consequent upsetting of the social régime resulting from the licence granted, the person on whom the exasperated populace sought vengeance was the ruler who had by his despotism driven his distracted victim to prefer death to life.

A somewhat similar idea runs through the well-known custom of committing suicide, but before doing so ascribing the cause to some particular person who is thereby compelled to commit suicide himself, or again, the custom of swearing an oath on a person that he must kill you, when the person on whom the oath is sworn is in the predicament of having to choose between violating the oath or committing what will be considered and punished as murder.

497. *Obi mfi bea akyi ntu ne tam.* (170)
No one can pull the loin-cloth off a woman without her knowledge.

Mfi . . . akyi. Lit. to come behind one's back and do a thing, i. e. to do without one's knowledge.

498. *Obea kɔ aguare na wamma ntem a, na osiesie nehŏ.* (23)
When a woman goes to bathe and is a long time in returning, then (you can be sure) she is decking herself out.

Aguare. A verbal noun. See note on No. 353, *hohoro.*

499. *Obea tenten so abɛ a, ɔnwam di.* (25)
When a tall girl carries palm nuts, the toucan eats (them).

Obea tenten. The Ashanti women are shorter in stature than the men, and the expression 'tall girl' here implies a woman who does things unbefitting her sex, or who is shameless.

Ɔnwam di. The saying, *anwam bedi wo mmɛ,* 'the toucans will eat your palm nuts', is a common expression among the Ashantis, meaning 'some trouble will befall you'.

500. *Mmea nhĩnā yɛ bākŏ.* (27)
All women are alike.

501. *Mmea n'nyae ankā aguare, na ahohow hŏ bɔn.* (28)
Let women cease to bathe with limes, for even the (*ahohow*) red ant has an offensive smell.

Ahohow. A small red ant that lives in the branches of trees and which is found in lime trees. They have a nasty smell. The native women are very fond of using limes to rub their bodies with, perhaps to get rid of the smell that seems inherent in the black man and woman however clean they may be. The saying means, anything inherent in one cannot be got rid of by artificial means.

502. *Mmea pe nea sika wo.* (29)

Where the gold dust is, that is where the women like to be.

Sika. See note on No. 591.

503. *Mmea se, ' Wo hŏ ye fe' a, ene ka.* (30)

When the women say (to you) 'You are a handsome fellow', that means you are going to run into debt.

Ka. Ashanti. The Twi dialect has *kaw*, see No. 54.

504. *Ọbā hŏ ye fe a, efi ne kunu.* (19)

When a woman is beautiful, it is from her husband she gets her beauty.

Meaning perhaps that he has bought her the ornaments or fine clothes that make her look beautiful.

505. *Ọbā na onim kunu.* (20)

It is the woman who knows her husband.

Na. Here emphatic, see note on No. 1.

506. *Ọbā nyinsen na wanwo bā a, ọwo banin,* (21)

When a woman conceives and does not give birth to a girl, she gives birth to a boy.

507. *Ọbā twa bọmmā a, etiberi barima dan mu.* (22)

Even when a woman makes (lit. cuts) a drum, it leans against the man's house.

Twa. To cut; here refers to the tree from which the wooden portion of the drum has been made.

Women have nothing to do with drums in Ashanti, either the carrying or beating.

The following brief notes on drumming are only intended to draw attention to this interesting subject. The writer hopes to discuss the matter more fully in some other work.

' A great deal is heard in Africa about the wonderful way in which news can be passed on over great distances in an incredibly short space of time. It has been reported that the news of the fall of Khartum was known among the natives of Sierra Leone the same day, and other equally wonderful instances are quoted to show that the native has some extraordinary rapid means of communicating important events. It must, however, be remembered that most of the instances that one hears quoted are incapable of verification, and would, moreover, probably be found to have been much exaggerated. Having said this much, however, it must be admitted that these natives have a means of intercommunication which often inspires wonder and curiosity on the part of Europeans. One of such means of communication is by drumming.

This idea the European will readily grasp, and being familiar with various means of *signalling*, will suppose that some such a method might be adapted to drums; but among the Ashantis the drum is not used as a means of *signalling* in the sense that we would infer, that is by rapping out words by means of a prearranged code, but (to the native mind) is used to sound or speak the actual words.

That is, we have drum-talking as distinct from drum-signalling, a *tympanophonetic* as opposed to a *tympanosemantic* means of communication. Tympanophony, or drum-talking, is an attempt to imitate by means of two drums (a 'male' and a 'female') set in different keys the exact sound or words of the human voice.

(Such an idea does not appear nearly so far-fetched to the native mind as it might to a European, accustomed as the former is to ascribe even the sounds made by birds and some animals to attempts at human speech.)

We have all perhaps experienced the sensation that bells were ringing out *words*, and the classical example of 'Punch brothers punch' will occur to many, and children have a game where one plays a tattoo on another's back, beating harder and harder till the one who is acting the part of drum guesses the tune played.

These childish examples illustrate exactly what the Ashanti drummer strives to do with his drums.

Now the question naturally arises as to the limitations of this means of communication. Can the drum be made to say anything, or are the messages drummed restricted to certain preconceived and prearranged words or rather sentences? As far as the writer has been able to discover, the drummers' vocabulary is more or less restricted to the latter class of messages, but this point requires further investigation.

These drummers are trained from childhood, and must not only be experts in drumming, but also have learned the traditions and genealogies of all the kings, and the folk-lore of the tribe as contained in the proverbs, for it would seem that most of the sentences drummed come under these two headings.

The subject is one of absorbing interest, but only the briefest description can here be given.

The classes of messages sent come under several heads.

1. The names and deeds of each king or chief who has occupied the tribal stool as far back as tradition has any memory of. Drumming thus serves as an important way of perpetuating the tribal memory.

2. Messages addressed to the various materials from which the drums are made, the particular tree from which cut, the elephant from whose ear the tense membrane is made, the wood from which the pegs are made, the creeper used to tie down the skin. An appeal is also always made to a mythical divine drummer for permission to drum. This class of messages always precedes any drumming.

3. Many of the best-known proverbs are drummed, and among the commonest to be thus perpetuated are those in which ONYA-NKŎPǑN (a Supreme Being) figures. This the writer considers of considerable interest and importance as proving that the native name and conception of a High God is not derived from the Europeans. (See note on *Onyàmé*, No. 1.)

4. Alarms, especially fire.

5. War messages generally insulting, and not, as one might suppose, messages giving instructions as to movements of troops or orders to war captains. The Ashantis account for such messages not being, as it were, in 'the code book' by saying that any such orders would have to be delivered secretly, and not 'shouted out' for the enemy to hear.

A few examples taken from the hundreds of messages that an expert drummer can send will now be given.

The words and sentences are rapped out on two drums placed side by side. The drummer squats beside them with a drumstick in each hand. The tones of the drums are pitched in different keys. The message is rapped out with extraordinary rapidity and skill, the endeavour being to imitate the intonation usually given to the particular sentence to be drummed, each syllable of a word being represented by a beat on one or the other or both of the drums.

The following are drum messages beaten at the Wednesday and Sunday *adai* held in honour of the departed chiefs, on which occasion the ancestral stools are carried forth to the burial ground. (See note on No. 388, *akonnua*.)

First, as is always the case when the drums are brought out, the drummer propitiates or condoles with each separate part of which the composite drum is formed. (It is worthy of note that many words in these messages are now archaic and the meaning is not known even to the drummers.)

O-ba-yi-fo, o-do-man-ko-ma, kye-re-ma se, o-re-se-re, wo, ba-bi, a-gyi-na.

O wizard, the sacred drummer says he craves of you a place to stand.

The meaning is that the drummer asks permission from the wizard (see note on No. 56, *obayifo*) to drum. A drummer when he makes a mistake in the message he is sending, attributes the error to the interference of an evil spirit. Such an error on the part of a drummer is punished by the fine of a sheep. (It will be noted that this form of drumming is almost entirely ceremonial or religious.)

Twe-re-bo-a, Ko-di-a, Bi-rim-pon, o-do-man-ko-ma, kye-re-ma, se, o-ko-o, ba-bi, a, wa-ma ne hŏ m-me-re-so, fir-im-poṅ, da-mir-i-fa, da-mir-i-fa, da-mir-i-fa!

O cedar tree (from which the drum is made), the mighty one, the divine drummer says he had gone elsewhere for a while, but that now he has returned, pity, pity, pity.

Here the wooden portion of the drum is condoled with.

O-bu-a, yen-kye-re-du, o-do-man-ko-ma, kye-re-ma, se, o-ko-o, ba-bi, a, wa-ma ne ho m-me-re-so fi-rim-poṅ, da-mir-i-fa, da-mir-i-fa, da-mir-i-fa!

O *obua* tree (from which the pegs are cut that hold down the skin), the divine drummer says he had gone elsewhere for a while, but now he has returned, pity, pity, pity.

Bo-fu-mu, am-pa-se-kyi, o-do-man-ko-ma, kye-re-ma se, . . . (as before).

O *bofumu apasekyi* (the tree from which the bark is stripped to make the string with which the skin is fastened down to the pegs), the divine drummer says . . . (as before).

A-fe-ma, dun-si-ni, ne, a-sa-re n-kon-ta, o-do-man-ko-ma kye-re-ma, se . . . (as before).

O *afana* tree (from which the drumsticks are cut), the divine drummer says . . . (as before).

Ẹ-so-no, o-bæ, a-ku-ma, o-do-man-ko-ma, kye-re-ma, se, . . . (as before).

O elephant (lit. the great one), breaker of the axe, the divine drummer says . . . (as before).

Here the elephant, from whose ear the membrane of the drum is made, is propitiated. This concludes the propitiation of the drum, and this prelude being over the real business on hand will begin, namely, the mentioning of each chief's name and his deeds; there are only given one or two examples out of the many that exist.

A-si-a-ma-Tọ-ku-A-sa-re, ọ-twe-a-du-am-poṅ, ọ-nyà-mé, ọ-do-man-ko-ma, kyẹ-re-ma, se, ọ-kọ-ọ, ba-bi, a, wa-ma, ne-ho, m-me-re, so, ọ-bọ-ọ, de-en, ọ-bọ-ọ ọ-seṅ, na, ọ-bọ-ọ, ọ-kye-rẹ-ma, na ọ-bọ-ọ, ọ-bra-fo ti-ti-ri.

Asiama-Toku-Asare (the first king who sat on the stool of Mampoṅ), Supreme Being, God (see note on *Ọnyàmé,* No. 1), the divine drummer says he had gone elsewhere, but has now returned. What did He create; He created the herald, He created the drummer, but above all He created the executioner.

It is worthy of note here that we have two of the names of the Supreme Being introduced in connexion with the name of the first ancestor of the chiefs of Mampoṅ. It is extremely unlikely that this would be so, did their names and the sense in which they are understood, date only from the advent of the missionary.

The drummer thus runs through the whole line of ancestors of the chiefs right down to the reigning king, now and again a word or a sentence throws a flash of light on some forgotten custom, and every message has stamped on it signs of having been handed down from a distant past.

Here is another example :

Ọ-do-man-kọ-ma, bọ-ọ, a-de, Bọ-re Bọ-re bọ, a-de, ọ-bọ de, e-beṅ, ọ-bọ-ọ ọ-seṅ, ọ-bọ-ọ, kye-rẹ-ma, ọ-bọ-ọ, Ku-a-ku, Ak-wa, bo-a-fo ti-ti-ri Ko-nin-sa-mo-agya, Gya-me, A-mo-a-gya ẹ-seṅ, be-gye, wo, fo-kye, o-gya, wo de e-beṅ ọ-gya, wo, a-ka-bu, ọ-gya, wo a-tọ-per-ẹ o-gya, wo, Gya-me, A-m-poṅ-sa-kyi, A-m-pon-sa, Mam-poṅ, A-som Gyi-ma, bi-rem-poṅ fi-rim-poṅ, da-mir-i-fa, da-mir-i-fa, da-mir-i-fa !

The Supreme Being created things, the Creator created things, what things did He create? He created the herald, He created the drummer, He created *Kwaku Akwa* (meaning unknown), but chiefly He created the executioner, *Koniṅsamoagya, Gyame, Amoagya* (meaning unknown), Herald, come and get your black monkey-skin hat, what did he leave you? he left you *akabu* (meaning obscure) he left you death of a thousand cuts, he left you *Gyame Amponsakyi* (a name?) *Amponsa Mampọ̀n, Asom Gyima*, mighty one, *firimpon* (?) woe, woe, woe!

(Asom Gyima was the 8th king of Mampọ̀n.)

A message to summon people when a fire is raging in a town runs as follows :

Mam-pọ̀n kon-ton-kyi, ọ-bo, a, ẹ-hĩ a-ku-mă, mo, m-mă, mo-hŏ, m'-me-re-so, o-gya hu-reṅ! hu-reṅ! hu-reṅ!

Mampọ̀n (an important town in Ashanti), *kontonkyi* (archaic), the stone that has worn out the axe, arise, fire raging! raging! raging!

Note, the allusion to a stone wearing out an axe almost certainly refers to the grinding of celts or axe-heads, though the Ashantis have no recollection of a stone age, calling all such stone axes, ' God's axes '.

Finally, the following is selected out of many messages used in time of war. As already stated, in an actual engagement messages to the various companies are sent by the general by means of heralds and the *abrafo* executioners, the drums being used to encourage the men and insult the enemy.

. . . First come the names of famous chiefs, then, *wa-kum n-nipa mă n-ni-pa yẹ de-ẹ-beṅ, wa-kum, n-ni-pa, ma n-ni-pa yẹ sa-maṅ, a-boa-a, dom-po, se, ọ-da, wo, a-se, ne, m-mer-e-bo-sẹ-ẹ, n-yaṅ-kom-pa-sa-kyi, Kwa-ku, A-gyai, se, ọ-da, wo, ase ọ-n-wi-ni kọ, dwo, a, ọ-da, wo, ase, u-de kọ-kye, a-no-pa-nso, a, ọ-da, wo ase A-ku-ran-tọ, ọ̀-kye-na, ye-be-kum, wo, a-no-pa he-ma, he-ma, he-ma.*

. . . Men are slain that they should become what? men are slain that they should become ghosts, the animal the dog says he is very grateful to you for that thick lump of your liver, the vulture too, he says he thanks you very much, he thanks you in the evening when the sun is cool, when the day dawns he thanks you, hailing you, *Akurantọ!* We shall kill you to-morrow early, early, early.

508. *Wo yere a onye no, na ẹtẹ sẹ obi aguamaṅ.*
When your wife is a woman of no morals, then she might as well be some one else's harlot.

509. *Wo yere anyiǹ a, wuntutu 'mirika na ekohyia no.* (3649)

Before your wife has reached puberty you do not run to meet her.

Anyiǹ. Lit. has not grown. Euphemistically used for a girl reaching puberty. Quite little girls are married and go to live with their husbands, cooking and engaging in the household work, · though the man does not usually have sexual intercourse till she ' grows up '.

510. *Wo yerenom anum a, wo tekrema anum.* (3650)

When you have five wives, you have five tongues.

511. *Wo yere apem a, wo asem apem.* (3651)

When you have a thousand wives, you have a thousand ' palavers '.

512. *Obea nè ne kunu asem, obi nnim mu.* (24)

The conversation between husband and wife no one knows about.

513. *Oyere te se kũntũ; wódè katá wo sò a, wo hõ keka wo, wuyi gu ho nso a, awow de wo.* (3652)

A wife is like a blanket; when you cover yourself with it, it irritates you, and yet if you cast it aside you feel cold.

514. *Oyere nye nãm na woakyekye amãnã.* (3653)

A wife is not meat that she should be parcelled up and sent out to others.

Woakyekye. The original has *woakyekye*, but the common word in use is, *kyekye amãnã,* to tie up and send.

515. *Wo yere nye a, ente se wo ǹkõ wo da.* (3654)

Even if your wife be a bad lot, that is not to say you are going to sleep alone.

Nye. Lit. is notgood, meaning she is unfaithful.

516. *Asem a wontumi ǹkã no abonteǹ so no, wo nè wo yere te fie a, ǹkã ǹkyere no.* (2858)

When you have anything to say which could not be spoken on the street, do not tell it to your wife when you and she are together at home.

517. *Woko na obi nè ne yere rekõ a, mpe ntem mmua, na ewo nea waye no.* (1580)

When you go (to a man's house) and find him fighting with his wife, do not be in a hurry to interfere, for there is probably a good reason for his doing so.

518. *Nea ɔrefʋefʋɛ yere nto mmea hõ mpɛ.* (2162)
One who is looking out for a wife does not speak contemptuously of women.

519. *Aware foforo sa ɔde.* (3434)
On the honeymoon the yams always taste sweet. (Lit. (in) a new marriage, the yams mix well.)

520. *Wowo ba bone a, wofa ɔkasabɛrɛ.* (3463)
When you give birth to a bad child, you (will) grow weary of speaking.

521. *Wɔwo nipa, na wɔawo ne tamfo.* (3464)
A man is brought forth; his enemy has (already) been born.
Wɔwo, wɔawo. Note the different tenses, present, and aorist.
Tamfo = Taṅ and fo.

522. *Wɔwoo tafoni ba no, na onkura ta.* (3465)
When the archer was born, he did not hold a bow.
T'afoni. In the original this is written with a capital, which would give it the meaning of a *Tafoni* man, (there is a town of this name). The Ashantis, before the introduction of flintlock guns from Europe, fought with bows and arrows and shields. There is even now a street in Coomassie known as *ɔkyɛm* (shield) street. Bows and arrows are now only seen as 'survivals' in the toys the little children play with, and a shield is a royal emblem of the paramount king of Ashanti. (See No. 29.)

523. *'Mawo wo mabɛrɛ,' wokyi.* (3467)
'I am weary of having born you' is something no one ever wants to say.
Wokyi. See note on No. 89, *akyi,* and No. 132, *wokyi.*

524. *Obi ṅhyeɛ da ṅwoo panyiṅ peṅ.* (194)
No one ever yet fixed on a particular day to give birth to an elder (i. e. a man who was to be of importance some day).
Ṅhyeɛ ... ṅwoo. Past tenses. For the negative see note on No. 33, *mfa, nsisi.*

525. *Wowoo ' Wɔ di amim' Kwasida, na wowoo ' Wo yi adĭbow' Dĭboda.*
  (3466.)

The greedy person was born on Sunday and the extortioner on Monday.

(That is, the greedy person and the extortioner are very much akin to each other; or perhaps it may mean the greedy person may find what he has stored up by his greed taken from him by the extortioner   Both interpretations are found given.)

Wo di amim. The literal translation runs, 'You are greedy' was born, &c., &c.; 'You are an extortioner' was born, &c., &c.

Kwasida . . . Dĭboda. There are seven days in the week and twelve months in the year.

The origin of the names of these days the writer has been unable to trace.   This origin probably dates back to remote antiquity. Every Ashanti child born has, as one of its names, a name derived from the particular day on which he or she was born.

CHAPTER X

STRANGERS, EUROPEANS AND EUROPE.

526. *Ọhọho akyi mpa asẹm.* (1403)

After a stranger has gone there is always something to be said about him (good or bad).

Ọhọho. A stranger. Deriv. perhaps the reduplication of the demonstrative *ẹhọ*, there, in the distance, far away; lit. 'one from over there '.

Akyi. See note on No. 89.

Mpa. Lit. to be wanting, (*pa*).

527. *Ọhọho amă woanyă sika amă woanyă kaw.* (1404)

A stranger causes one to get money (but) he also is the cause of one getting (bad) debts.

Sika. See note on No. 591.

Kaw. See note on No. 54.

528. *Ọhọho ani akẹse-akẹse, nanso eñhũ mañ mu asẹm, na nea ọde kŭrow aniwa ñkete-ñkete na ohũ mu asẹm.* (1406)

A stranger may have big big eyes, but he does not see into what is going on among the people he is among, whereas the town's man, with little little eyes, *he* knows all the town's affairs.

Akẹse-akẹse. Note the plural form of the adjective; as also *ñkete-ñkete.*

529. *Ọhọho nsoa funu ti.* (1408)

A stranger does not carry the head of the corpse.

Nsoa funu ti. For note on the custom of ' carrying the body ', see No. 77. *Funu,* see note on No. 185.

530. *Ọhọho soẹ wo fi na wannyaw wo biribi a, ogyaw wo kaw.* (1409)

When a stranger stops at your house and does not leave you anything else, he leaves you debts.

Fi. See note on No. 262, *fie.*

Wannyaw. Lit. has not left, neg. of *gyaw.*

Kaw. See note on No. 54.

531. *Ọhọho te sẹ abofra.* (1410)
A stranger is like a child.

532. *Ọhọho te sẹ sunsüansu.* (1411)
A stranger is like unto the water running over the ground after
a rain storm (which soon dries up and leaves little trace
behind.)

533. *Ọhọho ntõ mmảra.* (1412)
A stranger does not break laws.

Ntõ mmảra. Tõ mmảra, to break a law; *hyẹ mmảra,* to make
laws; *di mmảra so,* to keep laws. This saying shows that ' igno-
rance of the law' *does* excuse, according to native custom.

534. *Ahọhoduan yẹ wo dẹ a, wo anuonyam yẹ ketewa.* (1413)
When you accept the hospitality of a stranger, your dignity is small.

Anuonyam. Anim-yẹ-nyam, lit. in the eyes makes bright.

535. *Abürokyiri nyẹ kọ-nã, na po na ehïa.* (665)
It would not be difficult to go to Europe, if it were not for the sea.

Abürokyiri. For deriv. see note on No. 268.
Kọ-nã. See note on No. 157, *nyẹ-nã.*

536. *Abürokyiri a merekọ eñhïa me, mpoãno na ehïa me.* (666)
(The thought of) Europe, where I am going, does not distress me, it is
(surf on) the beach that is the difficulty.

Mpoãno. Lit. the edge (mouth) of the sea. The West Coast of
Africa is of course notorious for the surf which thunders along its
beach, making landing often a difficult and dangerous proceeding.

537. *Nnipa ñhïaä pẹ Abürokyiri akọ, na onyã na wonnyã.* (2431)
All men would like to go to Europe, it is the opportunity they lack.

Akọ. Note the construction in the subordinate noun clause,
after the verb *pẹ;* see note on No. 2, *wopẹ.*
Onyã na wonnyã. Lit. getting (*onyã,* a verbal noun), they do
not get.

538. *Obüroni a ẹte abantenteñ mu, sẹ owu a, na ọda fam'.* (668)
The white man who lives in the castle, when he dies he lies in the
ground.

Obüroni. A European; deriv. *büru,* dirty, filthy. This seems
a decidedly unflattering etymon till one remembers that in Africa

dirt is white, clay, dust, or earth coloured, hence the white man was christened ' the dirty one '.

Qte. See note on No. 366.

Abantenteṅ. Deriv. perhaps *ǫbo,* stone, *ǫdaṅ,* house, and *tenteṅ,* long, high, i. e. a house built of stone. The old Coast castles are so called. ' The white man who lives in the castle ', is the Governor. *Abaṅ, (ǫbo 'daṅ)* is the common word used for ' the Government ', lit. ' the castle '.

539. *Obǔroni tǫṅ asekaṅ na ne ti afuw.* (669)
It is the white man who sells knives, yet his head is overgrown with hairs.

A native, when he wants his hair cut, uses a sharp knife or razor; the white man, as the purveyor of these, might, so the native thinks, have been expected to make more use himself of his unlimited supply.

Afuw. See note on No. 709.

540. *Brǫfo adaworoma na yeṅ ṅhĩnã furafura ntãmã.* (644)
It is thanks to the white man that we all wear cloths.

Brǫfo. Plu. of *Obǔroni,* q. v. No. 538.

Adaworoma. The word *nti* is probably understood after *adaworoma.*

Furafura. Reduplication of *fura.* The Ashanti dress is a cloth wound round the body up to the breasts and the end thrown over the left shoulder, (if a left-handed man, the right). When coming into the presence of, or addressing, a chief or superior, the shoulder is bared as a mark of respect, the right hand placed on the hip, the right foot advanced, the sandal slipped off and the foot set on it, but not in it.

541. *Brǫfo de nyansa na ǫforo po.* (645)
By virtue of wisdom the white men mount the sea.

542. *Qbrǫfotefo na ǫmã obǔroni yę ayę.* (646)
It is the native who knows English who directs the white man whom to praise (and whom to blame).

Qbrǫfotefo. Lit. ' one who hears English ', here, the native interpreter. This saying pretty shrewdly sums up the position, in the native mind, of the official or other European who has to rely on an interpreter in his dealings with them.

543. *Obi nim sε ɔhῐa behῐa no a, aṅkᾱ ɔkɔ Brɔfo mᾱ 'yewo no.* (264)

    If any one had knowledge previous to his birth that he was going to
        have to suffer from poverty, then he would have gone to the
        white men that he might have been born of them.

    In the native mind all Europeans must be prosperous and rich.

    Aṅkᾱ. See note on No. 733.

    'Yewo. See note on No. 641, *'yedi.*

544. *Wudi Bῠreni ade a, wokᴏ̌ aprεm ano.* (876)

    When you eat the white man's pay, you fight at the cannon's mouth.

545. *Wo nᾱ te Abibirim' na wo agya te Abῠrokyiri, na wopε ade a,*
      woṅkyε nyᾱ. (2065)

    When your mother lives in Africa and your father in Europe, and
        when there is a thing you want, you do not have to wait for it.

    Te. See note on No. 366.

    Abibirim'. Africa, lit. among the blacks, the black man's country,
deriv. *biri*, black.

    Abῠrokyiri. See note on No. 268.

CHAPTER XI

546. *Okom de aberewa a, na ose, 'Tŏtŏ biribi mă mmofra na wonni'.* (1685)
When an old woman is hungry, then she says, 'Roast something for
the children that *they* may eat'.

547. *Okom de hoho a, oda, na odidi mě a, obisabisa ṅkůrofo yerenom.*
(1686)
When a stranger is hungry he sleeps, but when he has eaten his fill
he goes about accosting the town's folks' wives.

Hoho. See note on No. 526.

Ṅkůrofo. For note on suffix *fo*, see No. 78, *kontromfĩ.*

548. *Okom de hoho a, ode fi ne kůrom'.* (1687)
When a stranger is hungry, he brought it (hunger) with him from
his own village.

549. *Okom de akoa, na okom de hene.* (1688)
Hunger is felt by a slave and hunger is felt by a king.

550. *Okom de wo a, ede wo ṅkŏ.* (1690)
When you feel hungry, it is only you who feel hungry (one does not
feel hungry for another).

551. *Okom de wo a, womfá wo nsa abieṅ nnidi.* (1691)
When you are hungry, you do not use both your hands for eating
with.

Womfá . . nnidi. For note on double negative see No. 33,
nsisi ; nnidi, neg. of *di.*

552. *Okom nè ka, na efanim ka.* (1692)
Of (the two) hunger and debt, debt is preferable.

Ka. See note on No. 54.

553. *Oyare a ebekum wo bo wo a, woṅkae duruyofo.* (3540)
When the illness that is going to kill you comes upon you, you for-
get the doctor who could have cured you.

Duruyofo. Duru-ye-fo; some one who makes medicine.

554. *Ọyare, woḱŏ no ahohora.* (3543)
Illness is driven off by insults (fear of insults) ?

Physical defects or abnormalities among the Ashantis such as
lameness, having lost a finger, arm, or foot, &c., &c., preclude a man
from ever becoming a chief. An infant born with six fingers used
to be killed. The saying perhaps means that a patient is more
willing to submit to the treatment prescribed by the doctor as he
fears the slights he would be subjected to were he to be permanently
disabled.

555. *Ọyare nsãe a, wonnye ayaresade.* (3545)
The physician's fee is not paid till the sickness is over.

Wonnyȝ. Neg. of *gye*, to receive, lit. they do not receive.
Ayaresade. *Sa ọyare*, to cure an illness, lit. something given for
curing an illness.

556. *Ọyare see akyẽafo.* (3546)
Sickness destroys even he who is most worthy.

557. *Woyare ɔnomdẹw a, na woyare ntotọ.* (3548)
If you suffer from a complaint that is always crying out for deli-
cacies, then you (also) have a complaint that is always calling
for buying.

Anomdẹw. Lit. 'a sweet mouth', cf. 'sweet tooth'.

558. *Oduruyẹfo nnŏm aduru mmã ọyarefo.* (1045)
The physician does not drink the medicine for the patient.

Aduru. See note on No. 13.
Mmã. See note on Nos. 727 and 14.

559. *Wopa opꜟayare a, ọyare pa gye wo mu.* (2579)
When you make pretence of being ill, a real illness lays hold on you.

Wopa. See note on No. 254, *oboa.*

560. *Obi nyaré ayamka ńkye akyebüro mfa nsa nehŏ yare.* (394)
No one who has belly-ache tries to cure himself with parched corn.

Nyare, ńkye, mfa, nsa. A good example of the idiom noted
under No. 33, *nsisi.*

561. *Nnua ńhãnã yẹ aduru, na wunnim a, na wuse, ẹyẹ bone.* (1021)
All plants are medicinal, but you do not know and say this one is
(useless) bad.

Aduru. See note on No. 13.

562. ' *Mà me aduru mprempreñ,*' *nyẹ aduru.* (1972)

'Give me medicine at once,' you cannot expect that to be good medicine.

The meaning is that the native herbalist must be given time to go and search for the suitable plant or root.

563. *Suro nea ọbẹñ wo.* (3124)

Fear him who is near you.

564. *Suro nea ose, obegye, na nsuro nea ose,* ' *Meremã wo* '.   (3125)

Fear him who says he will take from you, but do not fear him who says, ' I am going to give you '.

565. *Misuro kum nti na mayẹ me kọñ tiã.* (3126)

Because I fear to be killed I have made my neck short.

The common method of executing people in Ashanti was for the executioner (*ọbrafo*) to seize the victim, force his head forward and then slowly carve through the spinal column at the base of the neck. A small skewer-like knife (*ọsẹpọ*) was generally first run through the cheeks and tongue in order to prevent the swearing of the ' great ' oath or the 'king's ' oath. (See note on No. 496, *wokã*.)

566. *Yensuru dọm anim, na menne asẹm anim.* (3127)

We do not fear the front of battle, much less the front where words are weapons.

Dọm.   See note on No. 306.

Menne.   Neg. of *de.*

567. *Wusuro nnimmo a, wode wo sekañ gua ọnañkã.* (3128)

If you are afraid to incur unpopularity, you have your knife taken (borrowed) to flay a python.

Nnimmo.   Deriv. *Bọ din.*

Gua ọnañkã.   After the knife being so used it would be considered useless.

The proverb means, a weak man who panders to a cheap popularity is soon imposed on. This saying, in the eight words it contains, gives one perhaps as good an insight into the Ashanti character as might be otherwise gained in as many years, and might be taken as the motto of those whose lot it is to rule and guide the destinies of this people, or at least as giving a sound basis on which to work. No natives among whom the present writer has ever cast his lot, have sharper or keener wits, or are more ready

to take full advantage of weakness whether engendered by a real
and genuine desire to win their hearts by an exaggerated consideration and mistaken kindness, or merely in the hopes of gaining
a temporary and cheap popularity; for the recipient of any such
mistaken leniency will be the first to laugh at and take advantage
of the donor behind his back. Here, real firmness, tempered by
absolute fairness and infinite patience, commands in the long run
real and lasting respect long after the temporary abuse and
grumbling thrown at one ' who will *not* have his knife taken from
him to flay a python ', has subsided. The true Ashanti is at heart
' a strong' man and at heart respects the man who deals with him
as such.

Bacon's saying that no king was ever loved who was not feared,
is very true among this really fine and manly nation.

568. *Wusuro odeṅko biṅ a, wofwe no mprensā.* (3130)
When you fear (to remove) a slave's excrement, you look on it
many times.

Odoṅko. See note on No. 460, *nnoṅkofo.*
Mprensā. Lit. three times, see note on No. 767.

569. *Wusuro guamsem a, wo abaguade ye ketewa.* (3131)
When you fear to take part in public disputes, your share of fees
(for attending such ' palavers ') is small.

Guamsem = Gua-mu-asem.
Abaguade = Bo-agua-ade.

570. *Wusuro aḥeṅware a, wowo nnofowa ba.* (3132)
If you fear to marry a chief, you will give birth to a nameless child.

571. *Wotaṅ wo yoṅkō ba a, wo ba wu awusiṅ.* (3179)
When you hate your friend's child, your own child dies a sudden
death.

Awusiṅ. *Awu-siṅ; siṅ,* a part or fragment of a thing, hence
here, short, sudden.

572. *Wotaṅ nipa a, womā oye nneema ṅhīnā.* (3180)
When a man is disliked he is blamed for all kinds of things.

573. *Obi taṅ wo a, na oparuw wo mparuṅ̇woma.* (431)
When some one hates you, he makes malignant remarks about you.

Mparuṅ̇woma. *Paruw,* and *ṅ̇woma,* bitter, gall; *paruw* is, ' to
express an opinion on a person or matter '.

574. *Obi taṅ wo a, eṅworaṅwora wo.* (432)
When some one hates you, he scratches you.

Among the Ashantis it is considered a disgrace to have any
marks (tattoo) on the face or body, such being considered a mark
of slave origin.

When a child is born, all of whose brothers or sisters have died,
it has its face scarred over, the idea probably being that the
malignant spirit which has caused the death of this child's brothers
and sisters will consider it of no account. Such a child is even named
odoṅko, slave. See also No. 138.

575. *Obi taṅ wo a, na obo wo aboa ade.* (429)
When some one hates you, he reminds you of the promises you
made (and have not fulfilled).

Aboa ade. Bo ade, (cf. proverb No. 54), a thank-offering made
or promised to a *sumaṅ* or *obosom* (see No. 17).

576. *Wo atamfo abiesã ko agyina, na hena na abebu wo bem ?* (3169)
When three people who hate you go aside to deliberate on the
verdict to be given on you, who is going to find you innocent ?

Ko agyina. Lit. to go and stand (apart).

577. *Wo tamfo di wo asem ase kaṅ a, wokã ṅkyene a, edaṅ mako.* (3170)
When one who hates you gets the first chance to state a case he
has with you (before the elders), when you talk salt it turns
to pepper.

Wokã ṅkyene. Lit. to talk salt, i.e. speak well and truly. Salt
is greatly valued here as among all savages. A pinch of salt is to
the little African what sweets are to the European child. Much of
the salt used on the West Coast comes from the salt lagoons on the
coast.

578. *Wo tamfo sũa wo asaw a, okyeakyea ne pã.* (3173)
When one who dislikes you imitates you dancing, he bends his
waist sideways.

Sũa. To learn, also to copy.

579. *Otaṅ nni aduru.* (3174)
There is no medicine to cure hatred.

Nni. Neg. of *wo*.
Aduru. See note on No. 13.

580. *Wotaṅ bi a, na wofa ne yere.* (3175)

When you hate some one, then you seduce his wife.

Wofa ne yere. Lit. take his wife.

581. *Wotaṅ wo nĩ a, womfá no mmã dǫm.* (3176)

(Even) if you hate your mother, you do not hand her over to the enemy.

Womfá . . . mmã. See note on No. 33, *mfa, nsisi.*

Dǫm. See note on No. 306.

582. *Wo yǫṅkŏ di wo amĩm na wunni no bi a, na ęte sę wusuro no.* (3673)

When your friend helps himself to the larger share (when eating with you) and you (next time you are eating with him) do not do likewise, then it is as if you fear him.

Wunni. Neg. of *di, amĩm* being understood.

583. *Oyǫṅkŏ mu wǫ ǫyǫṅkŏ.* (3674)

Among friends there are some who are (greater) friends (than others).

584. ' *Yǫṅkŏ, yǫṅkŏ,*' *na ęmã asęm teręw.* (3675)

' Friend, friend (I will tell you a secret),' that is how news spreads.

585. *Ade tǫ wo ani so a, wo yǫṅkŏ na oyi mã wo.* (814)

When something gets in your eye, it is your friend who removes it for you.

Na. Here emphatic, see No. 1.

Mã. See note on No. 14.

586. *Wokǫ wo yǫṅkŏ ṅkyęṅ agoru na ne nã pam no a, na ǫde wo.* (1583)

When you go to your friend's house to play, and his mother drives *him* off, it is really you she means (to send home).

Agoru. Subjunctive.

Na. See note on No. 1.

587. *Wo ani bere wo yǫṅkŏ ade a, woyę bi, na wuṅwia.* (2291)

When you covet something belonging to your friend, you work for it, but you do not steal (it).

Ani. Eye reddens, see note on No. 34, *kǫṅ dǫ.*

Ade. See note on No. 85, *me dea.*

Woyę bi. Lit. you make, i. e. earn one by work.

CHAPTER XII

588. *Okwasea na ose, ' Wọde me yọṅkọ̄, na wọnnẹ̄ me'.* (1907)
It is the fool who says, 'They mean my friend, but not me '.

Okwasea. Deriv. *okwa,* in vain, foolish; and *se̱,* to say.
Na. Here an emphatic particle, translated by the definite article.
See No. 1.
Wọnnẹ̄. Neg. of *de.*

589. *Okwasea na wobu no be̱ a, wọkyere̱ no ase.* (1908)
When the fool is told a proverb, the meaning of it has to be
explained to him.

Wobu . . . be̱. See note on No. 258.
Wọkyere̱. Translated by passive.

590. *Okwasea, na ne guaṅ tew mpẹṅ abieṅ.* (1906)
It is the fool's sheep that breaks loose twice.

Guaṅ. See note on No. 17.

591. *Okwasea redi ne sika a, ose ne nsenĩa yẹ merẹw.* (1904)
When a fool is squandering his gold dust, he says his scales are out
of order.

Sika. See following note on *nsenĩa. Sika,* original meaning,
gold, gold dust, now stands for money (gold, silver or copper).
Nsenĩa. Scales. Light balances are used by the Ashantis for
weighing gold dust. The weights, commonly known as ' Ashanti
weights ', are cast from metal by the *cire perdue* process and often
show a high degree of aesthetic art. Each weight is designed to
represent some object; man, woman, animal, hunting-belt, pumpkin,
&c., &c. The process of casting is as follows: A rough model of
the object desired is worked in clay; when dry this is coated all
over with beeswax, and all the finishing touches added. The
whole model is then covered over with clay; a duct, or passage
being left, leading to the wax. The clay is now heated, when the
wax runs out leaving a space between the first and second layers.

Into this the molten metal is run. When the clay is broken away, the metal model is found. (For a full description, vide the Author's *Hausa Folk-Lore*.)

The names and equivalent values in English money of some of the Ashanti weights (for gold dust) are as follows:

Name of Weight.	Value in Gold Dust, (approx.) in English Money.			Remarks,
	£	s.	d.	
Powa. . . .			½	Smallest weight used.
Pésewa . . .			1	Lit. a small seed, perhaps originally used as weight.
Damma . . .			2	Also a small seed.
Takuță . . .			3	Lit. half a *taku* q.v.
Taku . . .			6	
Dommață (lit. half a *domma*).		4	0	There is a tree called the *domma* tree. Probably its seed was used originally.
Agyiràtibéfă .		4	6	One *ackie*.
Bodommô . .		10	0	*Bodôm*, a kind of bead.
Sowa		6	9	*Sowa*, also name of plant.
Agyiratibe . .		9	0	2 *ackies*.
Suru		18	0	4 *ackies*.
Asia	1	7	0	6 *ackies*, on which standard probably based as *asiá*=6.
Osiā	2	0	6	*Asuanu* = 2 *asiā* = £4 1s. ; *asuasa* = 3 *asiā*, and so on.
Bensā . . .	7	4	0	
Pereguan . .	8	2	0	36 *ackies*.
Tasuanu. . .	12	13	0	There is a tree with long seed-pods called *tā*, plu. *nta* (not to be confused with *tawa*, the tobacco plant); so in *tasuanu* we would seem to have, 1 *ata* + 2 *asiā*. Two *nta* = *ntanu*, as seen below = £16 4s. One *atā* therefore = £8 2s. + 2 *asiā* (= £4 1s.) ; total, £12 3s.
Ntanu . . .	16	4	0	See note above on *tasuanu*.
Ntasa. . . .	24	6	0	*Ntasa*=£24 6s. and so on.

It will be noted that many of the names of 'Ashanti weights' are also the names of plants or trees, and hence of their seeds, which would seem to point to these having originally been used as weights, and it would be most interesting to take, say two seeds from the *tawa* tree and compare the metal weight of that name, when the value of gold dust in ancient times might be roughly gauged. There seem to be three bases of currency, the *mpésewa*, the *taku*, and the *ackie*, corresponding (approximately) to our 1*d.*, 6*d.*, 4*s.* 6*d.* The designs used for weights would seem often to be symbolical (see proverbs Nos. 136 and 174).

Merew. Soft, yielding, here of scales, easily weighed down, hence out of order.

592. *Okwasea ani te a, nã agoru agu.* (1910)

By the time the fool has learned to play the game, the players have dispersed.

Te. Te, tew, lit. to be clear.

593. *Okwasea nnim biribi a, onim ne fufū tow.* (1911)

If the fool knows nothing else, he (at least) knows all about his plantain dumpling.

Fufū. See note on No. 14.

594. *Nea wuresisi kwasea no, na onyansafo te ho fiee wo.* (2238)

Where you are taking advantage of a fool, there a wise man is, looking on at you.

Onyansafo. For note on suffix *fo*, see No. 78, *kontromfi*.

595. *Okwasea na wotew ne ntorowa ton no.* (1909)

It is the fool whose own tomatoes (?) are plucked and sold to him.

Na. Translated by the definite article.
Wotew. Translated by passive.

596. *Nyansa nye sika na woakyekyere asie.* (2554)

Wisdom is not gold dust that it should be tied up and put away.

Woakyekyere asie. Lit. that they have . . . in order to.

597. *Onyansafo de pesewa gye okwasea nsam' pereguan.* (2555)

The clever man takes one penny worth of gold dust and receives from the hand of the fool gold dust of the value of £8.

Pesewa . . . pereguan. See note on 'Ashanti weights' under No. 591.

598. *Anyansafo banu goru a, ntŏtŏ ba.* (2558)

When two men of equal wisdom play together, discord arises.

Bānu. See note on No. 781.

599. *Anyansafo banu kye mensã, obākŏ dan si ho, na obākŏ redan butuw ho.* (2559)

When two wise men are dividing up a yam between them, one turns a piece over and puts it down (for the other), but the other again turns it over and exposes the other side.

Mensã. A variety of yam which is very liable to attack from an insect pest which bores into the yam and spoils it; the turning of the yam mentioned in the saying is to cover up the diseased portion.

600. *Obi nkyekyere nyansa-kotoku mfa nkoto adakam' mmegyina adiho, nse no se, 'Kyere me asem'.* (223).

No one ties up a wisdom-bag, and takes it and puts it away in a box and comes and stands in the courtyard and says, 'Explain the matter to me'.

Nyansa-kotoku. In the original this is written with a hyphen, making the word a compound noun, lit. 'a wisdom-bag'; without the hyphen, and with *mu* added, it would mean,—'wisdom in a bag'.

Mfa, nkoto, mmegyina, nse. Note that all these verbs are in the negative following the first verb *nkyekyere*. See note on No. 33, *nsisi*.

601. *Nokware mu nni abra.* (2475)

In truth there is no deceit.

Nokware. Deriv. *ano* = mouth, and *kware* (?).

Nni. Neg. of *wo*.

602. *Nokware nye ahã (nnŏsŏ) na woatiba mu nkontompo.* (2477)

There is not so much of truth that it should be cut off by falsehood.

Woatiba. Lit. that they should have cut it. *Tiba nkontompo*, lit. to 'cut a lie' (from truth?), i. e. to tell a lie.

603. *Wutiba nkontompo a, wusuro Kumase.* (3403)

When you tell a lie, you fear Coomassie.

The king of the Ashantis used to be resident in Coomassie, hence important cases would be taken to be tried there.

Kumase. Deriv. *Kum*, to kill, and *ase*, under. Lit. ' under the kill tree ', from a tree in the centre of the town under which human sacrifices and executions took place.

604. *Otŏrofo de mfe apem tu kwan a, ɔnokwafo de dakoro tiw no to no.* (3338)

Whereas the liar takes a thousand years to go a journey, the one who speaks the truth follows and overtakes him in a day.

Otŏrofo. A liar ; the root would seem to be *tŏro, tŏrotŏro,* slippery, hence metaphorically ' smooth-tongued ', ' oily-tongued '.

605. ' *Otŏrofo gye agua* '; *ose,* ' *Manyă ɔbo* '. (3339)
' Smooth-tongued one take a seat ' ; he says, ' I have got a stone '.

Otŏrofo. See note above, 604.
Agua. As *akoṅṅua,* stool.

606. *Otŏrofo na ose,* ' *Me dansefo wɔ Abŭrokyiri* '. (3341)
The smooth-tongued one says, ' My witness is in Europe '.

Abŭrokyiri, See note on No. 268.

607. *Wode ṅkontompo kă asɛm a, wobĕrɛ.* (754)
When you speak falsehoods in stating a case, you become weary.

The antithesis of this saying is often added, i. e. *wode nokware kă asɛm a, awu* ; when you speak the truth the matter dies, i. e. is quickly settled.

608. *Wode ṅkontompo pɛ ade mfe apem a, onokwafo de nokware gye wo nsam' dakoro.* (755)
When you seek for a thing for one thousand years by the aid of falsehood, the truthful man, using truth, takes it from your grasp in a day.

609. *Atokoro sɛe nokwapem.*
One falsehood spoils a thousand truths.

Atokoro = Atoro-koro.
Nokwapem = Nokware-apem.

610. *Ehĭa bateni hĭa păni.* (1330)
When the hirer is in want, the hireling is in want.

Ehĭa. An impersonal verb, ' it lacks, there is need of to '. *Ehĭa me sika,* there is need of money to me, I lack money.

Batani. Deriv. *bata*, trade, and *ni*, the personal suffix. *Di bata* = to trade.

Pāni. Deriv. *pa* to hire, also to give one's services for payment, *ni* the personal suffix.

611. *Eh̃ia onipa a, ǫda wuram'.* (1331)

When a man is in want, he sleeps in the forest.

That is, he is compelled to go far afield, hunting or fishing, in order to find food.

Wuram'. See note on No. 92.

612. *Eh̃ia wo a, na worewe sumǎnǎ-diwe.* (1333)

When in want, then you eat the palm nuts off the refuse heap.

Worewe. Present continued action expressed by *re*, lit. you are eating.

613. *Eh̃ia wo a, ṅwu.* (1334)

When you are in want, do not die.

That is, do not give up hope.

614. '*Ah̃ia me na fwe mǎ me,*' *nti na obi yęę akoa.* (1335)

'I am in want, so look after me,' it is thus some became slaves, (lit. one became a slave).

Yęę. Past tense, formed by lengthening of final vowel.

Akoa. See note on No. 443.

615. *Oh̃ia, wodi no fie, na wonni no gua so.* (1337)

When you are a poor man, you remain at home and do not mix in public affairs.

Wodi no . . . na wonni, &c. Lit. poverty, you eat it at home, but do not eat, &c. *Wonni,* neg. of *di*.

616. *Oh̃ia h̃ia wo a, wowe aberekyi wĕre.* (1339)

When you are in want, you chew a goat's skin.

Aberekyi wĕre. In times of scarcity the skins of goats and sheep are cut up and boiled.

617. *Oh̃ia h̃ia wo na wutĩ abeté a, ędaṅ' fáṅ.* (1340)

When you are in want and pick out the maize from the pot, that even turns into a leaf.

Abeté. Roasted maize, which only the poor eat. *Tĩ,* lit. to pinch between the finger and thumb, hence pick out with the fingers.

Fán. A leaf, hence vegetable, like spinach. Many leaves of various plants are boiled and eaten in time of great scarcity. The natives derive Fantee from this word.

618. *Ohĩa hĩa wo na wotǫ nsu-onẁinim' a, ęhye wo.* (1341)
When you are suffering from poverty and happen to fall into cold water, it scalds you.

619. *Ohĩa ṅhye da.* (1342)
Poverty does not fix on a day (to come upon one), (i. e. its arrival will be unexpected).

620. *Ohĩa na ęmã ǫdehye yę akoa.* (1344)
It is poverty that causes the free man to become a slave.
Na. Here emphatic. See No. 1, *na.*
Ǫdehye. See note on No. 430.
Akoa. See note on No. 443.

621. *Ohia na ęmã ǫtẁea kǫ anǫpa-bę sǫǫ.* (1345)
It is poverty that causes the dog (i.e. the dog's master) to have to turn out for the early morning palm-nut cutting.
Ǫtẁea. A bitch, also used generally for both male and female, =*okramaṅ*=dog.
Anǫpa-bę. Anǫpa-abe, lit. morning palm nut. There are two recognized times for the cutting of palm nuts, very early in the morning, called *anǫpa-bę* and again late in the afternoon, called *anume-be (anumere-abe).* Hence these two expressions are often used to mean generally the hours of about 5-6 A.M. and 4-5 P.M.

622. *Ohĩa ne gyimi.* (1346)
Poverty is stupidity.
That is, a poor man is reckoned a fool. Cf. No. 627 below.

623. *Ohĩa nni Abŭrokyiri a, aṅkã Obŭroni ammęhata ne ntama Abibirim'.* (1347)
If there had been no poverty in Europe, then the white man would not have come and spread his cloths in Africa.
Abŭrokyiri. See note on No. 268.
Aṅkã. See note on No. 733.
Obŭroni. See note on No. 538.
Ammęhata. Note the auxiliary, *bèra.*
Abibirim'. See note on No. 545.

624. *Ohĩa te sẹ 'wo, ẹnnọ fãkõ.* (1348)

Poverty is like honey, it is not peculiar to one place alone.

> *'Wo = Ewo.*
>
> *Ẹnnọ.* Neg. of *dọ.*

625. *Ohĩa nti na aseredowa sisi abũrobia so.* (1351)

It is want that causes the little ' *aseredowa* ' bird to alight on the ' *bũrobia* ' plant.

> *Nti = Enɔ ti.*

626. *Ohĩa tumi nyẹ tumi-pa.* (1353)

The display of power exhibited by poverty is not real power.

A poor man having nothing to lose and becoming desperate, sometimes commits acts which some one having anything at stake would hesitate to do.

627. *Ohĩa yẹ adãmmọ.* (1354)

Poverty is madness.

> Cf. No. 622 above.
>
> *Adãmmọ.* Derive. *bọ dam.*

628. *Ohĩa-da na wohũ nipa.* (1357)

On the day of poverty it is then you perceive who is a man. (a friend)

> *Na.* Emphatic particle, see No. 1.

629. *Ohĩani abãwa koro ṅkyẹ bẹrẹ, nso waṅkọ a, yennidi.* (1359)

The poor man's only slave girl soon gets wear, but if she does not go (and work) we do not eat.

> *Ṅkyẹ bẹrẹ.* Lit. does not delay tiring. ' Soon ' is thus expressed in the Ashanti idiom.

630. *Ohĩani bo mfuw.* (1360)

The poor man does not get in a rage.

> *Bo mfuw.* See note on *kọn dọ,* No. 34.

631. *Ohĩani bu bẹ a, ẹṅhye.* (1361)

When a poor man makes a proverb, it does not spread abroad.

> *Bu bẹ.* See note on No. 258.

632. *Ohĩani di pọwade a, ẹyẹ sẹ odi diwane.* (1362)

When a poor man eats something of the value of a halfpenny, it is as if he partakes of a sheep.

Pǫwade. Pǫwa ade, see note on No. 591, *nsenīa.*
Dibane = Ọguaṅ.

633. *Ohïani fura kyěmě a, eyɛ sɛ efura dunsiṅ.* (1365)
When a poor man wears a silken robe, it is as if it decked a tree stump.

Dunsiṅ = Dua siṅ. For derivation according to natives, see No. 57, *odum.*

634. *Ohïani hyɛ sika a, wobu no aḃowa.* (1366)
When a poor man is decked out in gold, people say it is brass.

Sika. See note on No. 591, *sika,* here 'golden ornaments'.

635. *Ohïani nɛ ǫdefo ṅṅoru.* (1367)
The poor man and the rich man do not play together.

Ọdefo. Plu. *adefo,* lit. the possessor of things. For note on suffix *fo,* see No. 78, *kontromfï.*
Ṅṅoru. Neg. of *goro.*

636. *Ohïani nni biribi a, ǫwǫ tɛkrɛma a ǫde tutu ka.* (1368)
If the poor man has nothing else, he at least has a tongue with which to defer the payment of his debts.

Ọde. This verb (*de*) is used to express the English 'by means of', with.
Tutu ka. See note on No. 54.

637. *Ohïani nni yoṅkŏ.* (1369)
The poor man has no friend.

638. *Ohïani nom tawa-pa a, eyɛ sɛ tāsɛṅfï.* (1370)
When a poor man smokes good tobacco, it is as if he were smoking the remains of some old tobacco in a pipe.

Tāsɛṅfï = Tawa-oseṅ-fï.

639. *Ohïani pam akorogow a, na eyɛ no sɛ odidi sānyăm'.* (1372)
When the poor man mends his broken wooden bowl, it serves him just as well as if he ate off a pewter dish.

Akorogow. Gow, old, useless, cf. *ntamagow,* an old cloth. Suffix *fï* expresses the same idea.

640. *Ohïani mpaw dabere.* (1373)
A poor man does not chose his sleeping-place.

Dabere. Suffix *bere* = place where.

641. *Ohiani asem', 'yedi no ntiantiam'.* (1374)

The complaint a poor man brings is investigated briefly.

'Yedi. *'Ye* is probably the Akem dialect, 3rd person plural, Ashanti *wo, wo.* Here translated by passive.

642. *Ohiani asommen ne batafose.* (1375)

The poor man's elephant tusk is the wart-hog's tooth.

Asommen. See note on No. 94, *se.*

643. *Ohiani yane gorow a, 'yese oyane nnbahama.* (1378)

When the poor man wears a necklace of the soft silky ' *gorow* ' leaves, it is said he is wearing a sheep's halter.

Gorow. A plant with particularly soft silk-like leaves, also called *afase.* *Gorowo* also means weak, perhaps from same root.

'Yese. See note above, No. 641, *'yedi.*

Nnbahama = Oguan hama.

644. *Obi mfa ohia ntow adotebe.* (146)

Not even poverty will make a man fell a palm-tree that stands in a swamp.

Adotebe = Dote-abe. *Abe,* the palm wine (*palma vinifera*) tree. On felling, that the wine may be drawn off, the tree is not cut down as a rule, but the roots dug under. When so felled the wine lasts much longer without drying up than when the tree is cut down in the ordinary manner.

645. *Obi mfa ohia nsi apempem.* (147)

No one can extort from another by using his poverty as a threat.

Mfa . . . nsi. Note the two negatives, see note on No. 33, *nsisi.*

646. *Obi bo wo dua se, 'Ma onwu !' a, enye yaw se ose, 'Ma ohia nka no !'* (116)

If any one invokes a fetish against you, saying, ' Let this man die ', he is not harming you as much as he would were he to say ' Let poverty lay hold on him '.

Bo dua. To knock a piece of wood into the ground and at the same time to invoke a curse and call on the fetish to harm the person against whom evil is intended.

Onwu, nka. Imperative.

647. *Wunni ntrama a, na wuse, nsa nye de.* (919)

When you have not a cowry shell, then you say that wine is not sweet.

Wunni. Neg. of *wo.*

Ntrama. Cowries, still to be seen in the markets of the interior. At Ejura in 1913, 160 cowries went to 1*d.* ; 40 cowries=1 *oban* ; 50 *mman* (plu. of *oban*)=1 *otiri*, (head). The small ' subsidiary ' coinage introduced in 1912 to the Gold Coast Colony, and previously to that into Nigeria (tenths and halfpennies) will soon banish the cowry altogether from these regions.

648. *Osikani ne panyin.* (2960)

The rich man is the elder (i.e. man of importance whose words carry weight in council).

Ne. See note on No. 1.

Panyin. See note on No. 1.

649. *Wonni sika a, anka wofre no nhwea kwa.* (917)

If one could not make use of gold dust, then it would merely be called sand.

Wonni. Neg. of *di.*

Sika. See note on No. 591.

Anka. See note on No. 733.

650. *Sika nni adagyew a, womfa mpe bosea.* (2935)

When one has just sufficient money for one's own needs, one does not let it out at interest.

Nni. Neg. of *wo.*

Adagyew. Lit. when money has no ' opportunity '.

Womfa mpe. For double negative see note on No. 33, *nsisi.* *Pe bosea*, also *bo bosea*, to lend, or to borrow.

651. *Sika nni, ' Ka wo nsa pe '.* (2936)

With gold dust (money) it is not (a case of), ' Put forth your hand and find '.

652. *Sika nko adidi nsan mma kwa.* (2938)

Money does not go out to earn its livelihood and come back empty-handed (i.e. it earns interest).

Nko, nsan, mma. For the negatives see note on No. 33, *nsisi.*

653. *Sika kyen nkrante nnam.* (2939)

Money is sharper than a sword.

Kyen. Note the comparative degree formed by using the verb *sen* or *kyen*, to surpass.

654. *Sika peregwan da kŭrom' a, ęwǫ amansań.* (2942)

If there is a *pereguan* worth of gold dust in a town, it is for the whole people.

Peregucń. See note on No. 591, *nsenia.*

'This saying points to a system of communism having existed even with regard to what would now be considered as more or less private property. There are many survivals of a communistic state still in evidence ; it is seen in their system of land tenure, and in that the private debts of one person are recoverable from the entire family of that person. This last is a relic of collective responsibility of the whole clan for the acts of a single member.

655. *Wo sika resă a, na wo ani tew.* (2944)

When your gold dust is becoming finished, then you become prudent.

Ani tew. Lit. your eyes become open, wide.

656. *Sika seńe, biribi ańseń bio.* (2945)

Wealth (is) beyond everything, nothing is beyond that again.

657. *Sika te sę akoa, woańhŭ no so fŏę a, oguań.* (2946)

Gold dust (money) is like unto a slave, if you do not look after it well, it runs away.

Woańhŭ. Lit. have not. Aorist tense.

658. *Sika yę fę na ǫpegyafo yę nă.* (2950)

Wealth is a fine thing, but to find an heir is not easy.

Ǫpegyafo. Lit. *pę-(nea)-gyaw-fo,* some one to leave to.

Nă. See note on No. 157, *nyę-nă.*

659. *Wo sika rę wo yaw a, ǫkǫm de wo.* (2951)

If (spending) your money gives you pain, you will go hungry.

660. *Wo sika rę wo yaw na wokŏ a, wunyi dǫm.* (2952).

If (spending) your money gives you pain and you go to war, you will not win.

Dǫm. See note on No. 306.

661. *Sika-diǔma biara nyę aniwu.* (2953)

It is no shame at all to work for money.

Aniwu. See note on No. 753.

L 2

662. *Osikafo nom nsā bow a, wofrę no yare.* (2954)
When a sick man is drunk, he is merely said to be unwell.

663. *Osikafo wǫ hǫ yi, ofura ntamagow.* (2955)
When a man is wealthy, he may wear an old cloth.
Ntamagow. See note on No. 639.

664. *Osikani de, wǫṅwǎnsī no bone ara da.* (2957)
As for a rich man, *he* is never sneezed at unluckily.
Wǫṅwǎnsī. Ṅwǎnsī, a good example of onomatopoeia. In
Ashanti when a subject sneezes before a chief his nose is immediately rubbed with white clay, and during that particular day the
sneezer will be held accountable for any bad *or good* luck the chief
may have, and punished or rewarded accordingly.

665. *Sika bęṅ wo a, ęhoa.* (2931)
When gold is close to you, it is pale (no longer glitters).

666. *Wunyā ade a, wǫtaṅ wo ; wunnyā ade a, wofrę wo bone.* (2516)
When you are rich, you are hated ; when you are poor, you are
called a bad man.

CHAPTER XIII

FIRE, WATER, RIVERS, RAIN.

667. *Ogya a ẹbẹdẹw nè ne ẇisie ṅkŏ.* (1245)

The fire which is going to blaze up has a different smoke (from other fires).

Ogya. Fire, also firewood, fuel.

Nè ne. The first *nè* is the conjunction, 'and, with' (from the verb *de*), the second *ne* is of course the possessive pronoun. Lit. 'the fire and its smoke', &c.

Wisie = Owisiw.

668. *Ogya a eyẹ nnam ṅkyẹ́ afuw so.* (1246)

The firewood which is good for fuel does not remain long in the plantation. (It is soon carried home for fuel.)

Nnam. Has various meanings; 'sharp, brave', and here 'quick', i.e. to catch alight.

Afuw. See No. 709.

669. *Ogya dedæw ano nyẹ sọ-nä.* (1247)

Wood already touched by fire (and rendered dry) is not hard to set alight.

Dedaw. Da, dada, reduplication.

Sọ- nä. See note on No. 157, *nyẹ-nä.*

670. *Ogya hye wo a, woperẹw to wo ba so ansä-na woayi afi no so.* (1249)

When a spark from the fire burns you, you shake it off on to your child before you (finally) take it off him (again).

Woperẹw. To jerk off, to shake off; not to be confused with *pirẹw,* to roll. See No. 672, below.

Afi. Translate by 'from, off'; really a verb, *fi,* to come out. Cf. use of the verbs, *wọ* and *mä,* as prepositions.

671. *Ogya hye wo a, enyẹ́ wo dẹ, na woretafo.* (1250)

When fire burns you, you do not find it sweet, but you keep licking the place nevertheless.

Woretafo. Re, present continued action ; *tafo = taforo.*

672. *Ogya pirẹw a, ẹhye nea ọda ano.* (1251)
When a firebrand rolls out from the fire, it burns the one sleeping nearest to it.

Pirẹw. In the 'Tshi Proverbs' this is written *pẹrew* (see note above, No. 670, on *woperẹw*). The present writer has always heard the saying as here given.

673. *Ogya nè atudŭru nna.* (1252).
Fire and gunpowder do not sleep together.

Atuduru = *Otuo-aduru,* lit. gun medicine.

674. *Yenim sẹ wọde gya bẹkọ akogu sumăna so, nanso wọdc fi wuram' ba a, wode ba ofie ansă.* (2350)
We know that ash is taken and thrown out on the ash heap, yet when it was brought from the bush (as firewood), it was first of all taken to the house.

Fi wuram'. *Fi,* translated by 'from' (but in Ashanti a verb, see above, No. 670, *afi*). *Wuram',* see note on No. 92.

675. *Asu a yenni mu adŭene no, yẹmfá mu pọw.* (3067)
From the river whose fish we do not eat, we do not (even) take a nugget. (Cf. No. 676, below.)

Asu. See note on No. 26, *nsu.*
Yenni. Neg. of *di.*
Pọw. A lump, here of alluvial gold. This proverb shows how strong a taboo can be considered. See note on *Tannọ,* No. 55.

676. *Asu a woṅṅuare no, wọnnom.* (3068)
A river (lit. water) you would not bathe in is not drunk from. Cf. No. 675, above.

Woṅṅuare. Neg. of *guare;* see No. 353, *hohoro.*

677. *Asu et ẹtă họ diṅṅ na ẹfa onipa.* (3069)
It is the water which stands there calm and silent that drowns (lit. takes) a man.

Na ẹfa. *Na,* emphatic particle; *ẹfa,* used euphemistically, lest perhaps the spirit in the river might be offended and be avenged on the speaker.

678. *Asu a ẹte sẹ bosõrõpo na ṅkyene aṅbam᾽ yi, na ẹwọ ase.* (3070)

A body of water like the great sea, which is so very salt, there
  must be a reason for that.

  Ase. Lit. bottom, foundation.

679. *Asu biara bọ po mu a, na ne diṅ ayera.* (3071)

Whatever the river that falls into the sea, its name is lost.

  Ayera. Aorist tense.

680. *Asu bọ biriḃi diṅ na ẹṅvow.* (3072)

Water adjures the name of some thing (utters a spell) and then
  dries up. (Water does not dry up without a cause.)

  Bọ biribi ḋiṅ. Lit. to speak the name of some thing, i. e. (1) gives
  or has some reason for a certain action, or (2) adjures some one or
  some thing to give it power to perform a certain action.

681. *Asu fa wo a, ẹhõ ṅhama ṅhĩnā taṅ wo.* (3073)

When a river is taking you (i. e. drowning you), then all the creepers
  on its bank (you clutch at) hate you (and will not let you get
  a hold).

  Fa. See note above on No. 677, *na ẹfa.*

  Ehõ ṅhama. Lit. the ‘about it creepers’, i. e. on the banks.
  Note how nature is given human attributes, cf. proverb No. 680.

682. *Asu nyiri ṅwam.* (3079)

A river does not flood out the toucans (which roost on the tops
  of high trees).

683. *Nsu a wọdẹ redum gya, wọmpẹ no kroṅkroṅ.* (3080)

Clear water is not sought for to quench a fire.

  Nsu. See note on No. 26.

  Wọmpẹ. Translated by passive.

684. *Nsu fa wo a, wonom bi.* (3086)

When water is drowning you, you nevertheless drink some of it.

  Fa. See note on No. 677, *na ẹfa.*

685. *Nsu-hunu yẹ ọmẽ a, aṅkā akā mfa darewa.* (3087)

If plain water was satisfying enough, then the fish would not take
  the hook.

  Aṅkā. Vide note on No. 733.

Akā. A kind of fish.

Darewa. Dade, iron, and the diminutive suffix *wa,* lit. 'the little piece of iron'.

686. *Nsu kyɛ toam' a, ɛboṅ.* (3089)

When water remains long in a calabash, it stinks.

Ɛboṅ. Boṅ, of a disagreeable smell only; *huăm,* of a pleasant smell.

687. *Nsu potopoto! tiatia mu na kosaw nsu-pá!* (3090)

Muddy water! pass through it and go and draw the pure.

Potopoto. An onomatopoetic word, of walking and sinking in mud.

688. *Nsu asã asum' nti na osánsá refa apatā.* (3091)

Because the water has dried up in the river the fish eagle is catching the fish.

Nsu, . . . asum'. Note the difference in meaning. See note on No. 26, *nsu.*

689. *Nsu ansŏ aguare a, ɛsŏ nom.* (3093)

Water which is not sufficient for bathing in, is sufficient for drinking.

Aguare. See note on No. 353, *hohoro.*

690. *Nsu-nsu ṅhĩnā dŏsŏ, na bŏsonopo ne panyiṅ.* (3094)

Of all the many waters the sea is the old man among them.

Ne. See note on No. 1.

Panyiṅ. See note on No 1.

691. *Nsu yiri a, na apatā ayɛ ahantaṅ.* (3097)

When the water is in flood, the fish is proud.

692. *Osu a ɛto Krobow no, ebi ato Siade.* (3051)

Of the rain that falls on the Crobo hills some has fallen on the Shai mountains.

Osu. See note on No. 26, *nsu.*

Krobow. The 'Crobo' hills to the west of the Volta; 'Siade', part of the same range (?).

693. *Osu boro bo a, etim' nea etim'.* (3053)

Though rain beats on a stone it (the stone) stands firm where it stands.

Etim = Ti mu.

694. *Osu ибе fво a, wuse, ' Wafвe me ', na wunse se, ' Opetëë me so '.*
(3055)

When the rain beats you, you say, 'It has beaten me', but you
do not say, 'It drizzled on me'.

Se. See note on No. 66.

. Perhaps the idea in this proverb is that seen in Nos. 681 and
677, where a euphemistic expression is used so as to avoid giving
offence. In the case of the rain, it not having any particular ' mana '
' we can afford to speak our mind ', they would say.

Opetëë. Past tense ; *wafibe* is Aorist.

695. *Oso to a, wokum komfo; osu anto a, wokum komfo.* (3056)

When the rain falls, the fetish priest is killed; (and) when the rain
does not fall, the fetish priest is killed.

Komfo. See note on No. 22, *okomfo.*

696. *Oso beto a, mframa na edi kań.* (3057)

When the rain is going to fall, it is the wind that comes first.

Na. Emphatic particle, trans. by 'it is the . . .' See No. 1.

697. *Oso ato aboro asense, ' Monnserew me, me hŏ bewo'.* (3059)

The rain has fallen (and) beat on the ' *asense* ' fowl (and she says),
' You need not laugh at me, I shall get dry '.

A to aboro. Note the two finite verbs unconnected by any prepositions.

Asense. A kind of native hen, the feathers on which look very
scanty and as if constantly ruffled.

698. *Osu to fibe wo na oibia fi hye wo a, na wuhü abrabo yaw.* (3060)

When the rain falls and beats upon you and the sun comes forth
and scorches you, then you behold (as it were) the troubles of
life.

Oibia. See note on No. 1, *asase.*

Abrabo. Deriv. *bo* and *bĕra* (?) a state of being or coming (into
the world), hence events that befall one in life.

699. *Osu to gu po mu.* (3061)

The rain falls, pouring into the sea.

(The saying is often continued by an explanatory sentence
which runs, *yenim se epo sŏ, nanso nsu to gum.* We know the sea
is large, but the rain falls into it notwithstanding.)

700. *Oso to na egu biribi so ansã-na ekã wo a, enyé yaw.*   (3063)
When the rain falls and drops on something else first before touching you, it does not hurt.

701. *Osu to anadwo na woanhũ a, adekyẽẽ, woanhũ fam ana ?*   (3065)
When the rain falls at night and you have not known of it, at dawn
have you not seen the ground ?

Adekyẽẽ.   See note on 203, *ade ansã.*

CHAPTER XIV

General Precepts and Maxims.

702. *Obi abẹsẹbйrow mmá (nyẹ yiye) a, womfá woṅ anaṅ ase akumsúmáṅ ṅkofa mù (asе).* (115)

When some one's October maize crop does not promise well, no one is fool enough to go and walk through that plantation with a bad charm fastened to his legs (and thus get the blame of causing the crop to fail, which was obviously going to happen in any case).

Abẹsẹbйrow. Derivation, *bẹsẹ* (to pluck ?) and *abйrów*, Indian corn. Hence, crops planted from October onwards, which are naturally very uncertain, as the rains proper are then over, such crops being dependent on chance showers. Such a second crop is also sometimes known as *adom-mйrow*, lit. 'corn got by grace'.

Womfá . . . ṅkofa. For the double negative see note on *mfa, nsisi,* No. 33.

Akumsúmáṅ. Lit. a charm to kill, i.e. counteract another charm, good or bad according as the charm which it is to neutralize is bad or good. In this case the owner of the farm would have a good charm to promote the growth of his crops, hence the counteracting charm would be a bad one. For note on *súmáṅ* see No. 17, *obosom.*

Ṅkofa mù. Lit. to go and take (the way) in, i.e. walk there.

703. *Obi bọ wo aẁerẹkyekyé súmáṅ ná ọde ṅkọmmọ́ dйé wò anó à, na wannyй́ papa bi anyẹ wo.* (117)

When some one fastens a charm of comfort (on your wrist) but finishes up by securing it with a knot of mourning, he has not really benefited you at all.

Aẁerẹkyekyé. Lit. 'to bind up, tighten the skin', i.e. to solace, to comfort. See note on *koṅ dọ,* No. 34.

Súmáṅ. See note on *obosom,* No. 17.

Ṅkọmmṍ. From *bọ.*

Wannyй́ . . . anyẹ. For double negative, see note on *mfa, nsisi,* No. 33.

704. *Obi abusudé yę obi akãradé.* (118)

What is bad luck for one man is good luck for another.

Abusudé. Deriv. *mmusu ade.*

Akãradé. Lit. something for the soul. Deriv. *ǫkra ade.* See note on *ṅkrabea*, No. 9.

705. *Obi busuyefoǫ ne bi nipa-pa.* (119)

A knave for one is a good man for another.

Busuyefoǫ. Deriv. *mmusu-yę-fo.* For suffix *fo*, see note on No. 78, *kontromfî.*

706. *Obi ade-dedaw kǫ obi nsam' a, eyę no foforo.* (121)

When an old thing belonging to one person gets into the hands of another, it becomes a new thing for him.

Ade-dedaw. Dedaw, reduplication of *da*, = *dada.*

707. *Obi afom akum a, wo nso mfom ṅñua!* (126)

When some one has killed something by mistake, as for you, do not flay it by mistake!

Afom akum. Note these two finite verbs, both Aorist tense, used without the conjunction (and), which is necessary in English. The Ashanti idiom runs, '... some one has made a mistake, some one has killed'. The same idiom is seen in *nfom ṅñua*. It is this form of speech, short principal clauses unconnected by any preposition, which accounts for the confusing double negative, see note on *nsisi*, No. 33.

Ṅñua. Neg. of *gua.*

708. *Obi frę wo Sęwósé a, mpę ntęm nserew; ebia wo agya yę ǫbonnãtófǫ.* (127)

If some one remarks you are like your father, do not be in too great a hurry to laugh (i.e. be flattered); for all you know, your father may have been a ravisher of women.

Sęwósé. Lit. *sę-wo-ǫse* = like-your-father.

Mpę, nserew. Note the negatives, see note on *nsisi*, No. 33.

Ǫbonnãtófǫ. For the suffix *fo*, see *kontromfî*, No. 78.

709. *Obi afuw sõ a, wǫmfá mpampã na ęfow.* (128)

Though some one may have a very large plantation, that is not to say people are to bring their bowls and loot.

Afuw. A farm; deriv. *fuw*, to shoot up from the ground.

Mpcmpā. Sing., *apampā*, a flat, wooden dish used for carrying plantains, yams, &c., from the farms to the house.

Efow. Note the use of the 3rd pers. neuter pronoun for the 3rd pers. plural.

710. *Obi gyina obi 'mati, na ohū-guam'.* (130)
When one stands on another's shoulders, then he sees over the market.

    'Mati. Deriv. *ba, basa,* and *ti.*

711. *Obi kuan nkye na esi bi de mu.* (134)
One man's road does not go far without meeting another's.

    Nkye. Lit. is not long.

712. *Obi kye wo ade a, (na) woda n'ase.* (135)
When some one gives you a present, (then) you thank him.

    Ade. See note on No. 85, *me dea.*

    Woda n'ase. Lit. you lie at 'his down', i.e. feet. This is the Ashanti idiom for ' to give thanks ', and well expresses the real root idea of 'thank you', which is now hardly recognized perhaps by us; i.e. I am *under* an obligation to you, I lie down before you; said and understood in its literal sense in the days when the world was young and politeness for politeness' sake unknown.

713. *Obi mfa obi ade nhoahoa nehŏ.* (137)
No one boasts of what belongs to another.

    Obi. Some one, and with neg., lit. some one not, i.e. nobody.

    Mfa . . . nhoahoa. Note the two negatives, see *mfa, nsisi,* No. 33. *Hoahoa* is to praise, and with the reflexive pronoun (*nehŏ*) to praise oneself, i.e. boast about.

714. *Obi mfa obomū nhow gya so.* (138)
No one takes a whole animal and dries it over a fire.

    Mfa, nhow. Note the double negative. See *nsisi,* No. 33.

    Obomū. *Aboa-mū* (*mū* = whole), i.e. an animal that has just been killed but not yet flayed and cut for drying and roasting on a rack over the fire.

715. *Obi mfa ade nkoyi mmusu wo kurotia, na onsan nkofa bio.* (140)
No one places his propitiatory offering at the entrance of the village, and turns back again to remove it.

Ade ṅkọyi mmusu. Lit. something (i. e. eggs, &c.) to take away harm; perhaps here an offering for an *ọbayifo*, q. v. No. 56.

Wọ. Really a verb. Here rendered by the preposition 'at'. See note on No. 240.

Ọnsaṅ ṅkọfa. All negatives after the first verb *mfa*. Note the auxiliary verb *kọ* in *ṅkọfa.*

716. *Obi mfa adidi mfa adepẹ.* (141)
One cannot both feast and become rich.

Adidi. A noun. From reduplication of verb *di*, to eat, much eating, i.e. feasting.

Adepẹ. Lit. a thing sought after, wealth.

717. *Obi mfa dọkonsiṅ kwáṅkyẹṅ mmisa nea otŏaa so.* (142)
One does not take half a loaf from the wayside and then inquire who cut the other half.

Mfa . . . mmisa. See note on *nsisi*, No. 33. *Mmisa*, neg. of *bisa.*

Dọkonsiṅ. Ọdọkono-siṅ, ọdọkono, cakes made of maize, *siṅ,* a piece, a part of anything.

The writer has heard this proverb quoted à propos of a case where a man complained that some one had seduced a prostitute he was living with.

718. *Obi mfa fẹre ṅware obi ne nua a ne păm pọw.* (145)
No one, lest he should be called shy, would marry some one's sister who had a lump at the base of her spine.

Mfa, ṅware. For double negative, see note on *nsisi*, No. 33.
Fẹre. See note on No. 155, *mfẹre.*
Obi ne nua. Lit. some one, his sister.
Păm. Pă, the base of the spinal column.

719. *Obi mfa ahina hunu mu ṅkyerẹ opanyiṅ.* (148)
One does not show the inside of an empty pot to an elder. (Cf. No. 382.)

Opanyiṅ. See note on No. 1.

720. *Obi mfa ṅhŏma nto nsu mu ṅkọ ahemfi.* (149)
One does not put a hide in water and then go off to the king's palace (where one has been summoned).

Ahemfi = Ohene-fi.

This proverb is spoken by a tanner, who, summoned to the chief's house, does not know how long he will be detained.

721. *Obi mfa hyirew ntiw nea wato wuram'.* (150)

No one takes white clay and follows some one who has run off to the forest (in order to rub it on him).

Hyirew. White clay, used to rub on the body and face (in various designs) on certain ceremonial occasions, and also when a person accused of a crime has been acquitted. This is the sense in which it is used here. The man 'who has run to the forest' has been found 'guilty', and escaped to avoid punishment.

It is a quaint belief among these people that the Milky Way is white with the myriads of clay-decked bodies of the dead.

722. *Obi mfa amanne a wahũ ntutu kaw.* (155)

No one tells how bad a state his affairs are really in, when asking for time to settle a debt.

Amanne a wahũ. Lit. the trouble he has seen. *Amanne*, not to be confused with *amannẹ?* what news? *Amanne=ọman-ade.*

Kaw. See note on No. 54.

723. *Obi mfa n'afuru mmutuw bŭropatá so na ne mfefo ntũẽtũẽ mfa n'ase.* (156)

No one uses his own belly to cover up his corn store, that his friends may pull some out from under him.

Heard in the sense of, 'a chief is not going to allow his prestige to be used by others in order to extort and rob'.

Mmutuw. Neg. of *butuw.*

Bŭropatá. Abŭrów, corn (maize), and *páta*, a rack to store crops on.

724. *Obi mfa nɛ nan abien nsusu asu.* (158)

No one tests the depth of a river with both his feet.

Asu. See note on No. 26, *nsu.*

725. *Obi mfa nɛ nsa benkum ṅkyerẹ n'agya amamfõ so.* (159)

No one takes his left hand to point out his father's old village.

Nsa benkum. Among the Ashantis it is considered particularly insulting to put out the left hand to take anything from another. It is also insulting to point out a thing with the left hand. The left hand, never the right (as is the case among the Hausas), is used to hold the stick they generally use to wipe the anus with. The left hand is also used to blow the nose.

Amamfo. The suffix *fõ* (nasal) is not to be confused with personal suffix *fo*, plur. of *ni*.

726. *Obi mfa ne nsa nto bi anom' na ompae n'atifi.* (160)

No one puts his finger in another man's mouth and then beats him over the head.

Nsa. Hand or finger, the latter is also *nsatẽā*. See note on No. 355, *nsa*, for names of the fingers.

727. *Obi mfa ne sĕ mmobo adŵe,mmã ne yonkõ.* (161)

No one cracks a palm nut with his own teeth and gives it to his companion.

Mmobō. Neg. of *bobo*, reduplication of *bo*.

Mmã. Instead of translating this by a verb, which it really is (as is seen by its agreement with the other negative verbs), it might be rendered by 'for'. See No. 14, *mã*.

728. *Obi mfa toamũm mfa nkosĕrɛ nno.* (168)

No one takes a calabash without an opening in it to go and ask for palm oil.

Toamũm. Toa, a gourd out of which calabashes are made; *mũm,* having no opening, the same word as *mũm,* deaf or dumb. Cf. curiously enough, our own word 'mum', and also the Latin and Greek *mu*, representing the least sound it is possible to make with the lips.

729. *Obi mfi agyama so mma fam' mmɛpɛ okŏtokŏro.* (172)

No one descends from the '*gyama*' shrub to the ground and then says he wants a forked stick.

Agyama. A tree with many of its branches forked.

730. *Obi njŵefŵeɛ odabere na ade nkyĕe da.* (182)

No one ever kept looking for a sleeping-place (and continued the search) till dawn.

Nfŵefŵeɛ . . . nkyĕe. Past tenses.

731. *Obi nhintaw nso gya.* (185)

No one hides himself and (then) lights a fire.

732. *Obi nhinti prɛkŏ mmo ahina.* (186)

No one breaks the water-pot the first time he stumbles.

Ńhinti. Hintiw, cf. Hausa *funtwa.*

Mmo. From *bọ.*

733. *Obi ńhũ 'Ańkănă', ńkita 'N'ańkănă', nnyā 'N'ańkănă', na onse se, 'Mĩhũi a, ańkănă'.* (189)

No one who has seen 'Had I known, I should not . . .', who has laid hold of 'Had I known, I should not . . .', who has (ever) possessed 'Had I known, I should not . . .', would ever say (again) 'Had I known, I should not . . .'

Rather a quaint and pretty proverb this. 'Had I known . . .', that is, remorse, regret, 'of all sad words, it might have been', is here personified in the native mind.

Ańkănă. Ańkă, used in the protasis and apodosis of a conditional sentence.

734. *Obi ńhũ nimdeẹ ńkọ ayi (ase) na ọkọsọre a, waserew.* (191)

No one has any sense (who) goes to attend a funeral custom, and on rising up to take his departure, laughs.

Nimdeẹ. Knowledge, here, sense of the fitness of things. Deriv. *nim*, to know; and *ade*, a thing.

Waserew. Lit. has laughed.

735. *Obi ńhũ onipa dakoro nse no se, 'Woafọń'.* (192)

One does not see a man for one day only (or for the first time), and say to him, 'You have become thin'.

Se. Note, *se* is here of the nature of a true preposition, as seen by the absence of the negative.

Woafọń. Aorist tense.

736. *Obi ńhũ onipa awia na anadwo ọnsọ kanea ńfwe n'anim.* (193)

No one sees a man by day and at night lights a lamp to look at his face.

Awia. See note on No. 1, *asase.*

Kanea. Portuguese (?).

Ńfwe. Note the distinction between *hũ*, to perceive, see, and *fwe*, to look at. See No. 390, *hũ.*

N'anim. See note on No. 80, *aniwa.*

737. *Obi ńkọ obi akurā ńkyerẹ n'ase.* (204)

One man does not go to the village of another and tell (the chief of that village) its origin (history).

Akurā. A diminutive, for *ọkŭrow-wa.*

738. *Obi ṅkǫ obi kūrom' ṅkǫfrę nehŏ sę, 'Agyemaṅ'.* (205)
One does not go to another's village and call himself '*Agyemaṅ*'.

Agyemaṅ. Deriv. *Agya, ǫmaṅ,* lit. father of a nation.

739. *Obi ṅkǫ ahǔā ná ǫṅkǎ ṅkwǎṅ.* (207)
No one (who) goes begging a meal is the one to serve out the soup.

Ahǔā. A verbal noun, lit. a scraping; *hǔǎ,* to scrape the burned portion off a yam or plantain; hence perhaps from this part being given to a beggar, by metonymy, 'to beg for food'.

Ǫṅkǎ. Kǎ, to touch, handle, perhaps to stir, 'dish out'.

740. *Obi aṅkǫ ná obi amma a, aṅkǎ yębęyę deṅ ahǔ sę ǫkwaṅ mu nye ?* (208)
If no one had gone and no one had come, what should we have done to find out if the road were safe (or not) ?

Aṅkǎ. See note on No. 733.
Ahǔ. Subj. mood.

741. *Obi ṅkose sę, 'Putu ṅhyew ! Putu hyew a, yehǔā bi adi'.* (213)
No one says (when the yam store is on fire), 'Let the yam store burn ! When it does we shall scrape roasted yams to eat.'

Yehǔā. See note above, No. 739, *ahǔā.*
Adi. Subjunctive.

742. *Obi ṅkǫtew bisekyim mfa mfra bisetŏro ṅkǫtǫṅ mmǎ ne mǎnni.* (214)
No one picks good kola nuts and mixes them with spurious ones and goes and sells them to his own countrymen.

Nkǫtew, mfa mfra, nkǫtǫṅ mmǎ. A good example of the idiom explained under note on *mfa, nsisi,* No. 33, q. v. See also note on *mmǎ,* No. 727.

Bisekyim. Bise, the kola nut and tree (*Cola acuminata*), Hausa *goro.* The greater part of the kola consumed in the two Nigerias (N. and S.) is grown in the dense Ashanti forest. *Kyim = pa.*

Bisetŏro. Lit. false kola nut ; *toro* ɛame root as in *atoro,* a lie.

743. *Obi nkwati kokǔrobeti mmǫ pǫw.* (221)
No one dispenses with the thumb in tying a knot.

Kokǔrobeti. The thumb, deriv. *kokuro,* big. For names of the fingers see note on No. 355, *nsa.*

Mmǫ. Neg. of *bǫ.*

744. *Obi ṅkyerẹ ɛbi se, ' Tọ ṅkyene di '.* (226)

No one shows another, saying, ' Buy salt and eat '.

Ṅkyene. See note on No. 577.

745. *Obi nnim a, obi kyerẹ.* (265)

If one man does not know, another man explains.

746. *Obi nnim adekyɛe mu asẹm.* (272)

No one knows the story of to-morrow's dawn.

Adekyɛe mu asem. Adekyɛe mu, is an adjectival phrase, qualifying *asẹm.*

747. *Obi mpe ọbi yiye.* (317)

No one wishes well for another.

One might be tempted perhaps to translate this, ' There are some
(lit. is one) who do (lit. does) not wish well for others ' (lit. for
another), but this would be a distortion of the literal words and of
the sense. On second thoughts, the saying is not quite so callous,
selfish, and wanting in feeling as it might appear to us. Primitive
man had very little scope for sentimentality or even sentiment, and
the rough, wild, dangerous life gave a man plenty to do to think of
his own welfare without troubling overmuch about his neighbour's
affairs, nor does it necessarily mean he wished his neighbour evil,
but simply expresses the *natural* wish that any luck going might
come his own way.

748. *Obi ntó ntasu nto fam', mfa ne tẹkrẹma mfa.* (360)

No one expectorates on the ground and then takes his tongue and
licks it up (lit. takes it up).

749. *Obi ntwɛn Firaw ansã-na wahoro ne tãm.* (390)

No one waits (to reach) the Volta river before washing his cloth.

Firaw. The Volta, one of the largest rivers in the Colony, forming its eastern boundary.

750. *Obi se, ọbɛɛoa wo a, wunse sẹ, ' Mẹnantew'.* (408)

When some one says he will carry you, you do not say, ' I shall
walk '.

Mẹnantew. Future tense; *menantew* with a narrow instead of
a broad sound to the vowel *e* would be Present tense.

751. *Obi se ọkyɛn wo amirika a, huruw fwe kwaṅkyeṅ, na fa akyiri nè
anim to no họ.* (413)

When some one says he can run faster than you, jump (and) fall to the road-side and leave the way open for him behind and before.

So typical this perhaps of the African mind, enervated (one must remember) by a climate that even at times converts the European to this sad philosophy. Cf. also No. 752.

752. *Obi seṅ wo a, mǎ ọnseṅ wo ; na ọno nso wọ obi a ọseṅ no.* (422)
When some one excels you, let him excel you; as for him, he again has some one who excels him.

 Ọnseṅ. Imperative.

753. *Biribiara nyẹ yaw sẹ aniwu.* (464)
There is nothing that hurts like shame.

 Aniwu. Deriv. *ani* and *wu.* Lit. death of eye, i. e. shame.

754. *Biribi wọ soro a, etịba sẹ ẹbẹba fam'.* (472)
Whatever is above must come down to the earth.

 A dimly conscious recognition by some native Newton of one of nature's great laws. Cf. Proverb No. 241.

755. '*Bọ me na memmọ wo,' nyẹ agoru.* (481)
'Hit me, but I must not hit you,' is not play.

 Memmọ. Neg. of *bọ.*

756. *Wobọ ahina hõ a, na wuhũ nea ọkǎm da.* (485)
When you tap the pot, you see where the crack is.

 Da. Lit. lies.

757. *Wode tẹkrẹma si awowa a, wuntumi mpọṅ no.* (770)
When you place your tongue in pawn, you cannot redeem it. (A word once spoken cannot be unsaid.)

 Mpọṅ. *Pọṅ* means literally to pull off or strip off, hence to remove, take back. A common use of the word is to 'dismiss' from work or parade, 'to break off'. Cf. the Scotch, 'to scale', meaning 'to disperse'.

758. *Ade ketewa na wọde susuw kẹse.* (807)
It is a small thing that is taken to measure a big thing.

 Ade. See note on No. 85, *me dea.*
 Wọde. Translated by the passive.

759. *Ade-pa na ẹtọṅ nehõ.* (809)
The good thing sells itself.

Na. This particle marks the subject as being definite or emphatic and is here rendered by the definite article.

760. *Ade yera a, na ewo nipa nsam'.* (819)
When a thing is lost, then it is in some one else's hand (possession).

761. *Wo ade ye fe a, obi na okǎ kyere wo, na enye woankasa na wokǎ.* (822)
When you possess something that is beautiful, it is some one else who tells you (so) and not you yourself who speak (about it).

Na. Emphatic, translated by 'it is'.

Okǎ kyere. To tell ; *kasa kyere,* to instruct, teach. *Kyere* in conjunction with another verb almost takes the place of the English preposition 'to'. In common with the genius of many African languages, in Ashanti verbs take the place of prepositions.

762. *Wo de anye yiye a, wonkofa obi de nye wo de.* (824)
When what *you* have is not good, you do not go and take what belongs to some one else.

Wo de. See note on *me dea,* No. 85.

763. *Dua a ebewo wo ani no, wobu so, na wonsen āno.* (994)
You break off the point of the stick that is about to pierce your eye ; you do not sharpen the point.

No. A particle introducing an adverbial clause of time (as *y i*).
Lit. 'when (*no*) a stick. . .' &c.

764. *Dua a etõ nǎm na āno hyew.* (999)
It is the stick that the meat is roasted on that gets the end burned.

Na. Emphatic particle.

765. *Dua biara nsow nnyā nfwiren da.* (1004)
No tree ever bore fruit without first having flowers.

766. *Dua biakõ nye kwae.* (1006)
One tree does not make a forest.

Kwae. See note on No. 92, *wuram'.*

767. *Dua mfa mfe aduasǎ nkyea, na womfa afe koro ntěe no.* (1011).
A tree does not grow bent for thirty years that one should (expect to) straighten it in one.

Mfe aduasǎ. Lit. thirty years, but thirty is also used to mean a number greater that can be conveniently reckoned, and, curiously enough, the number 3 is sometimes used in a similar sense. The gap perhaps represents an immense period of progress.

768. *Dua kęse bu a, brofere na esi anaṅmu.* (1012)

When a great tree breaks (and falls), the papaw tree takes its place.

Brofere. Deriv. *Obŭroni* (European) and *ęfere*, (a native indigenous gourd).

Anaṅmu. Lit. in the foot (marks), i.e. instead of.

769. *Dua kęse bu a, ne mma bubu wǫ ne hŏ kwa.* (1013)

When a great tree has fallen, its children (young shoots or seeds) burst forth from it in vain. (They will soon die once the sap has dried up.)

Wǫ. See note on No. 240.

770. *Dua si akurā a, ne ntini wǫ fie.* (1016)

When a tree stands in a small village, its roots are in the houses.

771. *Dua taṅ wo a, na ebu bǫ wo.* (1020)

When a tree hates you, it breaks (and) falls on you.

Here the idea is of a (to us) inanimate object (possibly in connexion with its being the abode of a spirit), being endowed with a human attribute, perhaps not till something happened that *demanded a reason*, here the falling of the tree.

772. *Wǫmfá ade anum nto aduonum hŏ.* (1083)

Four things are not compared with forty.

Aduonum. Lit. 4 × 10, four tens, the numbers from 20 to 90 being so formed, 20 = two tens, 30 = three tens, and so on. The origin of almost all the numbers seems lost, as is usually the case. 4, *anan*, is probably the same word as *anan*, feet, i.e. 2 hands + 2 feet = 4. *Edu*, plur. *adu*, is in all probability the same root as *du*, to reach, to arrive at, meaning all the fingers and all the toes have been 'reached', i.e. counted. 11, 12, &c., are expressed by 10 + 1, 10 + 2, &c.

773. *Wo fi ne wo fi.* (1121)

Your house is your own house.

774. *Afisęm nyę atamagow na wǫasi ahatá gua sŏ.* (1136)

A private matter is not like the old cloth that has been spread to dry in the market-place.

Afisem = *Ofie asem.*

Ahatá. Subjunctive.

775. *Wobeforo dua a, wofi n'ase na womfi soro.* (1145)
When one would climb a tree, one begins from the bottom and not from the top.

776. *Mframa mmae a, na fiberee mu ye kránä.* (1152)
It is before the wind comes that the long grass is motionless.

Mmae. Aorist; when used as here negatively and with the particle *a*, translated by, 'before' or 'not yet'.

777. *Afuw mu nni biribi a, ewo kránänä.* (1174)
If a plantation has nothing else in it, it has at least silence.

Nni. Neg. of *wo*, to have, to possess; see note on No. 240.

778. *Agoru, wogoro no tipén.* (1214)
Play, you play with one your own size.

Wogoro. *Goro* is here transitive, governing the pronoun *no*, in the accusative. Lit. 'play you play it . . .'

779. *Ahina hö ayehyē no, na nsu na ewom'.* (1383)
When the surface of a pot glistens, that is because there is water on it.

Ahina. A baked clay pot, black and shining when wet, used for carrying water chiefly.

780. *Ahina bo a, na kora ata hö.* (1381)
When the water-pot breaks, the calabash in it remains (unharmed) beside it.

The woman going for water carries *inside* the water-pot a small calabash for a scoop to take the water to fill the pot; on returning, this is left inside and helps to prevent the water splashing about.

781. *Wo hö ye den a, wonye bänu adiuma.* (1390)
Though you may be strong, you do not do two men's work.

Bänu. The numerals from 1 to 9 when qualifying a noun which denotes a person have the prefix *ba* added, e.g. *bako, banu, basa*, &c. Cf. the prefix *ba* in Hausa, *Ba-hausha, Ba-ture* and *Ba-ntu.*

782. *Wo hö nye den a, na wuse, 'Kahiri nye'.* (1391)
When you are not strong, then you say, 'The head-rest is no good'.

783. *Ahōǫfę ntua kaw.* (1397)
Personal beauty does not pay a debt.

Kaw. See note on No. 54.

784. *Wohyę afiri a, wuṅwu agyaṅ.* (1469)
When you stand on (fall in ?) a trap (and are killed), you do not die
from an arrow (wound).

Agyaṅ. See note on No. 522, *tafoni,* and No. 29.

785. *Wokaṅ nantvbi a, wokaṅ nɛ dùa.* (1522)
When you count cattle, you count their tails.

Dùa. Tail, lit. stick.

786. *Wokǫ obi fi, na ǫkotow hǫ a, wummiza no agua.* (1566)
When you go to some one else's house, and the owner is squatting
there on the ground, you do not ask him for a stool.

Ǫkotow. See note on No. 367.
Wummiza. Neg. of *biza.*

787. *Wokǫ kŭrow bi mu na wuse, 'Mammęto nnipa bi wǫ ha' a, wose wo
sę, 'Yeaṅhŭ onipa a waba'.* (1578)
If you go to some one else's town and say, 'I have not met any one
here so far (of importance)', they (the town's people will retort
and) say, 'We have not been aware that some one has come (to
our town)'.

Mammęto. Lit. I have not come and met.
Yeaṅhŭ. Aorist tense.

788. *Woṅkǫǫ obi afum' da a, wuse, 'Me ṅkŏ ne kùafŏ.* (1587)
If you never went to any one else's farm, (you would) say, 'I alone
am a farmer'.

Woṅkǫǫ. Past tense, formed by lengthening of final vowel.
Afum'. See note on No. 709.
Kùafŏ. For suffix *fo* see note on No. 78, *kontromfĩ.*

789. *Yekum bi ansǎ-na yęapam bi.* (1816)
Some are killed before others are put to flight.

790. *Woṅkŭm mmarima a, wǫmfá mmea.* (1819)
If the men are not slain, the women are not carried off.

791. *Ǫkwaṅ a wunsuro mu, na aboa kyere wo mu.* (1888)
It is the path you do not fear that the wild beast catches you on.

Na. Emphatic particle. See No. 1.

792. *Ɔkwantenni nim asɛm-kã, na onnim asekyerɛ.* (1901)

The traveller (may) tell all he has seen (on his journey), but he cannot explain (all).

A sekyerɛ. Ase, lit. down, bottom, base; hence origin, meaning.

793. *Ɔkwaṅ wo asõ.* (1893)

A path has ears.

794. *Ṅkyene fi nsum' na wohata, na wode gu nsum' ho ara bio.* (1940)

Salt is procured (by evaporation) from water, yet it is taken and put back there in the water again.

Ṅkyene. See note on No. 577.

795. *Ṅkyene nsɛ nehõ sɛ, ' Meye dɛ'.* (1942)

Salt does not address itself and say, ' I am agreeable (to the taste)'.

796. *Akyene anim da ho a, wonnyae nyaṅ ṅkyeṅ.* (1937)

When the face of a drum is there (to beat), you do not leave that to beat the side.

Nyaṅ. Yaṅ, an onomatopoetic word, well illustrating the 'yang yang' (cf. twang) given forth by the native drum. Drums are here not beaten with the padded stick we generally use, and hence do not give out the booming sound usually associated with them. The drumstick is generally one bent somewhat in the shape of the figure 7, the face of the drum being hit with the short end.

797. *Wokyerɛ oṅipa akunse na wokum no a, ɛnye no yaw.* (1951)

When you have a just reason for seizing a man and killing him, you do not hurt him (by doing so).

Akunse. Deriv. *kum* and *ase.* Lit. ' a foundation for killing '.

798. *Nãm nni ho nti na wode mmerɛ ye ṅkwaṅ.* (2077)

It is because there is no meat that mushrooms are taken to make soup.

Nni. Neg. of *wõ.*

799. *Nea wadi bɛm nsoaa oguaṅ da.* (2150)

He who has won his case never yet carried the sheep.

Nsoaa. Past tense.

Oguaṅ. A fine, and so many sheep, is a usual judgement in native courts.

800. *Nea wadi fo na okasa.* (2151)

He who is guilty is the one who has much to say.

Na. Here rendered by 'the one', emphatic.

801. *Nea oko anadwogoru nnyă kaw a, nea oda anadwo dan mu na onyă kaw ana ?* (2186)

When he who goes out to dance all night does not get into trouble (lit. debt), is he who sleeps in his bed-chamber likely to ?

Anadwogoru. Lit. play by night.

802. *Nea wobekum wo nne ne se wobekum wo 'kyěna no ; mă wonkum wo nne na kohome prekŏ.* (2195)

They who were coming to kill you to-day, but say they will come to kill you on the morrow (instead), rather let them kill you to-day and rest the sooner.

Wobekum, kokome. Note the auxiliary verbs ('come' and 'go').
Wonkum. Imperative mood.

803. *Nea wompe no, wonsan nkofa.* (2226)

What is not wanted is not turned back for.

804. *Nea osew kete okwan mu, nè nea okotiaa so no, hena na oyee bone ?* (2236)

Who is in the wrong, he who spread a mat on the path, or he who trod upon it ?

Okotiaa, oyee. Past tenses.

805. *Nne-mma se, tete asoee, wonsoe ho bio ; na den nti na wontu tete 'muka abiesă no biakŏ na enka abien ?* (2285)

The children of to-day say they will not any more halt at the ancient halting-place (where their forefathers were wont to alight) ; why then do they not pull up one of the three from time immemorial hearth-stones and let but two remain ?

Asoee. A noun formed from the verb *soe*, to alight. The suffix *e* or *ee* means, a place where. Cf. *anomee*, a drinking-place, &c.

'Muka abiesă. The three conical hearth-stones, made of clay, on which the cooking-pots are placed, also called, *mukia, bukyia.*

806. *Wo ani tra wo nton a, woyera.* (2302)

When your eyes are higher than your eyebrows (i.e. puffed up with pride), you get lost.

Ani tra wo ntọṅ. 'Eyes higher than eyebrows', that is, proud, conceited, exactly our own idiom 'supercilious', (*super*, above, and *cilium*, eye id).

Tra. To go beyond, reach beyond, not to be confused with *tĕna*, *trã*, to sit.

807. *Wunnim aʒaw a, na wuse, 'Akyene nyẹ dẹ'.* (2337)

When you do not know how to dance, then you say, 'The drum is not sounding sweetly'.

808. *Wo nua sĕrẹ sŏ a, na ẹnyẹ wo na woda so.* (2504)

Your sister's thigh may be plump, but it is not you who lie on it.

Nua. See note on No. 37, *abusũa.*

809. *Nsátĕā biakŏ butuw fa ade wọ fam' a, entumi.* (2793)

If one finger tries to pick up something from the ground, it cannot.

Nsátĕā. For names of fingers see note on No. 355, *nsa.*

Wọ. See note on No. 240.

810. *Asẹm a wọkã serew wọ bābi na wọkã sũ wọ bābi.* (2854)

A matter which in one place is a subject of mirth, in another place is the cause of tears.

Wọkã serew . . . wọkã sũ. Lit. talk (and) laugh about . . . talk (and) cry about.

811. *Asẹm a wobẹse na wobẹsaṅ no, fa sã mã ẹnka wo tirim.* (2856)

A word that when spoken you would wish back, let it remain (unspoken) in your head.

Sã. This word is rather difficult to explain here, perhaps, 'thus'.

Mã ẹnka. Imperative.

812. *Asẹm-pa nẹẹ ọkã-nã.* (2873)

A good case is not difficult to state.

Ọkã-nã. See note on No. 157, *nyẹ-nã.*

813. *Asẹṅ-kẹse bẹba a, ọfraṅkã nsi so.* (2901)

When some really big business is on hand, no flag is flown.

Asẹṅ-kẹse = Asẹm-kese (?)

Ọfraṅka. Probably a corruption of the English word 'flag', applied to the emblem of the various companies.

814. *Wọso adakc a, na wọso ne mu ade.* (2976)

When a box is carried, what is inside the box is carried.

Ne mu. An adjectival phrase qualifying *ade.*

815. *Asŏ te sę nsęnǐa ; woto mu to mu a, ęda.* (2986)
The ears are like a pair of scales ; when more and more are put in,
they are weighted down (lit. sleep).

Asŏ. This may be either singular or plural, as both have the
same form, nor does the singular pronoun *ę* in *ęda* give any real
clue, as the Ashanti idiom commonly uses this third person neuter
pronoun for the third person plur.

Nsęnǐa. See note on Ashanti scales and weights, No. 591.

816. *Osram de bĕrębĕrę na etǐba oman mu.* (3043)
The moon moves slowly, but it crosses the town.

Osram. The moon, also *obosom.*

817. *Ata-panyiṅ nni ṅkyene mmã ęntere ata-kŭmã anom'.* (3148)
The elder twin does not eat salt that it may trickle into the
younger's mouth.

Nni. Neg. of *di.*

Ata-panyiṅ. The first twin to be born is called *ata-panyiṅ,*
=elder twin ; the second is known as *obi wom',* i.e. some one is
(left) inside. In no case is one of the twins killed (the ninth child
among the Nkoranzas was killed). The second of the twins to be
brought forth is considered as having precedence over the first, ' the
first merely has been sent to prepare the way for the second '.
Twins when born are put in a basin and carried on a woman's
head through the town, women following and singing :—

'*Wa wo nta* ',
'*Wa wo nta abien* '.
Lit. She has borne twins,
She has borne two twins.

Every Friday the parents of twins mash yams and eggs (*oto*), in
which the usual oil is not added, in order that the mash may be
white. White clay is then rubbed on the wrists, and shoulders,
and heads of the twins. The parents of twins never partake of any
firstfruits without first making an offering to the special fetish of
twins, Abamu.

An Ashanti chief has always the right to claim twins as his wives.

An attempt is always made to dress twins alike.

818. *Wo ntama biri a, wohoro, na woṅhyew.* (3163)
When your cloth is dirty you wash it, but you do not burn it.

Wohoro. See note on No. 353.

819. *Wote nsu kõ reguare na obodamfo fa wo tãm a, fibefibe bi ansã-na woatiw no; nà wumfura bi a, obi besusuw se mo bānu ye abodamfo.* (3202)

When you are down bathing at the water and a madman runs off with your cloth, look for another before you follow him, for if you follow him naked, some one will suppose you are both of you mad.

Wote. See note on No. 366, *te.*

Reguare. Present continued action, expressed by *re.* See a so note on No. 353, *hohoro.*

Obodamfo. Bo dam, to be mad. For suffix *fo* see note on No. 78, *kontromfi.*

Woatiw. Aorist tense.

Bānu. See note on No. 781.

820. *Tete abe, womfá nye ṅkwaṅ.* (3236)
Old palm nuts are not used to make soup.

Womfá nye. For double negative see note on No. 33, *nsisi.*

821. *Tete ara ne nne.* (3239)
History repeats itself. Lit. The very same ancient (things) are to-day.

Tete. Deriv. perhaps *te,* to be, to live, hence by reduplication, to express emphasis, lasting, old.

822. *Eti nye brofere na woapae mu ahũ mu asem.* (3265)
The head is not the papaw fruit that it should be broken to see the thoughts inside.

Brofere. See note on *brofere,* No. 768.

823. *Owia wo soro na ehyehye sã yi, na menné se ebeben fam'.* (3524)
The sun is up above and it can burn like this, but how much more (could it scorch) if it came down near to earth.

Owia. See note on No. 1, *asase.*

Menné. Neg. of *de.*

824. *Wiase wotrã no bānu bānu.* (3525)
In the world all things are two and two.

Wiase. See note on No. 1, *asase.*

Bānu bānu. See note on No. 781.

825. *Obi ṅkyi koko na onni ne mma.* (239)

No one makes a fowl taboo and then eats its chickens.

Ṅkyi . . . onni. For double negative see note on No. 33, *nsisi.*
Ọnni from *di.*

826. *Obi ṅkyi pete nni ne ṅkesua.* (240)

No one makes a vulture taboo and then eats its eggs.

Pete. Also *kokosakyi.*

827. *Aduaṅ bi a wuṅhũũ bi da wọ wo nã nè wo ọgya muka so no, na nea*
  wukyi neṅ. (1030)

Some food, the like of which you have never seen on your mother's
  or your father's cooking hearth, that is the kind you make taboo.

Nã . . . agya. Note the mother is given precedence in speech as
in reality. See notes on No. 37, *abusũa.*
Muka. See note on 805.
Neṅ = Ne no.

828. *Nea ahõọdeṅ kyi ne kọm.* (2172)

What strength makes taboo is hunger.

Kyi. See note on No. 89 and No. 132.

829. *Obi nsõ dae, ṅkọ nea wọbekum no.* (339)

No one dreams of going to where they will kill him.

Lit. no one dreams (and) goes to . . ., i. e. no one dreams he is going to be killed at a certain spot and deliberately goes there ; but
the expression appears to be understood also in the loose sense in
which we use it in English ' no one dreams of ', &c.

830. *Tete ka asõm'.* (3238)

Ancient things remain in the ears. (Tradition survives).

Tete. See note on No. 821.

By the same Author.

HAUSA FOLK-LORE, CUSTOMS, PROVERBS, &c.

Collected and Transliterated, with English Translation and Notes.
With a Preface by R. R. MARETT. With some 300 facsimiles.
2 vols. 8vo. 30s. net.

WESTMINSTER GAZETTE (Sir H. H. JOHNSTON).—'There can be no question but that Mr. Rattray's book is a valuable contribution to the study of African peoples, and except that the writer of this review dislikes sensational titles and gush—gush that seems to be more called out by the superficial study of Africa than by that of any other Continent—he would have headed his review with 'The Soul of an African People'. For it seems to him that Mr. Rattray does more in this work to open to us the minds of the folk who dwell in the Nigerian Soudan than Clapperton, Barth, Schon, Robinson, and Vircher—and the greatest of these was Barth—have yet achieved in their setting forth of Hausa Tradition and Literature. . . . This book will be a mine for the researches of the philologist and an indispensable accompaniment to the study of the Hausa language.'

MORNING POST (A. C. HADDON).—'We need not be anxious about our Protectorate and Dominions in Africa or elsewhere when the Civil Service can receive and retain the men who, in addition to the effective exercise of their administrative duties, find time to give scholarly accounts of the people over whom they are put in charge. Some, like C. W. Hobley, formerly of British East Africa, are interested in customs; others, like A. C. Hollis, of B.E.A., and R. S. Rattray, of Ashanti, are more particularly concerned with linguistic folk-tales and the like; while history claims the attention of such scholars as H. R. Palmer, of Nigeria, and H. A. MacMichael, of the Egyptian Soudan. . . . The author, the Clarendon Press and the Government of the Gold Coast are to be congratulated on the admirable way in which this valuable book has been produced.'

THE ATHENAEUM.—'The foundation of this valuable work is a voluminous MS. prepared at the request of Mr. Rattray by Shaihu, a malam, or learned scribe of the Hausa people. The liberality of the Government of the Gold Coast in granting a subvention for the present publication has enabled what is virtually a facsimile of a selection from the MS. in Arabic characters to be given. . . . Mr. Rattray's work has a definite value of its own.'

THE COLONIAL JOURNAL.—'An important result of this laborious work is to bring to light some features of the Hausa language which the spoken word did not reveal. . . . The text, in fact, places Hausa on a literary basis for the English student, and this achievement by itself fully justifies the grant made by the Gold Coast Government towards the expense of the work. . . . The notes appended by Mr. Rattray are mostly grammatical, and will be of great service to those who are learning Hausa. The work will, it may reasonably be expected, facilitate the understanding of the language, and lead to a higher standard among its students.'

MAN (A. WERNER).—'Mr. Rattray's little book on Chinyanja folk-lore is so exceedingly valuable that this specimen of his West African researches scarcely needs any other recommendation than a reference to his authorship.'

EAST AND WEST.—'Mr. Rattray's two volumes, which are attractively got up, provide both in Hausa and English a large collection of instructive legends, stories and descriptions of Hausa customs which form a valuable addition to our knowledge of the subjects with which they deal. The writer has not himself been in the Hausa country, but has studied Hausa in the Gold Coast Colony, where he was in constant touch with Hausas. A Hausa version of the whole contents of the volumes, written in modified Arabic characters, is provided.'

PRINTED IN ENGLAND
AT THE OXFORD UNIVERSITY PRESS

Milton Keynes UK
Ingram Content Group UK Ltd.
UKHW022249080124
435706UK00005B/318

9 781015 438644